GRAHAM GREENE'S COMIC VISION

Graham Greene's Comic Vision

The highest art must have a metaphysic:
the final satisfaction of man's creative
desire is only to be found in aesthetic
formation of some credible correspondence
between perceived existence and a conceived
absoluteness of reality.

Lascelles Abercrombie

... in the course of the blackest book
I have written I had discovered comedy.

Graham Greene

GRAHAM GREENE'S COMIC VISION

V.V.B. RAMA RAO

RELIANCE PUBLISHING HOUSE

ISBN: 81-85047-59-6

Published by: –
Lion Dr. S.K. Bhatia
For
Reliance Publishing House
3026/7H, Ranjit Nagar
New Delhi-110 008. Ph. 5722605/586889.

Lasertypeset by:
Jay Compusoft,
H-296, Uday Niketan,
Narain Vihar
New Delhi 110 028.

Printed at:-
Efficient Offset Press
Naraina, Phase II
New Delhi-110 028.

CONTENTS

PREFACE

i. Some years ago I happened to read *The End of the Affair* and developed a liking for Graham Greene's fiction and read all his novels. When I came to *The Comedians*, his distinctive comic vision made an impact on me. A study of the critical material on Greene made me understand that his comic vision did not receive the attention it deserved from the British, American or Indian scholars. I have been studying this aspect of Greene's art off and on. The award of a Teacher Fellowship enabled me to stay at the Andhra University and study Greene's comic vision in depth. I limited my study to the novels till *The Human Factor*(1978).

i.i This book is a modest attempt to trace the maturation of Greene's comic vision in his novels through an intensely tragic phase. The unusually complex responses his novels evoke have their origin in the skill with which Greene combines the tragic and the comic. It has been my sincere attempt to study the tragic and the comic strands that progressively intertwine in various ways to bring out the complex blend of the comic with several shades of the tragic.

i.ii I thank the University Grants Commission for the award which made this work possible, as also the Principal and the management of the Maharajah's College, Vizianagram, for permitting me to accept the Fellowship. I thank Emeritus Professor K. Viswanatham, the supervisor of my research, and Professor N. Krishna Rao, Member of the Doctoral Committee, for going through my script at various stages and for helping me with their comments and criticism. I am also grateful to the professors who discussed my project with me and made a number of suggestions, particularly to Professor R.A. Malagi of the Gujarat University. My thanks are due to the librarians of the Utkal University, Karnatak University, Gujarat University, and librarians of the British Council Library and American Centre, Madras, and those of the American Studies Research Centre and Central Institute of English and Foreign Languages, Hyderabad. I also thank the librarian of De Nobili College, Poona. My thanks to the staff of the Andhra University library for having given me the maximum help and co-operation in my work. I must thank Professor (Mrs) Ila Rao, Head of the Department of English, Andhra University, who has been a constant source of help and encouragement and was kind enough to requisition, for my use, xerox copies of several unpublished dissertations on Greene produced in the U.S.

Chapter 1

Introduction

> *Perhaps the most important discovery in modern criticism is the perception that comedy and tragedy are somehow akin, or that comedy can tell us many things about our situation even tragedy cannot.*
>
> *Wylie Sypher*

1.1 At a point in the middle phase of Graham Greene's career as a novelist, a critic[1] wittily accused him of joyfully reversing Browning: "God's in his heaven, all's wrong with the world." Greene closes his *Travels With My Aunt* (1969) with the principal character proposing to read Browning with his fiancee in the warm scented evenings:

> *God's in His heaven*
> *All's right with the world.*

The author of *The Man Within* (1929) is not just the same as the one of *The Human Factor* (1978). Heraclitus says that the water in the river is not the same at two different points of time. Greene himself states in the introduction to *Collected Stories* (Collected edition, 1972): "With a novel, which takes perhaps years to write, the author is not the same at the end of the book as he was at the beginning." This should be more so at the end of several books and several decades.

1.1.1 The aim of this study is to trace the growth and the full flowering of Graham Greene's comic genius and the emergent comprehensiveness of his vision. The tragic aspect of his vision has always a comic vein lurking in it even in the early novels and progressively the comic seems to have pervaded the whole of his later fiction ultimately attaining full bloom in the novels of the third phase. *Brighton Rock* (1938) marks the end of the first phase, while *A Burnt-out Case* (1961) marks the transition between the second and the third phases. Greene's novels may be analysed in terms of the artistic exploration of modes of experience; tragic, comic and tragicomic. Greene has a tendency to combine the stereotypes of

---

1. Sean of Faolain. Quoted by Francis Kunkel in "The Theme of Sin and Grace", R.O. Evans (Ed), *Graham Greene: Some Critical Considerations* (Lexington: Univ. of Kentucky Press, 1967), p. 53

the tragic and the comic thus helping the audience into responses less easy than the conventional ones. It is worth tracing the apparently contrary strands of tragedy and comedy in Greene's novels. While tragedy reveals the human spirit ready to sacrifice itself in confrontation with evil and unreconciled to things, comedy envisages a reconciliation with things after confrontation with the mystery of evil. The preoccupation with evil sharpens Greene's tragic sense which in its turn leads him to delve into the reason for the 'aboriginal calamity' in which Newman saw the human race implicated. For establishing a contact with reality a profound tragic sense is needed. Tragedy proves in the end that even though evil is a strong contender, it is powerless before a strong soul. Greene's chief characters in the early novels as well as those in the novels of the middle phase are undeniably tragic The Whisky priest realizes in a moment of tragic illumination that it would have been easy to be a saint and that he has missed his tryst with God in a matter of seconds. The missed sainthood marks the tragic centre of the novel. The tragic protagonist is a trapped individual and the tragedy lies in his being a little too late. The fruits of his achievement are not readily palpable and that is the reason why tragedy leaves us with a sense of loss and waste. If tragedy exaggerates to press a point of view, comedy too does the same though there is no rushing to the precipice in it. There is an intensity of the tragic sense in the novels up to *A Burnt-out Case* but even the darkest of Greene's tragedies do not usually exclude the comic. There is a delicate sensibility in the way the two strands are interwoven. The tragedies are not unmixed with the comic spirit and the comedies do have tragic undertones. In a way every novel creates an antithesis in itself. There are forces which are harnessed to modify the purely tragic by, for example, sentimentality and a divided mind in *The Man Within*. The deflation of the purely tragic is at times deliberate. The undercurrent of comedy surfaces first in *Brighton Rock* and dominates progressively in the later novels. The comic forces crop up to modify what could otherwise have been a tragedy. At a point the comic seems to take over leaving the tragic only as an undertone. This does not imply that Greene is an imperfect artist. He has found a way of presenting the one in the other in complexly varying combinations, alternating the tragic and the comic strands with the express purpose of communicating his intensely felt 'sense of life'. In all his moments of great insight Greene appears to be at the intersection of the tragic and the comic. It is a balance of the two that makes for the most significant penetration into reality and the communication of 'livingness'. The deeper the one, the deeper also is its counterpart and the deficiency of the tragic sense is clearly a deficiency of the comic. A failure in the one entails a failure in the other and the novel gets reduced in stature in the sense that it does not have the right contact with reality. In Greene's fiction the maturation of the vision has always meant a progress of the comic sense. Tragedy and comedy are parallel forces and the depth in one necessarily implies depth in the other. They are co-extensive, co-terminous and they never mutually exclude each other. If we present in a graph the progress and development of the tragic and the comic, the peaks of achievement would show peaks in the tragic as well as in the comic. In the highest literature, as in a Dante, a Cervantes, or a Shakespeare, the comic and tragic are integrated.

1.2 Aesthetics, the philosophy of the beautiful, discusses the different kinds and degrees of communicating joy and related feelings through different genres. As Susanne Langer writes: "the novel is peculiarly suited to formulate our modern life by taking our most pervasive interest for its theme— the evaluation and hazards of personality .... a novelist intends to create a virtual experience, wholly formed, and wholly expressive of something more fundamental than any 'modern' problem, human feeling, the nature of human life itself."[2] The novel as much as drama evokes the same kinds of responses in terms of the tragic, the comic and the tragi-comic. The novel, as Dawson points out, is not a narrative form with dramatic moments, but a dramatic form within a narrative framework. It would be impossible to illustrate the full dramatic range of which the novel is capable. Dawson concludes: "*Mutatis mutandis*, almost everything significant that can be said about plays can be said about novels."[3] The novel has replaced drama as the most popular literary form because of its flexibility. The tragic, comic or tragi-comic import is to be estimated in the light of certain questions suggested by Cyrus Hoy: "How final are the contradictions conceived to be? On what conditions, if any, are they to be reconciled? How ironically are they rendered? How conscious are the dramatic protagonists of the incongruities that compass them round? In differentiating the various responses everything turns on the level at which the issue is joined between the moral or ethical, the psychological or the metaphysical elements that are in opposition."[4] In this context the generic distinctions like comedy and

---

2. Susanne K. Langer, *Feeling and Form* (New York: Scribner's 1953), pp. 287-88
3. S.W. Dawson, *Drama and the Dramatic* (London: Methuen, 1970), p. 82
4. Cyrus Hoy, *The Hyacinth Room* (London: Chatoo and Windus, 1954), p. 7

tragedy belong merely to the mode of presentation while as fictional modes they act and react in innumerable degrees of combinations. Tragedy and comedy need not necessarily refer to forms of drama. F.L. Lucas writes: "It seems to me a mistake to consider the effects of tragedy in such isolation and apart from the epic and the novel, as if we felt essentially different when we read the death of Hector or of Hamlet, of Desdemona or of Tess of the d'Urbervilles."[5]

1.2.1 The tragic has always referred to some aspect of man's concrete involvement with evil and with his efforts to comprehend it and deal with it. Evil is not objectively presented for our inspection and understanding and as such it is to a large extent subjective. The evil could be either from external sources or from within the individual himself or of some cosmic origin as subsumed under the concept of primordial evil. The peculiar tragic character of the protagonist's struggle turns upon his perception of evil and upon his possible creative use of it. In the treatment of evil in literature a necessary correlation has always been sought to be established between the action of the tragic hero and the fruits he plucks thereof. The tragic view of life has its value in the faith or at least the hope that the struggle will be followed by an illuminating insight, the noetic quality. The value is affirmed only in an ironic sense as when Edgar realizes "Ripeness is all", where the illumination will be of little avail to Lear. In a tragic action the outcome leaves the impression of undeviating heroism, a willed failure to make unheroic adjustments. The final disaster in tragedy entails magnificent obsession in spite of change of fortune and does leave an impression of heroism though accompanied by misery and emotional distress. Geoffrey Brereton points out: "The main point at which the tragic can enter is through the 'imperfect Christian'. This is the man who is aware of the religious virtues but is unable to practise them in living, or possibly the man who seeks to reinterpret them in an unorthodox way."[6] The schism, between what ought to be and what is, gives rise to many a tragic dilemma, not necessarily among Christians as Brereton's remark would seem to suggest. Fulke Greville, a contemporary of Shakespeare, exclaims:

Oh, wearisome condition of humanity
Born under one law, to another bound
Vainly begot and yet forbidden vanity
Created sick, commanded to be sound.

5. F.L. Lucas, *Tragedy* (London: Hogarth Press, 1946), p. 51.

6. Geoffrey Brereton, *Principles of Tragedy* (London: Routledge and Kegan Paul, 1968), p. 52.

The schism between the flesh and the spirit is a well-nigh primal split. In his Epistle to the Romans St. Paul speaks of it: "For the good that I would I do not: but the evil which I would not, that I do."

1.2.1.1. The tragic sense may sometimes exist in inchoate forms but is always held to consist in an awareness that human destiny is affected by uncontrollable factors and that its usual condition is unhappiness. Miguel Unamuno finds the source of the tragic in the contradictions in man's nature. He thinks that the root of the tragic vision of life is in the hunger of man's heart for personal immortality which his noblest faculty, his reason, told him was a dream. Kierkegaard also sees in 'contradiction' the essence of life and the tragic according to him is the 'suffering contradiction'. Schopenhauer holds that it is the finality of tragedy that satisfies us -- that the end brings peace because all is over, the story is complete, "the rest is silence; there is no more to saye."[7]

1.2.1.2 Many writers on tragedy have indeed affirmed that there is a deep discord between the tragic and the Christian view of man and his destiny. *Tragedy is not Enough* is the title of a book and *The Death of Tragedy* is another. Helen Gardner quotes Macneil Dixon who asks whether tragedy be at all possible under the protection and in the light of revealed religion. It is argued that the Christian doctrine of a life in the world to come and of reward and punishment after death is destructive of tragic finality and that a true Christian could write no tragedy. But Helen Gardner argues: "The concept of rewards and punishments after death is held very strongly in other religions than the Christian, nor is Christianity unique in believing in an after life. Its uniqueness lies, as I have said, in the doctrine of Resurrection: 'Behold I make all things new.'"[8] In this context one has to agree that tragedy presents the historical, the course of life in *this* world. There is an interesting and exhaustive entry on the tragic sense in *The Dictionary of the History of Ideas* where the point is mentioned: ". . . Jaspers (*Tragedy is not Enough* (tr.) Reiche, Moore and Deutsch, Boston, 1952) and others have argued that tragedy is no longer possible in a Christian universe because evil is transcended. Yet Original Sin remains to place this transcendence in question. Evil, then for the Christian tradition is both human, an externally determined Fate, and Adamic or human

7. Quoted by Helen Gardner, *Religion and Literature* (London: Faber, 1976), p. 30.

8. Helen Gardner. p. 95.

and ethical."[9] Joseph Wood Krutch writes that the term tragedy is a misnomer since it is obvious that the works in question (modern works) "have nothing in common with the classical examples of the genre and produce in the reader a sense of depression which is exact opposite of that elation generated when the spirit of Shakespeare rises joyously superior to the outward calamities."[10] For the great ages, he writes, tragedy was not an expression of despair but the means by which they saved themselves from it. It is a profession of faith, and a sort of religion; a way of looking at life by virtue of which it is robbed of its pain. It is perfectly clear that tragedy is profound and that it puts man in direct confrontation with the profundities of human reality. But one does realize that even while it enjoys the privilege of probing deep into life, it becomes exclusive, it becomes chemically pure as Aldous Huxley puts it, narrows the focus even like a lens which is focussed only to burn. We are left with a charred human spirit. Nietzsche's wild prophecy that 'God is dead' can lead us to the modern fact of the death of tragedy. At least in Greene, God and tragedy have gone together. A modern tragedy has almost come to be a contradiction in terms, an oxymoron.

1.2.2 A movement from tragedy to comedy is an empirical phenomenon when one turns to poets like a Dante, or a Chaucer, or a Shakespeare, or a Goethe. Moelwyn Merchant writes: "It would be hazardous and unbalanced to press the argument too far, but it is certainly a modest and justifiable conclusion that the progress from tragedy to comedy (from *Troilus* to *The Canterbury Tales*) was for Chaucer in no sense an anticlimax, a movement from a serious game to a mere literary trifling ... It is certainly no overstatement to regard the cosmic sequence from *Inferno* to *Paradise* by way of *Purgatorio* as a progress towards 'an agreeable ending'".[11] Comedy tends to adjust the individual towards the ideal. These three alternatives, mentioned in *The Dictionary of the History of Ideas*, point to three kinds of contrast which are enlivened by the comic vision of life. This comic vision implies an acceptance of life which includes an acceptance of man as well. One must be prepared to forgive the weaknesses, or even the treachery, even the downright depravity, which in spite of man's best intentions seem to be inherent in his behaviour. To accept and to forgive, one must be, above everything

9. *The Dictionary of the History of Ideas* (New York; Scribner's, 1973), Vol. II, p. 417.

10. Joseph Wood Krutch, "The Tragic Fallacy", Schorer et al (ed), *Criticism* (New York: Harcourt, Brace, 1948), p. 77.

11. Moelwyn Merchant, *Comedy* (London: Methuen, 1972), p. 5.

else, clearsighted about what man is, and what could properly be expected of him. Comedy in this sense is realistic about the nature of man and the nature of human life. It can be compassionate in its forgiveness and in its acceptance of human failings. It does emphasize the need for man to undeceive himself about the limitations of humanity; but it asks him to refrain from making a bid for the impossible and plunging into the depths of tragic despair when the impossible may not be achieved. Even in the realm of comedy, the effort to transcend human limitations can never be regarded as mere folly. Comedy works through a perception of the inherent incongruities of human existence. Cyrus Hoy says that the special province of comedy is to view the incongruities in perspective. The mess of incongruities of life, unorganized by a comic imagination, is more likely to baffle than amuse. Comedy adjusts the right perspective on the apparent contradictions of life by enlarging our awareness of things. That is the reason why Feibleman writes: "... comedy is an antidote to error. It is a restorer of proportions, and signals a return from extreme adherence to actual programmes, in so far as these programmes are found to be faulty."[12] If great tragedy consists in the invention of platitudes, great comedy consists in their destruction. Though it is a great game it is an extremely hazardous one, for like all art, "it is a matter of dancing on the edge of the abyss or hiding it with flowers."[13] The perception of incongruity does not breed contempt for things. Comedy teaches both sympathy and tolerance. Jean Paul Richter holds that true humour springs from the heart and that its essence is love. The thing itself of course existed long before it was named humour. Hegel described this kind of humour which he found in shakespeare: "Inseparable from the comic is an infinite geniality and confidence, capable of rising superior to its own contradictions and experiencing therein no taint of bitterness or sense of misfortune whatever. It is the happy frame of mind, a hale condition of soul, which, fully aware of itself, can suffer the dissolution of its aims."[14] The sense of humour may be regarded as the consummation of the instinct for laughter. Though the profounder appeal may be reserved to tragedy, the ministrations of comedy are to be viewed as essential to emotional health and spiritual sweetness. When Joseph

---

12. James Feibleman, *In Praise of Comedy* (London, Allen and Unwin, 1939), p. 181
13. Elie Faure, *The Spirit of the Forms* (New York: Garden City, 1937), p. 175. Quoted by Feibleman, p. 272.
14. Quoted by A. Thorndike, *English Comedy* (New York: Macmillan, 1929), p. 5.

Wood Krutch says: "All works of art which deserve their names have a happy end"[15] he seems to include all art under a sort of universal comedy. If comedy conveys to us an often harrowing sense of external changeableness of human nature and of life, it also makes clear to us the higher sense in which nothing ever really ends, in which indeed every end is a new beginning viewed in a fresh way. Reinhold Niebuhr rightly brings tragedy and comedy together when he observes laughter as a kind of no man's land between faith and despair. We preserve our sanity by laughing at life's surface absurdities, but the laughter turns to bitterness and derision is directed towards the deeper irrationalities of evil and death. "That is why," he concludes, "there is laughter in the vestibule of the temple, the echo of laughter in the temple itself, but only faith and prayer, and no laughter, in the holy of holies."[16] The comic vision penetrates the secret of man's condition vigourously when it is seen in relation to the structure of the traffic. Comedy reaches its greatest stature not in independence from but in association with the darker insights of tragedy. Indeed, comedy confronts us with its own especial way of life, its peculiar insight alongside of the intensity of the tragic vision. *The Dictionary of the History of Ideas* gives a fine summing up of the comic sense:

> The comic sense, in sum, is an awareness of the ironic character of man's involvement with social evil. In form it may mostly briefly be described as the catharsis of folly by folly. Comic action has been regarded as a means for disciplining the foolishness inherent in pretensions to social respectability by exhibiting and indulging the foolishness of the 'lower' and disreputable self. Consequently it depends upon the possible unity of the traditional duality of "that amphibious creature", man. This unity may be seen in the tendency of the comic sense to bring the deviating individual into accord with social norms, or to bring the deviating society to awareness of the ideal, or, finally, to reconcile the individual and his social milieu with the ideal by way of a productive and unifying insight into a more authentic vision of human possibilities. (*p. 490*)

1.2.3. F. H. Ristine, in his *Tragicomedy*, writes: "Between the extremes of pure tragedy and pure comedy of the Aristotelian formulas there was always a 'tertium quid', a something that

---

15. Schorer *et al*, p. 78
16. Qluoted by Merchant, p. 8.

manifestly overstepped the bounds of the one or of the other. The two forms were continually overlapping, blending one into the other, and creating an intermediate type so obviously neither tragedy nor comedy that classical writers were at a loss to name it."[17] In 1764 Fontenelle distributed the emotions aroused in a play in a sort of prismatic scale as the terrible, the sublime, the pathetic, the tender, the amusing, the absurd: allotting the first two divisions of the spectrum to tragedy, the last two to comedy, assigning the intermediate neutral spheres properly neither to the one nor to the other but mingled of both, to which one might give a special name. The Italian Guarini, in 1737, formulated a theory of 'tragi-comedy'. "Far from being a discordant mixture of tragedy and comedy, (tragi-comedy) is a thoro (*sic*) blend of such parts of each as can stand together with versimilitude, with the result that the deaths of tragedy are reduced to the danger of deaths, and the whole in every respect a graduated mean between the austerity and dignity of the one and the pleasantness and ease of the other."[18] The Germans called this genre *Schauspiel*, distinguishing it from *Lustspiel* and *Trauerspiel*, which is a comic pattern playing with the tragic. *The Dictionary of the History of Ideas* considers tragicomedy a kind of comedy. "Perhaps the seeming two arts of tragedy and comedy may at this point become parts of one and the same whole." (p. 470) Tragicomedy is more illuminating than tragedy. Quiller Couch expresses a similar opinion about the tragicomedies of Shakespeare:[19]

> Yes, as I can bravely imagine, yet can justly imagine, a world in which the murder of Desdemona, the fate of Cordelia, will be considered curiously as brute happenings proper to a time outlived. And again, while I reverance the artist who in *Othello* or in *King Lear* purges our passion, forcing us to weep for present human woe, *The Tempest*, as I see it, forces diviner tears.

As in the tragicomedies of Shakespeare, we find in Sanskrit drama a comedic or happy ending. Perhaps the aesthetic motive is that the comedic mode is inclusive and that the ending implies a tolerance of the incongruities, absurdities, and illogicalities in life's happenings.

17. F.H. Ristine, *Tragicomedy* (New York: Columbia Univ. Press, 1910), p. 2.
18. Ristine, p. xi.
19. Arthur Quiller Couch, *Shakespeare's Workmanship* (London: Benn, 1930), p. 299.

1.2.4 Many fundamental thinkers have felt and even enunciated theories that the tragic and the comic are inseparable. We are told in the *Symposium* of Plato that "the genius of comedy was the same as that of tragedy, and that the writer of tragedy ought to be a writer of comedy."[20] Socrates was speaking to the revellers and Aristodemus did not hear the beginning of the discourse. Plato, however, makes in his *Republic* an utterance opposed to that of Socrates: "For even when the two species of limitation are nearly allied, the same person cannot succeed in both, as for example, the writers of comedy and tragedy." But in *Laws* he admits that the understanding of the one leads to a better understanding of the other: "for serious things cannot be understood without laughable things, not opposites at all without opposites, if a man is really to have intelligence of either."[21] Writers on the tragic and the comic modes have tried to shed light on the remark of Socrates and elucidated it. Feibleman writes: "In Plato's theory we see that comedy is never free from tragedy, since the logical inexorability of fate which in tragedy has the power to make good its threat, in comedy is seen to be weak; yet by outward form at the beginning of any sequence of events they are both the same. So comedy becomes the avoidance of the terrible outcome of events which were threatened in tragedy. Thus as Plato says 'the true artist in tragedy was an artist in comedy also.'"[22] Cyrus Hoy gives another elaboration to the statement:[23]

> Comedy and Tragedy alike are the limitations of men and the crucial fact about man is his dual nature. His duality makes him an incongruous figure, and if there were nothing incongruous in the human condition, there would be nothing to dramatize. The union of the spiritual essence and a corporeal existence poses the initial incongruity, and from this all others flow. Infinite aspirations are subject to a finite capacity for achievement, immortal longings break upon the fact of mortality; the rational purpose gives way to irrational impulse. Incongruities such as these are the warp and woof of human experience and the fabric of human life reveals a pattern shot through with discrepancies: the discrepancy between the ideal and the reality, between the

20. Plato's Dialogues, Vol. I: *The Symposium*, (Tr. Jowsett, New York; Scribner's, 1874), 223.
21. Ibid., 5, 199.
22. Feibleman, p. 77.
23. Cyrus Hoy, p. 22.

intention and the deed, to name those which subsume all others. To dramatize these is the purpose of tragedy and comedy and this is the reason that the true artist in the one will be an artist in the other as well.

1.2.4.1 Great tragedy and great comedy underlie each other. While tracing the flowering of Greene's comic vision, this work also aims at explicating the progressive blending of the 'tragic rhythm' with the 'comic rhythm', to borrow the terms of Susanne K. Langer. She defines: "... the deathward advance of the individual lives has a series of stations that are not repeated: growth, maturity and decline. That is the tragic rhythm."[24] Comic rhythm is "the contest of men and women — the most universal contest, humanized in fact, civilized, yet still the primitive challenge, the self-preservation and self-assertion."[25] In terms of the philosophy of art she writes, "As comedy presents the vital rhythm of self-preservation, tragedy exhibits that of self-consummation."[26] The intermingling of the two rhythms is a mark of excellence in great writers like Dante and Shakespeare. This is so since the two rhythms are capable of various combinations incorporating elements of the one in the other. To quote Langer again, "the matrix of the work is always either tragic or comic, but within its frame the two often interplay. Dante calls his poem a comedy, though it is entirely serious, visionary, religious and sometimes terrible."[27] Dante's poem is an example of the sublime intermingling of the two rhythms. As Moelwyn Merchant writes: "Dante's poetic achievement of the beatific vision, after the secular power of Virgil had taken him to the limit of insight granted to human reason, gives the most substantial ground for the subsequent nature of comedy, an intellectual and spiritual standpoint which gives the literary form its claim to insights as grave and weighty as those of tragedy."[28] The intermingling of the tragic and the comic in a single work or in a single character definitely evokes a very valuable and complex aesthetic response. The two are not essentially different since they have the same ontological phenomena to deal with and the same metaphysical issues to face. The two shade off into one another, sometimes imperceptibly since contradiction is the common denominator to both. Kierkegaard writes: "The tragic and the comic

24. Susanne K. Langer, p. 351.
25. Ibid., p. 346.
26. Ibid., p. 351.
27. Ibid., p. 334.
28. Merchant, p. 5.

are the same, in so far as both are based on contradiction, but the tragic is the suffering contradiction, the comical, the painless contradiction."[29] Since comedy and tragedy emerge from the same ontological problem, the relation of the logical order to the historical order, Feibleman rightly observes "there is nothing which does not have its tragic as well as its comic aspect."[30] Ronald Peacock notes that comedy and tragedy spring from the tension between imperfect life and our ideal aspirations. "They exist together in their dependence on the contradictions of life. They are parallel expressions, in different keys, of our idea of what is good."[31] Styan points out that "experience of life and art compel us to be aware of the blood relationship of the tragic and comic senses, of the interbreeding of tears and laughter."[32]

1.2.4.2 It is the novelist's task as much as it is the poet's or the dramatist's to convey a sense of life by means of organisation and articulation of life. Different phrases have been used to signify this. Henry James in the *Art of Fiction* writes: "The only reason for the existence of a novel is that it does attempt to represent life." For him a novel is valuable for its 'felt life'. Susanne K. Langer writes that a novel, to be vital, "requires an illusion of the world, a history perceived and felt -- 'a corner of life seen through a temperament' as Zola said."[33] In organization one rhythm always dominates the dynamic form, while the other may underlie it is in contrapuntal fashion. The master of such a practice is Shakespeare and it is for this reason that Shakespeare has been the ideal against which the achievement of later artists is measured and evaluated.[34]

1.2.4.3 Scholars who have thought deeply on the inter-relationships of tragedy and comedy have always stressed the unity of the two genres. The prevalence of one even in a predominant degree does not exclude the presence of the other. Susanne K. Langer writes: "... The fact that the two great rhythms, comic and tragic, are radically distinct does not mean that they are each other's opposites, or even incompatible forms. Tragedy can rest squarely on a comic

29. Quoted by Helen Gardner, p. 32.
30. Feibleman, p. 198.
31. Quoted by J.L. Styan, *The Dark Comedy* (Cambridge: Cambridge Univ. Press, 1968), p. 36.
32. Styan, p. 36.
33. Langer, p. 299.
34. cf., Walter Allen's statement: "Shakespeare has always been the ultimate standard of comparison for imaginative writing." *The English Novel* (Harmondsworth: Pelican, 1958), p. 24.

substructure and yet be pure tragedy. This is natural enough, for life, from which all felt rhythms spring, contains both, in every mortal organism."[35] In his classic *The Tragic Sense of Life*, the Spanish thinker Miguel Unamuno concludes his exploration of Don Quixote: "The mortal Don Quixote, in dying, realized his own comicness, and bewept his sins; but the immortal Quixote, realizing his comicness, superimposes himself upon it and triumphs over it without renouncing it."[36] The point deserves to be stressed again that the tragic and comic commingle in the Don's life and activity and final consummation. Comedy when it embraces the tragic and integrates it into itself becomes 'high' comedy. 'High' comedy, as Wylie Sypher writes, chastens man. Sypher cites examples from Cervantes and Shakespeare to argue that the range of comedy is more embracing than the rage of tragedy. He further points out: "... if tragedy occurs at some middle point in ethical life where failure is weighed against man's nobility of spirit, comedy ventures into the further extremes of experience in both directions, towards the bestial or 'obscene' and at the other end of the spectrum toward the insane heroics of Nietzsche or the vision of Prospero, who sees sin as the last mistake of all our many mistakes, dispelled before our clearer reason whenever hate seems more absurd than charity."[37] It is being recognized that comedy is a maturer form than tragedy. The comic sense teaches tolerance. As Maugham puts it: "Humour teaches tolerance and the humourist, with a smile and perhaps a sigh, is more likely to shrug his shoulders than to condemn."[38] The world of *The Winter's Tale* is more comprehensive than that of *Othello*. Evil also is a part of life and there are more things in heaven and earth than our philosophy dreams of.

1.3 That existence is comic has been a fundamental tenet in Greene's thinking is evident in the epigraph he chose for *Stamboul Train* (1938): "Everything in nature is lyrical in its ideal essence, tragic in its fate, and comic in its existence." (George Santayana) In the *Confidential Agent* (1939) the principal character goes to a film and sees the blonde heroine weep. He feels that the tears, for people predestined for success by popular choice, are all extraordinarily sad and obtuse. "If we lived in a world, he thought, which guaranteed a happy ending, should we be as long in

35. Langer, p. 362.

36. Quoted by Merchant, p. 79.

37. Wylie Sypher, *Comedy* (New York: Doubleday Anchor Books, 1956), p. 213.

38. Somerset Maugham, *The Summing Up* (New York, Mentor Books, 1959), p. 45.

discovering it? Perhaps that's what the saints were at with their incomprehensible happiness they had seen the end of the story when they came in and couldn't take the agonies seriously." Though there has been a phase in which Graham Greene seems to have viewed the sins of his characters seriously, he seems to have progressively developed a saint-like sympathy for them. The comic sense digests incongruities and absurdities and recognizes like Keats that the worm that eats the rose is as much a part of the world as the rose. If one hates the worm one writes a tragedy; if one recognizes it as a part of life, one writes a comedy. In *The Ministry of Fear* (1943) Greene tells us of the principal character: "The grand names stood permanently like statues in his mind: names like Justice and Retribution, though what they boiled down to was simply Mr. Rennit, hundreds and hundreds of Mr. Rennits. But of course if you believed in God — and the Devil — the thing wasn't quite so comic. Because the Devil — and God too — had always used comic people, futile people, little suburban natures and the maimed and warped to his purposes. When God used them you talked emptily of Nobility and when the devil used them of Wickedness, but the material was only dull shabby human mediocrity in either case."

1.3.1 Greene considers writing a form of therapy. He writes: "Sometimes I wonder how all those who do not write, compose or paint can manage to escape the madness, the melancholia, the panic fear which is inherent in the human situation."[39] The self-designed therapy has succeeded in curing him of the things he dreaded and in the process his world-view has undergone a healthy change. In his introduction to the collected edition (1974) of *A Burnt-out Case* he writes:

> Thirty years before I had read Unamuno's *Life and Death of Don Quixote* with no particular interest — it left no memories. But perhaps the book which I so quickly forgot has continued to work its way through the cellars of the unconscious; in the life of which I was fully aware, I was making my way with passionate curiosity through works of theology. Yet *The Heart of the Matter* offended the moral theologians ... Without knowing myself the course I had been taking I found myself, in "A Visit to Morin" and *A Burnt-out Case*,, in that tragicomic region of La Mancha where I expect to stay. Even my Marxist critics shared the

39. Introduction to *Collected Stories* (Collected Edition), London: Heinemann and Bodley Head, 1972), p. xii.

> characteristic with Waugh — they were too concerned with faith or no faith to notice in the course of the blackest book I have written I had discovered comedy.

Greene's own asseveration came after several critics made the point. William J. Rewak in his essay "Maturation of Graham Greene's Vision" in *The Catholic World* (December, 1957) notes this: "Real maturity does not stop at an insight into the tragic; it involves the tragic completed by and suffused with, a vision of joy." Philip Startford reviewing *A Burnt-out Case* in his "Greene's Hall of Mirrors" in the *Kenyon Review* (Summer, 1961) notices the evolution in Greene's vision: "A new comic vision has been developing through the plays and entertainments of the 50s to replace the earlier melodramatic outlook and this is the vision which underlies this serious novel." The epigraph which Greene has for *The Comedians* bears further evidence to the evolution: "Aspects are within us, and who seems most kingly to the king." (Thomas Hardy) David Lodge who also notes the evolution quotes the central character's remarks in that novel: "Life was a comedy, not a tragedy for which I had been prepared, and it seemed to me that we were all ... driven by an authoritative practical joker towards the extreme point of comedy" and comments: "Without interpreting this passage as a personal confession we may perhaps see it as some kind of gloss on Greene's progress from fiction based on a tragic conflict between human and divine values to fiction conceived in terms of comedy and irony in which the possibility of religious faith has all but retreated out of sight in the anarchic confusion of human behaviour." A kind of merger of tragedy and comedy is found in *The Honorary Consul* (1973) which is suggested by the epigraph:

> *'All things merge in one another —*
> *good into evil, generosity into*
> *justice, religion into politics ...'*

A character in this novel says: "Contrary to common belief the truth is nearly always funny. It's only tragedy which people bother to imagine or invent." Reviewing a film Greene wrote as long ago as 1936: "The truth is seldom tragic, for human beings are not made in that grand way. The truth may be sad but truth is nearly grotesque as well." There has been a significant maturation in Greene's vision and his attitude towards life and reality. The glimmerings of the comic in the tragic novels of the earlier phase precede the intermingling and the flash of the comic in the middle phase which in turn gives way to the final development into ripeness in the third phase.

Chapter 2

The Novels of the First Phase

> *"... the symmetry of his thought lends the whole body of his work the importance of a system".*
>
> *Graham Greene*

2. *The Man Within* (1929), *The Name of Action* (1930), *Rumour at Nightfall* (1931), *Stamboul Train* (1932), *It's a Battlefield* (1934), *England Made Me* (1935), *A Gun for Sale* (1936) and *Brighton Rock* (1938) belong to the first phase of Greene's career as a creative artist. The first three form his juvenilia and *The Name of Action* and *Rumour at Nightfall* are excluded from the Uniform edition. In the novels of the first phase, Greene's tragic sense is predominant. As he matures the tragic is leavened by the comic.

2.1 Andrews, the principal character in Greene's first novel *The Man Within* (1929), has the makings of a tragic figure. He comes to a disastrous end trying to bring about a happy reconciliation of the opposing selves in him and also of the opposing forces of good and evil. By the time the good appears to have won and the evil to have been mastered, events beyond his control intervene and lead him to suicide. Greene's religion has not yet irradiated this first work in full measure but then his awareness of the unique duality in the nature of man is quite evident here.

2.1.1 Contradiction, duality, and conflict, inner or outer, are the essence of tragedy and Greene's intention is of a tragic purport in the first novel. The theme is one of the 'divided mind' and a split-personality. The epigraph, meant to highlight the theme, is from Sir Thomas Browne's *Religio Medici* (Part II, Sec. 7): "There is another man within me that's angry with me" which indicates the nature of the conflict. A knowledge of the source from which the quotation for the epigraph is taken gives the reader richer and wider associations. The sentence is from the spiritual autobiography of the philosopher-physician. The original passage reads:[1]

> The Devil that did buffet Saint Paul, plays methinks with me: let me be nothing if within the compass of myself I do

---

1. L.C. Martin (Ed); *Religio Medici and Other Works* (Oxford, Clarendon Press, 1964), p. 64.

> not find the battel of Lepanto, passion against reason, reason against faith, faith against Devil, and my conscience against all. There is another man within me that's angry with me.

Andrews is a schizophrenic torn between his sense of duty and natural cowardice; his aspiration for an ideal and his attraction for the sordid; his love for an innocent and aidless girl and lust for a slut. Ultimately the struggle resolves itself into the age-old conflict between good and evil. T.S. Eliot in *The Cocktail Party* makes one of the characters refer to a similar conflict between the willing self and the tougher self. In a way Stevenson's *Dr Jekyll and Mr Hyde* is a fictionalization of the same split-personality. Marlowe in *Dr Faustus* dramatizes a similar situation in the life of Doctor Faustus, the good angel and the bad angel of the protagonist advising and tempting him severally. Andrews succumbs to evil. By the time he determines to exorcise evil, events beyond his control occur and drive him to the single sad solution of suicide.

2.1.2 Greene makes us believe that Andrew's guilt is rooted in an unhappy childhood. The lines from AE (George Russell)[2]

> *In the lost boyhood of Judas*
> *Christ was betrayed*

had a powerful influence on Greene's mind and the theme of childhood is presented consistently in the light of this statement.[3] The betrayal psychology, summed up in the phrase "Judas-complex", is a favourite Greene abstraction, which stands for the idea that the cruelties and betrayals of adult lives are born in childhood. The guilt is rooted in childhood and Andrews is the victim of an unhappy childhood. The burden of his self-justification is in the self-pitying interior monologues, the source of resonance lying in this statement:

> "It's not a man's fault whether he is brave or ugly. It's all in the way he's born. My father and mother made me. I didn't make myself." (p. 52)[4]

Unhappy childhood vitiates his existence and leaves him a twisted being. The pale-faced, flower-loving mother, and the cruel bullying

---

2. Greene quotes these lines in two places: in his autobiographical essay 'The Lost Childhood' and in his short story 'The Basement Room'.
3. See my articles, "Graham Greene and the Burden of Childhood", in *The Literary Half-yearly*, Vol. XIX, No. 2, July 1978.
4. Page numbers refer to *The Man Within* (Penguin edn. 1971).

father leave unerasable memories on the young mind[5] and cleave his being into two. At school where his father sends him to be taught Greek and Latin[6], Andrews never forgets how his father had beaten his mother, his father's conceit, his ignorance and the beastly bullying ways. One possible reason why the educated boy with the delicate if ineffectual sensibility embraces, on hearing about his father's death, Carlyon's offer and becomes a smuggler, perhaps, is to find the happiness of freedom. But the freedom he thinks he has acquired does not hold out happiness for long. The past becomes a dead albatross round his neck; the bully he dreaded and hated continues to pester and haunt him in his own self as well as in the form of the comparison his mates would make between him and his dead father half-a-dozen times a day. His thirst for revenge is intensified. The motive behind the Judas-complex in him and the consequent first betrayal is his vengeful reaction to not being thought important[7]. The schism in him is occasioned by a moral sense but he fails to work out a synthesis of the multipartite schism. His education sharpens his moral sense and contributes to his awareness of finer values. He tells Elizabeth:

> "Oh I am not like you. I don't know what I want to do. You are so clear, so terribly sane. I'm twisted." (p. 182)

Greene sought to show the conflict in the principal character primarily through the theme of the divided mind. A victim of inaction, Andrew's ratiocinative, self-pitying self-communion fails to cover up his inability to act on a principle. The musings of the contorted and unintegrated mind on the one hand and the sensitive heart on the other, as well as the widely dispersed authorial guidance convince the reader of the sincerity of Andrew's quest for a solution. The reader does not fail to notice that Andrews is acutely aware of, and occupied with, the reasons for the split though he is not engaged in devotedly exerting himself to find a way of securing a harmonious synthesis. The consciousness of the rift weighs him down. He knows that he is "embarrassingly made up of two persons, the sentimental, bullying, desiring child and another more stern critic." (p. 24) There are multiple voices in him clamouring for sole attention,

---

5. Greene Tells us in his autobiography: *A Sort of Life*: "Unhappiness in a child accumulates because he sees no end to the dark tunnel." (Penguin edn. 1975, p. 78).
6. "It was so that", Andrews tells Elizabeth, "he could brag about it. He was proud of his success." p. 71.
7. Carlyon tells Elizabeth "he is a kind of Judas".

those of the 'stern critic', his heart and his reason. The author tells us :

> Always while one part of him spoke, another part stood on one side and wondered 'Is this I who am speaking? Can I really exist like this?' (p. 24)

After returning from the assizes at Lewes where he gives his deposition (not so much to keep his promise to Elizabeth as to pay the price for sleeping with the slut) he confesses to Elizabeth:

> "It is as though there were about six different people inside me. They all urge different things. I don't know which is myself". (p. 188)

2.1.3 The primary thing Andrews fights against is his bullying father and then the evil he experiences, 'the terror of life', the fear of soiling himself again and again. When he thinks that he has successfully exorcised his father in him he feels happy and at peace. The author comments:

> His father's had been a stubborn ghost, but it was laid at last, and he need no longer be torn in two between that spirit and the stern unresting critic which was wont to speak. I am that critic, he said with a sense of discovery and exhilaration. (p. 220)

What is deficient in Andrews is an understanding of the essential human condition. Passion, one is bound to conclude, confounds his reason. He does not come up victorious fighting against his self-pity and exaggerated romanticism. Self-pityingly he attributes his cowardice to factors beyond his control: "I didn't make myself." He justifies his sneaking letter telling the Judge "And unless I did something it [the bullying, the unsavoury comparisons] would have gone on for always and always. And I wanted to show these men that I was someone to be considered, that I had the power to smash all their plans." (p. 140) Again, in his relations with the two women in the novel, Elizabeth and Lucy, he wavers between a romantic ideal and degrading lust. After fouling himself with Lucy reason dawns on him again but very soon he falls into the slough of despond. The author comments: "He felt no fear of death, but a terror of life, of going on soiling himself and repenting and soiling himself again. There was, he felt, no escape. He had no will left." (p. 167). With an over-developed sense of self-pity he tells himself that there is no justice if a man is to be judged by the instinct and appetites of his body and not by the strength of the dream.

Ironically enough it is Elizabeth who is not given to cerebration that finds out what is fundamentally wrong with him: "Why do you always make little of the good you do and make much of the bad?" (p. 188). He broods overmuch on the schism between the willing spirit and the weak flesh: "... Only my heart wants to be good. But my body, this common, ordinary body, doesn't care for that ...(p. 201) (Fielding's Tom Jones too says that his indiscretions are sins of the flesh and not of the mind.) This goes on till the end of the book. The author describes the cerebration at length when Andrews goes to fetch a pail of water leaving Elizabeth alone in the cottage:

> Only when he reached the well did the prick of conscience bring him to a halt. Elizabeth was alone in the cottage. 'But she has the gun', he told himself and awaited for long seconds a shot which did not come. 'Go back, go back, go back', heart told the flinching flesh, but that single reiterated message was ineffective beside the host of reasons that the fearing body had at its call. 'They are looking for me, they will not hurt her', he told himself, and again. 'Carlyon must be there. He'll see that she's safe,' and last of all feeling of irritation against the responsibility forced on him. 'It's her fault,' he told himself. 'Why did she send me for water? Why did she leave the door open? She was asking for trouble. If she'd any thought for my safety, she'd have been more careful.' After all if he ran back now what could he do? He was unarmed. (pp. 205-6)

It is in this way that the sharp edge of realization gets blunted and Andrews fails to rise to the occasion, and to act. Consoling himself with false reasoning he goes to fetch some help and finds on his return Elizabeth dead, having stabbed herself with the knife he left behind before going to Lewes.

2.1.4 Andrews is really 'twisted' as he calls himself. 'You *are* twisted," (p.182) says Elizabeth to him. He fails to see the good in himself. He views the act of leaving the knife as an act of "sentimentality", while Elizabeth finds in it an act of bravery. Even after Elizabeth's death he continues to be a romantic fool playing an idealist's role and trying to come out as a moral and spiritual hero. His failure lies in his incapacity to have an insight into the dichotomy of the spirit and the flesh. Even his death which he must have thought a heroic sacrifice is a romantic illusion. As the reviewer in *The Times Literary Supplement*[8] puts it: "To the not psychoanaly-

8. June 20, 1929, p. 492.

tically minded it must seem incredibly perverse that Andrews should believe himself saved and not damned by his final exploits."

2.1.5 Andrews is the first exemplification of Greene's tragic sense though in his introduction to the Uniform Edition of the book Greene called the story 'embarrassingly romantic' and stated that he permitted its re-issue as a sentimental gesture towards his own past, 'the period of ambition and hope'. Andrews is an interesting combination of romance and melodrama. There is a good deal of romanticizing and dramatizing of his actions and motives. He is all the time subtly suspicious of theatricality though it is only once there is a specific mention of it. When Elizabeth asks him to go, Andrews says that it is easy for her to laugh; then follows this:

> But am I really bitter, the other part wondered. Am I play acting still? And if I am play acting, is it I who act or another who pulls the strings? But what a Pharisee the other part of him was. It never took control of his mouth and spoke its own words -- hard, real, trustworthy. It only stood on one side and listened and taunted and questioned. So now it let his voice go on, genuine or play acting dictated. (p. 24).

The author comments a few paragraphs later, "It was only to suit his own ends or his own self-pity that he allowed himself the pleasure of melodrama. (p. 26). But it is only in a rapid survey that Andrews may be seen as belonging to the realm of melodrama with his romanticizing and psychologizing. The problem of evil (which Andrews sees but does not quite understand and come to terms with-- the psychologizing self-pity only deepens the fog and mist in the book), the basic preoccupation in Greene, is here along with his persisting themes of lost childhood and betrayal. The unsavoury, unattractive details of external reality which are to become a compelling part of the tragic vision begin to get attention as in the description of lust and unbridled lechery. The seediness and squalor are yet to gain in intensity to merit becoming the aspects of reality in terms of the tragic sense of degeneracy and futility. The tragic sense is exemplified in the portraiture of the idiot boy Tim whom Andrews puts in the dock. Towards the end of the book he appears again only to be beaten by Andrews:

> The mouth creased with a cry of pain, the hand loosed the rein, and for a brief instant before the darkness separated them, Andrews saw a dog's eyes raised to him in pain and puzzlement. (p. 211).

This inexplicable pain and puzzlement recur time and again symbolizing the human condition and the terror of life. Andrews is a figure fraught with tragic potentiality analogous to Hamlet though he does not have the stature of Hamlet. Hamlet, of course, is involved in greater issues than one would expect in a novel like *The Man Within*. There are similarities between Hamlet and Greene's Andrews -- innate goodness, self-questioning and delay. Within its narrower compass, Andrew's is a painful tragedy of a person who does not engineer into play the positives in him.

2.1.6 *The Man Within* is a "tentative book"[9] but it does show the promise of a gathering tragic vision. Andrews brings himself to the point of illumination though the process of his self-discovery has been tortuous. The confusion in his mind is an outcome of the division in him, an explicit tragic device. Janet McCann writes:

> It may well be, of course, that Andrews has brought himself to the pinnacle of self delusion rather than of self-knowledge.[10]

But the ending of the book makes Greene's intention clear:

> Slowly his hand stole out unnoticed on an errand of supreme importance, for between the two candles there was a white set face that regarded him without pity and without disapproval, with wisdom and with sanity. (p. 221)

'The errand of supreme importance' is a way of ultimate reconciliation and the 'stars' and 'candles' hallow the act. Andrew's death by suicide is an attempt to prove his sincerity in trying to resolve the conflict by means of his love for Elizabeth which helps him discover his true self. In *The Comedians* (1966) the narrator Brown who considers everyone around him a comedian playing a role comments on the Negro lover of his mother when he ends himself after her death: "Perhaps he was no *comedien* after all. Death is a proof of sincerity."[11] Brown, of course, might be talking with his tongue in his

---

9. 'A writer,' Somerset Maugham declares in these "Variations on some Spanish themes", 'is not made by one book, but by a body of work. It will not be of equal value; his books will be tentative while he is learning the technique and developing his powers; and if, as most writers do, for it is a healthy occupation, he lives too long, his later work will show the decline due to advancing years, but there will be a period during which he will bring forth what he had it in him to bring forth in the perfection of which he is capable.'
 (quoted by Graham Greene in 'Some Notes on Somerset Maugham', Collected Essays (Penguin edn. 1970) pp. 148-49.

10. Janest McCann, 'Graham Greene: The Ambiguity of Death', *The Christian Century*, October 14, 1977)

11. Graham Greene, *The Comedians* (Bantam edn. 1967), p. 242.

cheek. A mass of contradictions as it is, the world presents more occasions for comedy than tragedy and it is only the very naive who choose death as a solution. Though there is very little of the explicit comic irony in the conclusion of *The Man Within*, one suspects a subterranean comic sense in the very way the conclusion is contrived: the suicide is a 'lamentable comedy'. Here is a simple intensification of a tragic situation which leads the hero into a self-devised duplicity with the result that the tragedy misses its mark.

2.2 Greene states: "In *Stamboul Train* for the first and last time in my life I set out to write a book to please."[12] Asked what he thought his contribution to modern novel was, the popular novelist in the 'entertainment' replies: "Surely that's for somebody else to state. But one 'opes, that it's something of this sort, to bring back cheerfulness and 'ealth to modern fiction. There's been too much of this introspection, too much gloom. After all, the world is a fine adventurous place." Greene's books, novels or entertainments, are never free from the serious note. In his essay on Edgar Wallace, Greene narrates how, as a very young writer, once he sat next to Arnold Bennet at a dinner. While he was taking a glass of "something" from the waiter (he was too frightened to refuse), Mr Bennet remarked sternly "A serious writer does not drink liqueurs." Greene adds in parenthesis that it doomed him, so far as liqueurs were concerned, to a lifetime of abstinence. He does belong to the class of serious writers not only by virtue of his "abstinence" but also by virtue of the vision that he has in him to project. *Stamboul Train* (1932), in the projection of the novelist's vision, is not very different from *The Man Within*. In the long railway journey are involved a girl on her first assignment in a chorus group, a businessman on his way to financial supremacy, an ill-fated revolutionary who is never to realize his dreams in action, a journalist pursuing her quarry of a sensational headline story, a thief and murderer on the run, a girl on her vacation, an elderly couple and a popular novelist who has been a shop assistant. The small circlets of individual worlds and individual existence intersect and the book represents the portion where the circlets intersect. Dr Czinner is the most meaningful character in the book, a committed man in marked contrast with the rich and successful Jew Myatt. He is a failure, a victim of his idealistic illusions. He is typical Greene hero, again a victim of unhappy childhood, like Andrews. In the framework of the plot, he is the famous Communist agitator who disappeared from Belgrade five

12. Greene's Introduction to *Stamboul Train* in the Collected Edition, 1974.

years earlier at the time of the Kamnetz trial. He is on the way home to Belgrade where he plans an upheaval. While he is on the way his followers prematurely ignite the upheaval and fail. He is shocked and disappointed. A bad Catholic (like several others to come in Greene's fiction), he has lost his belief in God. "He had blown that candle (of his own faith) out with his own breath, telling himself that God was a fiction invented by the rich to keep the poor content..."(p.114)[13] He had a clear conscience but he has not that faith which once he had. The author tells us:

> He remained aware nevertheless of the mixture of his motives; they had only begun to worry him since his knowledge of failure all his vanities, meannesses and small sins would have been swept to darkness in the thrill and unselfishness of victory ... My regret for what I have done is not less now than then, but I have no conviction that there is anyone to forgive.· He came near to sneering at his last belief: Shall I go and confess my sins to the treasurer of the Social-Democratic party, to the third-class passengers? (pp. 118-119)

Czinner, we are told, looks more like seventy than fifty-six and he shares the family likeness of all Greene's principals: the self-analysis, introspection, self-pity and self-condemnation. His death and Grunlich's escape: that is life. The author comments:

> It amused him to consider how hard it would be for a Christian to reconcile the escape with his own death ... He wanted to say to them that he had been damned by his faithfulness, that one must lean this way and that, but he had to listen all the way to their false comfort, falling and falling in great pain (pp. 190-191).

2.2.1 An intense realism is an essential part of the projected vision in Greene's fiction. While the train passes 'on the bank beside the line a man and a woman lay embraced.' While Janet Pardoe and Coral Musker emanate from the stock of harpies, the sex-starved bitch Anna and the Lesbian Mabel Warren deepen the squalor of the scene. Like Andrews in *The Man Within* Josef Grunlich overhears a bit of conversation:

> A door on the first floor was open, and as he passed he heard the petulant woman's voice: "Such drawers, I tell you. Well, I'm not the President's daughter, and I said to her,

13. Page numbers refer to *Stamboul Train* (Penguin edition, 1964).

> give me something respectable. Thin! You've never seen." (p. 91)

Coral's sense of chastity is modern. Modernity and virtue appear to be irreconcilable. With her exaggerated sense of modernity she painfully loses her virginity for a first class ticket. The authorial comment follows:

> Novelists like Ruby M. Ayres might say that chastity was worth more than rubies, but the truth was it was priced at a fur coat or thereabouts. One couldn't accept a fur coat without sleeping with a man. If you did, all the old women would tell you the man had a grievance. And the Jew had paid ten pounds. (p. 47)

The total picture of the seamy side of life presented in the book reveals Greene's tragic sense which is the outcome of his general attitude towards evil.

2.2.2 *Stamboul Train* is prefaced with a sentence from George Santayana: "Everything in nature is lyrical in its ideal essence, tragic in its fate and comic in its existence."[14] What emerges as the final impression about the book is the novelist's understanding of the nature of things in general. At this stage, Greene appears to be convinced of the truth of the philosopher's statement. He attempts to illustrate the truth of the statement in this novel. Dr. Czinner is 'amused' to consider how hard it would be for a believer to reconcile himself with the escape of the guilty and the suffering of the good. Greene underlines here for the first time the illogicality, absurdity and the farciality of existence.

2.3 The value of a literary work depends upon the sense of life which is infused into it. *It's a Battlefield* (1934) makes manifest Greene's tragic sense in yet more clear-cut terms than are evident in *The Man Within*. Puzzlement as much as a sense of waste of positives makes for the tragic sense and the Assistant Commissioner and Conrad stand for these diversely tragic impressions. The theme of the novel, mainly, is the injustice of human justice as in Kyd's *The Spanish Tragedy*. The title of the battlefield is opposite in the context of the violence and confusion of the events described in the book. The epigraph from Kinglake's Eothen not only emphasizes the motif but also gives the novel a form and a shape:

> In so far as the battlefield presented itself to the bare eyesight of men. It had no entirety, no breadth, no size, no

14. See my article, 'The Significance of Epigraphs in Graham Greene's Novels,' *The Journal of English Studies*, Nov. 1978.

> shape, and was made up of nothing except small numberless circlets commensurate with such ranges of vision as the mist might allow at each spot. ... In such conditions, each separate gathering of English soldiery went on fighting its own little battle in happy and advantageous ignorance of the general state of action, nay, even very often in ignorance of the fact that any great conflict was raging.

2.3.1 The epigraph indicates in a way the confused state the poet describes in "Say not the Struggle naught Availeth"; each combatant is compared to a small circlet and is ignorant of what happens elsewhere. Jim Drover, a bus driver, kills a policeman without meaning to do so and his execution or reprieve becomes a political question. The various efforts of his wife, Milly, his brother Conrad, and several others are frustrated in that each fights in a small circlet. For the Assistant Commissioner, who has been asked by the Minister to send a report on the possible effect of an execution or reprieve, things appear to be out of joint and he fails to see a purposeful pattern in life. Asked by Caroline Bury, what he hopes for, the Assistant Commissioner gives a bewildered reply and a long authorial comment follows:

> It was the nearest he could come to conveying his sense of a great waste, a useless expenditure of lives: Caroline in the operating theatre, Drover on the scaffold, the girl on Streatham Common, Justin in Spain. It was impossible to believe in a great directing purpose, for these were not spare parts which could be matched again. (p. 204)[15]

Drained by tropical fevers in the East and on the verge of retirement, the Assistant Commissioner is perplexed by the course which justice takes in the world. He tells himself time and again that he has nothing to do with justice. Morality, he thinks, is no more his business than politics. The remark of the minister's secretary "It's a battlefield" sticks in his memory. He finds the minister's tactful act an evasion of responsibility. He regards himself as a mercenary paid to fight. In terms of the battlefield motif:

> He was like a general left alone at head quarters to study the reports from every unit; they littered his desk. But he was not sheltered in a chateau behind miles of torn country; the front line was only a hundred yards away. (p. 136)

15. Page numbers refer to *It's a Battlefield* (Heinemann & Bodley Head, 1970.)

When Caroline, the influential society lady, tries to influence him, he tells her what has come to him at the moment in a flash of insight:

> "The truth is, nobody cares about anything but his own troubles. Everybody's too busy fighting his own little battle to think of the, the next man. (p. 201)

But he is aware of a greater pain than 'hope and fear in a cell'. When he takes the minister's secretary to show him round the prison he thinks of hell:

> "he had a dim memory that someone had once mapped hell in circles, and as the search-light swooped and touched and passed, and the bell ceased clanging for Block C to go to their cells, he thought, 'this is only the outer circle'." (p. 18)

If the course of human justice is incomprehensible to the chaplain, even divine justice is much the same to the Assistant Commissioner·

> The chaplain said, 'I can't stand human justice any longer Its arbitrariness. Its incomprehensibility.
>
> 'I don't mean, of course, to be, to be blasphemous, but isn't that very like, that is to say, isn't divine justice much the same?' (p. 214)

2.3.2 The confused Assistant Commissioner is introspective and self-searching. He convicts himself of cowardice. He tells himself towards the end of the book that he hasn't the courage of his convictions, he is not indispensable to the Yard, it is the Yard which is indispensable to him. He is puzzled by the contradictions like the criminal shaving every day carefully before his trial. The authorial comment runs:

> It was these contradictions, the moral maxims which did not apply, that made it impossible for a man to found his life on any higher motive than doing his job. A life spent with criminals would never fail to strip the maxims of priests and teachers from the underlying chaos. (pp. 82-83).

The contradiction presents itself poignantly only a moment later in the murderer who happens to be a member of the Salvation Army. As a man, the Assistant Commissioner (we are not told his name) has a sense of justice which he keeps private:

> ...in his secret life, he was troubled by the slightest deviation from the strictest justice. (p. 173)

But in his official life he relinquishes responsibility telling himself that justice is not his business. He wants to be content doing his job but that contentment does not give him either peace or satisfaction. He is conscious of his own battle for self-preservation:

> ...I am only a paid servant, doing what I am told; I am no more responsible than a clerk is responsible for the methods of the business he serves... It often occurred to him that he was less the general in control than the private soldier fighting in a fog, like the men at Inkerman, in a fury of self-preservation. (p. 177)

The solution which occurs to him is one of withdrawal into being an outsider. He acquires a kind of negative quality and the positive one of charity (like his impulse to help the beggar) gets dried up. There is a deeper confusion in him than meets the eye - his clumsiness of expression and half-finished sentences are symptoms of a deep befuddlement.

2.3.3 Conrad, the convict's brother, is exposed to injustice while for the Assistant Commissioner justice is only a notion. If puzzlement and incomprehensibility are exemplified in the officer, betrayal and failure find exemplification in Conrad. But it *is* all a battlefield; he fights in his own circlet, battling for retaining his own position as a chief clerk and staving off the possibility of being ousted by the director's nephew. Securing his brother's reprieve is necessary, he loves his brother, but then there is his own battle. Conrad is a much more complex version of Andrews in *The Man Within*. All that he succeeds in doing is to buy some flowers for his sister-in-law (they cheated him, the flowers were overblown) and later a revolver without exactly knowing what to do with it. He tries to console Milly and he goes to the extent of taking her to bed. He falls into a fit of disgust at the thought of going back to her. When Kay speaks of her going to bed with Surrogate he muses: "How simple she seemed to make it. ... it was only love which complicated the act". (p. 131) He too realizes that justice is a matter of influence. "We ought to use influence," he tells Milly.

> He heard the world humming with the voice of generals and politicians, bishops and surgeons and schoolmasters, who knew what they wanted, who knew what everyone wanted: 'I have a cousin, an uncle, a nephew, a niece' the world humming and vibrating with the pulling of wires. (p. 64)

Given to introspection and self-condemnation like Andrews, he convicts himself to lust, incompetence and ingratitude. He is more pathetically ineffectual than Andrews. His act of sleeping with his brother's wife is not mere lust as Andrew's sleeping with Lucy is. He wants to draw strength from it:

> When a cannibal ate his enemy, he received his enemy's qualities; courage or cunning. When you lay with your brother's wife, did you not become, receiving the same due as he received, something of the same man, so that if you were weak, you became strong, clever, you became stupid? For an instant last night he had been his brother, he became capable of killing a man. (p. 171)

The author is compassionate and he shows great understanding of the underlying pathos in the act of darkness. He comments: "One of them had injured the other, but it was not their fault. They had been driven to it." (p. 133) The physical exhaustion into which Conrad falls towards the end of the book is a result of his mental fatigue. He tells himself that if he had had enough sleep he would have known the uses of the revolver. With an uncertain mind he follows the Assistant Commissioner and when the latter comes out of his door to watch him across the street he wants to shoot but does not. Later he feels that he has missed happiness for ever in Great College Street. His betrayal of his brother and his abortive efforts to act lead him to an inevitable tragedy. His revolver loaded with blanks, he shoots at the Assistant Commissioner and gets hit by a car.

2.3.4 Conder, the journalist, has a better understanding of the way human justice works. Asked by Jules if Jim Drover is going to be hanged, he tells him:

> "One can't tell." ...They hanged this man and pardoned that, one embezzler was in prison, but the other men of the same kind were sent to Parliament. ...he knew well enough that it was not systematic enough to be called injustice. ..."You can't tell. You've got to try. None of us knows what motives they may have for hanging Drover or for reprieving him. Politics and religion are all mixed up in it." (pp. 36-37)

But the irony of it all is that Jim Drover is reprieved even before the Assistant Commissioner has written his report.

2.3.5 The world which the creative artist in Greene conceived of reflects the tragic sense. It is a chaos of conflicting interests where everyone fights for one's own self but then there is no confrontation between good and evil. The prison, the factory and the office are all mechanical and monstrously impersonal. As if rendered soulless, the characters who act against their respective backgrounds deepen the impression of chaos and futility. It is all a battlefield:

> *Swept with confused alarms of struggle and fight*
> *Where ignorant armies clash by night.*

In the words of Yeats, in a world of this sort, "Things fall apart; the centre cannot hold." What Greene avers tragically is what is stated in Shakespeare's *King Lear*:

> *Plate sin with gold*
> *And the strong lance of justice hurtless breaks*
> *Arm it in rags, a pigmy's straw does pierce it.*

Apart from the portraiture of justice, the tragic sense also inheres in the squalor that Greene portrays with realism. Kay Rimmer, Milly's sister, is a harpy driven by her sexual urges and stands as a representative of broken values. We are told that she never felt more at home than in bed or in a man's arms. Her lovers, the Communist Surrogate as well as the Catholic Jules, belong to the world of lust and lechery. They are mere brutes without any inquisitiveness about the deeper values. Happiness is a rare thing in the world and for these people pleasure is a cheap substitute.

2.3.6 *It's a Battlefield* thus portrays a world of lost values where justice and fairplay run away. The themes of the battlefield and justice are overlaid with the theme of puzzlement. The total effect of the books is one replete with a sense of bewilderment and confusion at the lack of a design and direction in the scheme of things. From *The Man Within* to *It's a Battlefield* it is a rapid stride towards a more convincing and more realistic presentation of man's helplessness in the face of a confusing uncertainty about the very fabric of justice, human or divine. There is a deepened tragic sense here, as compared to *The Man Within* since it is not merely a divided mind or conscience that causes the agony, but a large scheme of things suggestive of a metaphysical dimension. The comic vein figures prominently to deepen the tragic sense in this book. To begin with there are flashes of irony, a comic mode, in witty pieces of dialogue:

> "Is it the prison?"
> "A school for girls." (p. 12)

and

> "And that building there" the secretary asked. "What's that? Billiard room? Gymnasium?"
> "Execution shed," said the warder, quickening his step..." (p. 15)

Then there are several instances where the absurd, another comic mode, surfaces. Mr. Surrogate's Communist idealism not affecting his easy lecherous life, the Salvationist murderer's religious zeal, Conder's pursuit of the man who fled without paying his landlord, Conrad's pursuit by the Assistant Commissioner with a revolver loaded with blanks are all absurd. So is the act of Jules in making a spill of the petition he meant to send for Jim's reprive. Conrad's death in the circumstances described is grotesque in the light of his total harmlessness and befuddled ineffectuality. That life itself is absurd is realized by Mr Surrogate. When Caroline Bury says, "My dear Philip, don't be so defeatist. The whole thing is absurd and therefore something can be done," we are told, Mr Surrogate opened his lips to protest against this assumption that life of its nature was not absurd, but cleared his throat instead." (p. 91) *It's a Battlefield* reflects not merely the tragic sense. Greene seems to have become aware of a sense of the comic growing in his world-view by registering the impression that life is absurd.

2.4 In *England Made Me* (1935) the tragic vision is exemplified through the motifs of exile and alienation with a tangle of ill-realized incenstuousness of a hopeless pair of twins superimposed on it. The real significance of the novel lies in the portrayal of the tragic vision and the 'terror of life.' The world that is made manifest here is one of human fecklessness. The evil of life is very much here in a situation that is poignantly dramatized. To the much recurrent theme of depraved innocence is added the theme of exile. Greene holds that childhood impressions, specially the unhappy and painful, leave permanent scars and that growth into adulthood is a process of corruption. Krogh, the successful millionaire, as well as Anthony and Kate are corrupt. If wealth corrupts Krogh, it is insecurity that corrupts the twins. The tragic sense of life intensifies and reaches a further depth in this book for it is as much a tragedy of alienation and exile as it is one of depraved innocence, perhaps the taint of Original Sin. Here are a set of rootless exiles, whom Pryce-Jones calls declassé. The theme of justice (which runs as an undercurrent in *The Man Within* and is central to *It's a Battlefield*) is left behind; her are a set of thieves. Kate, the central character in the book, realizes it: "There is honour among thieves. No brotherhood in our boat. Only who can cut the biggest dash and who can swim." (p. 256)[16] If the life or death of Jim Drover becomes a question of politics in *It's a Battlefield*, the life or death of Anthony becomes

16. Page numbers refer to *England Made Me* (Heinemann & Bodley Head, 1970)

here a question of contributing to Krogh's success or prospective failure. The media for the portraiture of the tragic vision are the rootless wanderers, stealing a living here and there as best as they could. "All the world owes me a living", the quotation from Walt Disney chosen to be the epigraph, makes this clear. The characters are not merely rootless: they are soulless, mere clods of clay without the questioning sense or moral awareness. The exile motif is made plain in the very first chapter. Anthony goes on moving from place to place leaving one job after another. He tells Kate "I've promoted myself, It's Harrow" sporting a Harrow tie. At the end we are shown that he has given himself another promotion: 'Captain' Farrant. The series of charming lies, the eventual discovery and the moving on is symbolic of fecklessness. Aden, Shanghai, Bangkok, Stockholm -- whatever might be the milieu, Anthony is doomed to fail. Asking for a job is the thing he hated and that alone appears to be his life-work. "I haven't a future, Kate" is his sad but true realization. Kate knows what is wrong with her brother: "... he had a child's cunning in a world of cunning men; he was dishonest, but he was not dishonest enough. (p. 6) The smile which he turns to advantage is a deception; his smartness suspect. Kate knows it: "he carried it with him as a leper carried his bell; it was a perpetual warning that he was not to be trusted." (p. 10) A shabby and seedy adventurer, he knows that he has no future. Of the twins only he has an ever dim perception of respectability. He knows his weaknesses and gloats: "At least, no one can say I'm inhuman ... I may have my faults, but they are human faults. A glass too much, a girl now and then, there's nothing much wrong with that." (p. 91) The reason for Anthony's wordly failure is not that he is not depraved but that he is not depraved enough. Kate realizes the point. "He wasn't unscrupulous enough to be successful. He was in a different class to Krogh." (p. 178) When he tells her that he has given out the news of Krogh's marriage and threatens that he could sell the press the story about Young Andersson, she says that he is too innocent to live. His respectability appears to be awakened by Loo who thinks that his job under Krogh is not the right sort. It is this vague respectability rather than his moral awareness to be away from the incestuous tangle that draws him away from Kate. He knows that his desire to join Loo in Coventry is a mere lech but he tells himself that he is in love with her. He loves his sister no doubt and he tells her: "Love and in love, Kate. There's the difference."

2.4.1 The subtle tragedy that the book depicts lies in the relationship between the twins, in the tangle of the incestuous relationship. The fact that the whole cast is a set of exiles lends the book a special poignancy. The pursuits of all the characters are insignificant in any context beyond the immediate one of making a living in a seedy world. Greene's world-view as can be seen in this book is one starkly depressing and distressingly sad. The characters are pawns in the game of a millionaire aspiring to climb to global supremacy, the millionaire himself being an intellectual moron.

2.4.2 Minty is considered the hero of the book by David Pryce-Jones[17] but to consider him so is to miss the central point of the book. He is an essential minor character. He is a deformed young-old man leading a seedy existence like the spider he has kept trapped under his toothglass. He is shabby, crooked, and pigeon-chested. As elsewhere among Greene's characters he is stunted by the school which runs deep in his system. We are told: 'The school and he were joined in a painful reluctant coition." At odd times he remembers a gang of school boys. His Harrow tie is a harrowing scar on his memory, unforgettable and obstinate. His physical deformity is the poison that has vitiated his outlook on the world. He hates women ('tawdry little creatures, other people's sisters') he hates sex and he hates the body. But he has a secret devoutness with which he remembers St. Zephyrinus who, he believes, has saved his life. He draws pictures on the dirty glass of the telephone box, several crosses, a head wearing a biretta, a crown of thorns and a halo. The place of after-life, for him, is the place of no pain, no futures, no sex. His Catholicism is skindeep. He is said to have rushed into a Lutheran church with 'the passion and dry-mouthed excitement of a secret debauchee.' Doomed to his seedy existence on the monthly remittance and the occasional pickings from newspapers he is no better than the spider but he has his own moments of secret happiness, like the ones when he discovers that Farrant is sporting a Harrow tie, when he makes a scoop of the card which the reporter drops while throwing flowers to the actress, or when he bluffs Captain Gullie that Farrant is a Mac Donald. The spider symbolizes the existence of not only its captor but also of the whole cast. It is withered by its cunning - 'now blown out to twice the size, it was drooping to the floor on its invisible thread.' Minty, we are told, has withered like the spider, "blown out no longer to meet contempt; his body stretched doggo in the attitude of death, he lay there humbly tempting God to lift the glass." His religion is not a better alternative than the spurious respectability in Anthony. Anthony, Kate and Minty are in the same plight. Anthony can never find a

17. David Pryce-Jones, *Graham Greene* (Edinburgh: Oliver and Boyd, 1970) p. 26.

satisfactory job or a woman who holds his affection; Kate knows what she wants but she knows that it is a forbidden one and Krogh, for all his millions, is spiritually dead. His brilliant material progress from the bed-sitting room in Barcelona to the Palace in Stockholm dehumanizes him. Human relations baffle him and he is ill at ease with people: "One couldn't plan a human relationship like a graph of production." He is as dead as a robot, intellectually. Poetry embarrasses him for he cannot understand it. "Correctness was the quality he most valued: the correctness of a machine, the correcntess of a report. It was necessary at times, he thought, coldly, for men to go with women as it was necessary at times not to disclose certain assets, to conceal the real value of certain shares..." He cannot understand people and still less can he estimate the worth of a friend. Hall's fidelity is incomprehensible to him and he asks Kate when Anthony chose him ties: "Why does everyone give me things? I can buy them, can't I ?". Nationality and individuality are dim in him. Even the images of his mother and his own childhood no longer have any meaning for him and "he was like a man without a passport, without a nationality, like a man who could only speak Esperanto." In Kate's thought: "He's one of us, fighting for his own security like one of us, he's not the future, he's not self-sufficient, just one of us, out of his proper place."

2.4.3 The central figure among these exiles is Kate who is poignantly aware of her forbidden passion for her brother. The central point of the novel is her incestuous desire.

Greene himself states what the novel is really about:[18]

> The subject - apart from the economic background of capitalism staggering from crisis to crisis - was simple and unpolitical, a brother and sister in the confusion of incestuous love.

The very first sentence strikes the keynote: "She might have been waiting for her lover." Kate is Anthony's elder by half an hour. For her "he was all the experience she had missed." She knew his weaknesses, that sad ineffectuality and that pathetic pushfulness and bonhomie as well as that charm. Every move of his is calculated to charm and deceive. Eking out a living is as much a problem for him as for everyone else in the book. But it is Kate alone who is aware of the hopeless desire in her considering the 'respectability' and 'conventionality' in him. "He was weakness, but weakness could be very strong."

18. Introduction to *England Made Me*, Collected edition, 1970.

2.4.4 The climax of the sad drama in her mind comes in her interior monologue where she ruminates on Blake's Tiger. The incident of Anthony winning a blue vase and a tiger is cleverly juxtaposed. Besides adding a brilliant touch of characterization -- Anthony's ineffectual, flashy type of success -- the tiger that he wins, in a shooting booth sets off Kate's train of thought. The tiger that he wins, Blake's tiger and Anthony himself coalesce in Kate's consciousness -- the cheap prize for an unerring marksmanship, the mystery of God's creation, and the object of Kate's incestuous lust are all fused in one:

> Tiger burning bright in Tivoli, immortal eye, the hand against my side, feet touching mine; even there the women watched him when he turned, when he smiled, what shoulder and what art, to see the rockets throwing down their spears. I saw the girl's eyes on him in Gottenburgh, the badly-painted face, the trust, the innocence, the cunning that asks to be betrayed. Those we love we forget, it is those we betray we remember. Did she smile her work to see? He said: "I'll give her the tiger."... Don't be afraid. Don't hesitate. No cause of fear. No bulls on this exchange. The tiger bright. The forests. Sleep. Our bond. The new redemption. And we rise. And God who made the lamb made Whitaker and Lowenstein. ... No bulls, the tiger and the lamb. The bears. The forests. Sleep.... (p. 77)

The forest, the stock exchange and the redemption eddy in Kate's thoughts and the events in the book bear testimony to her having followed the inner voice: 'Don't be afraid. Don't hesitate." Even before this interior monologue, quite early in the novel we see she hints at the idea:

> "Tony, Kate said, "if you weren't my brother ..." She let the sentence drift away over the crumbs and the soiled glasses unfinished, meaningless. What was the good? (p. 23)

When she comes dangerously to the point and tells him that she loves him we are told that "he wriggled uncomfortably before her complete comprehension." When she tells Anthony of her plans for their being together he gets her idea in a flash of insight:

> It occurred to him with astonishment and pain that he had been wrong just now, that this after all was love, that he had been damned to bad luck from birth: she was his sister. He was conscious of a great waste, a great disappointment. Nobody, he thought, can put it over her own looks, she's got class, she's swell. The inadequate words fumbled at his heart. ... He wanted to tell her that he loved her, but a light

> went on above a door, and she said : "That's Erik. He's ready for you." (p. 93)

Both Kate and Anthony know what goes on in each other's mind and the author tells us several times that they might have been a married couple for thirty years:

> She was aware, having shared his thoughts for more than thirty years, felt his fears eat in her own body, of his incalculable nerves. (p. 6).
>
> They had as many memories in common as an old couple celebrating their thirtieth anniversary. (p. 8)
>
> Like an old married couple of thirty years. A silver copper what d' you call it golden wedding. (p. 12)
>
> The memories one turns over like an old couple after thirty years, who have shared first love, first hate, first drink, first treachery... (p. 76)
>
> "You know too much, Kate. One might as well be married," (p. 170)

When Erik proposes marriage to her she tells him that Anthony will be pleased and dwells on his name. The author comments: "... she might have been marrying Anthony and not Erik at all; ..." (p. 174) When Anthony tells her that she does not love Krogh and wonders why she is marrying him, she comes to the point:

> "I love you."
>
> That's not the point." He was worried; he was muddled; he said something under his breath about 'children' blushed with self-consciousness.
>
> Kate said, "I'm sterile. You needn't be afraid,"... (p. 177)

Desperate when she is told by Anthony that he would leave her for that girl Loo, Kate becomes furious:

> "I knew this was happening," Kate said, "I had my warning. Aren't I dressed to kill? But I expected it over the coffee. Your favourite lipstick, flowers," she said with her first sigh of weariness, "A sister's handicapped, isn't she? I can't appeal to you like Loo can; you'd think it indecent to say you loved me." 'But I do love you, Kate. Honestly." "Like that? In that tone? This is how I love you Anthony." He put his hand on their desk amiably, conciliatingly; she drove at his fingers with her penknife. He whipped them away."
>
> "For heaven's sake, Kate ..."
>
> "The lover's pinch, Tony, which hurts and ---" (pp. 229-30)

Towards the end of the book, in the eerie poker game scene (a memory of Greene's childhood reading as stated in 'The Lost Childhood') she thinks of a last plan to retain Anthony and be together with him and in this context comes the passage which unmistakably reveals her spiritual impasse:

> She knew she might have prayed; the temptation was there, to fall back on eternity, on other people's God, ... But she wouldn't pray, she took what comfort and credit she could for not praying; it wasn't that one disbelieves prayer: one never lost all belief in magic. (pp. 242-43)

Kate, in her emotional distress, thinks of magic and prayer along the same lines. There is no religious solution available to her, or even a moral one. There is a point in the novel where she thinks that Tony has all the moral consciousness that they could summon between them. The theme of incest is given a wider dimension with the rehearsal in the hotel where the Swedish translation of Shakespeare's play is rehearsed. The scene serves the double purpose of bringing the plot to a denouement while at the same time projecting the tragic vision. The point of the play is mentioned with slickness:

> With whom the father liking took
> And her to incest did provoke.

Even Anthony is plainly disgusted with it: "Frankly, I can't think why the professor's so pleased with the play. It seems vulgar to me." The whole scene is the finest that Greene has written so far. Adultery, superficial lecherous relationships and the suggested incest are portrayed in the whole scene where there is also a perfect fusion of imagery and incident. The professor drops his glasses down the blouse of the girl, goes on his knee and fished them out. Anthony takes a girl out for a walk and kisses her 'prehensile' lips:

> She was like a bundle of thin ropes when he kissed her; she pulled his hair with fingers which smelt of pear-drops; her mouth was sweet, synthetic, a laboratory fruit. She asked, 'Is that your sister?'
> 'Yes.'
> 'I don't believe you. You're in love with her.'
> 'Yes.'
> 'You naughty boy, "she licked his chin. 'You need a shave darling,' lick, lick mechanically like a match against emery-paper. (p. 211)

This mechanical response of the blonde (she has Garbo in her voice) and the unnatural urges of the twins are juxtaposed to heighten the effect. On one side there is the theme of incest, on the other there is synthetic, mechanical passion. Adultery and lechery are strikingly presented in this scene and Anthony's drowing is cleverly hinted at. "If there is one thing I hate, it's drowning," Anthony says and he is said to have 'walked' into the lake in the fog. "They are too rough that threw her in the sea." The tragic sense is made also poignantly manifest in Young Anderson who gets beaten for reasons incomprehensible to him:

> "I don't understand", he said, his breath bubbling on his lips, "understand, don't understand." (p. 218)

He is very much like the idiot boy Tims who gets beaten at the end of *The Man Within*. The Assistant Commissioner in *It's a Battlefield* repeats the statement "I don't understand." The objective correlative Greene finds for the experience of tragic befuddlement is found in the motifs of exile and incest. *England Made Me*, largely because of its theme of incest, makes us think of John Ford's play *'Tis a Pity She's a Whore* (1633). Both Ford and Greene have been exploring a somewhat novel theme in the process of their sensitive exploration of human nature. Just as Ford's play is in the pity, Greene's novel centres on the tragic uncertainties that cloud the thinking of the doomed pair. *England Made Me* is a significant document in cultural decadence, which is an aspect of the tragic vision Greene projects in the first phase of his career.

2.4.5 Shorn of nobility the tragic gets reduced to disaster and Anthony's death is a disaster. There is something grim and ominous in Hall's loyalty which should normally appear a virtue. Minty is too shabby and egotistic to be considered either a tragic or comic figure despite his physical deformity and seedy existence. *England Made Me* illustrates the tragic sense, though with a lesser intensity, and the comic sense in Greene, at this stage, is not much in evidence except possibly in Minty.

2.5 *A Gun for Sale* is a thriller in the 'cloak and dagger' genre. Raven is hired for a murder and paid in stolen currency. Angered by the double-crossing he pursues the agent. The central themes of the book are once again 'pursuit' and 'betrayal' Raven, the sensitive criminal, is a victim of betrayal. He is double-crossed by everyone: by Cholomondeley who hires him, by Dr. Yogel, the shady abortionist, and by Anne, the 'skirt' whom he believes against his habit and conviction. Raven is aware of a rough kind of justice and he is haunted by the sentiment of 'honour among thieves'. When he sees the nurse at Dr. Yogel's at the telephone he takes the knife from the doctor and hacks at the wire. He feels hurt by the fact that he has been betrayed by the lawless, by people who did not belong inside the legal borders. When, at the jumble sale, he spies Anne's bag in the hands of an old woman, he is worried. He feels that it is evil, people of the same class preying on each other. He does not trust anybody, still less a 'skirt'. He knows that women hate him for his harelip. What puzzles him is Anne's loyalty. When at the first chance she does not go to the police he begins to trust her. A few moments before his death he realises that Anne has betrayed him.

2.5.1 As has been noted earlier it is part of Greene's understanding of life that childhood memories leave powerful and indelible impressions: a man's personality is conditioned by the impressions of childhood. About Raven we are told:

> He had been made by hatred; it had constructed him into this thin smoky murderous figure in the rain, hunted and ugly. His mother had borne him when his father was in goal, and six years later when his father was hanged for another crime, she had cut her own throat with a kitchen knife; afterwards there had been the home. He had never felt the least tenderness for anyone; he was made in this image and he had his own odd pride in the result; he didn't want to be unmade. (p 67)[19]

As Greene himself writes, Raven belongs to the world of wounds and guilt. Son of a criminal and a social detritus, his childhood has been to him a single horrifying memory of his mother who hacked and sawed at herself with a kitchen knife. When he tells Anne that he has fixed up for himself a hiding place where there are a number of sacks he remembers his home and the way his mother committed suicide:

> She hadn't even troubled to lock the door: that was all she cared about him. He'd done some ugly things in his time, he told himself, but he'd never been able to equal that ugliness. (p. 104)

Unhappy childhood, early experience of horror, physical deformity, injustice and double-crossing -- these corrupt the outlook of the helpless man. He knows that he is a criminal, but he knows how his

19. Page number refer to *A Gun for Sale*, Penguin edn. 1965.

mind is made and how his impulses have been conditioned. Even the Christmas season does not evoke in him anything pleasant:

> ... He stood there with his face against the glass waiting for somebody to deny *that* reasoning, staring at the swaddled child with a horrified tenderness, 'the little bastard', because he was educated and knew what the child was in for, the damned Jews and the double-crossing Judas and only one man to draw a knife on his side when the soldiers came for him in the garden. (p. 91)

Life having not offered him anything pleasant or happy, he is a bitter example of the terror of life. In the shed when Anne tells him that in the event of a war babies shall have to die for gas-masks have not been invented for them, he says stubbornly:

> "The poor ones'll be lucky. And what do I care about the rich? This isn't a world I'd bring children into." She could just see his tense-crouching figure. "It's just their selfishness," he said. "They have a good time and what do they mind if someone's born ugly? Three minutes in bed or against a wall and then a lifetime for the one that's born. Mother love, "he began to laugh, seeing quite clearly the kitchen table, the carving knife on the linoleum, the blood all over his mother's dress. (p. 124)

These musings of the contorted mind are voiced aloud by the writer with a view to compelling possibly our comprehension, and hopefully, our compassion for the stunted man. All that Raven wants is a neat and expeditious death. When at least he is shot down the author comments:

> Death came to him in the form of unbearable pain. It was as if he had to deliver this pain as a woman delivers a child, and he sobbed and moaned in the effort. At last it came out of him and he followed his only child into a vast desolation out of him. (p. 174)

2.5.2 Raven's death is not far from being tragic in spite of his being a hired murderer. His introspection and self-analysis make him of a piece with Greene's principal characters. He knows what it is to be ugly. We are told: "he had been fed the poison from boyhood drop by drop: he hardly noticed its bitterness now." (p. 15) He tells Anne: "If a man's born ugly, he doesn't stand a chance. It begins at school. It begins before that." (p. 45)

2.5.3 There is not a single lovable character in the book, Apart from Raven being a criminal and so being not very pleasant, everyone else is an unpleasant person. Anne and Mather, for all their love, could not understand each other, Davis is a lecher and glutton, Sir Marcus a demoniac money-maker. There is nothing in life that is happy, pleasurable and lasting, or so this book makes it appear. Life is drab, dirty and gross. Anne is not a virgin and she makes no secret of it. ("It's no good looking for eggshell if that's what you mean", she tells Mr. Davis). The policeman expects to find couples even in December under the hail. The old woman at the soiree picks up a brassiere and tests its elastic with a malicious grin because it is made for someone young and pretty with breasts worth preserving. Ruby is prepared to have a good time with anybody if she gets so much as a meal. In a queue Raven observes a young man who looks at *Plasirs de Paris* furtively. The world is peopled with criminals, clergymen who have lost their vocation, lechers, brothel-keepers and abortionists. The entertainments Greene devises are subterfuges for comedy through their melodrama and horror. The very grotesqueness of the characters, like the Lesbianism of Mabel Warren and the harelip of Raven, and the melodramatic quality of the situations like the firing near the goodsshed and the gas-masks drill and its consequences point to a world at odds with itself. The world-view projected here is not tragic in the sense that there is no nobility in it. The world with all its sordidness reduces itself to a farce. Things seem to have come out of a wry joke, sometimes cruel and sometimes meaningless.

2.6 In his essay "Henry James: The Religious Aspect" Greene quotes T.S. Eliot:[20]

> It is true to say that the glory of man is his capacity for salvation; it is also true to say that his glory is his capacity for damnation. The worst that can be said of most malefactors, from statesmen to thieves, is that they are not men enough to be damned.

The lapsed priest in Greene's play *The Living Room* says: "Hell is for the great, the very great. I don't know anyone who's great enough for Hell except Satan." *Brighton Rock* (1938) is Greene's attempt to show a character hell-bent on damnation. As R.W.B. Lewis remarked it is a "deliberately pitiless book and partly because it aims, by moving beyond human pity, to evoke the far, faint light of

20. Graham Greene, *The Lost Childhood and other Essays* (Penguin edition 1966), p. 38.

an incomprehensible divine mercy. It is a pitiless book, with disaster lurking in every syllable."[21] The central character is Pinkie, a boy of seventeen, the leader of a Brighton race-course gang. Fred Hale comes to Brighton as Kolley Kibber hiding his cards which is part of the advertising technique of a newspaper. The person who finds the card and identifies the person as the one whose photograph is published in the paper is entitled to a cash prize from the paper. Hale who betrayed Kite, the leader of a gang, and who had been responsible for his murder meets with Ida Arnold, a blousy tart, and vaguely expresses his fear that he is going to be killed. The girl at Snow's knows that the person who left the card under the cloth on the table is not Kolley Kibber and Pinkie marries her to stop her from giving evidence. Later he proposes a suicide pact. Meanwhile Ida discovers that Pinkie is the murderer. Goaded into action by her ouija Board, she pursues Pinkie. The bottle of vitriol which Pinkie keeps with him breaks on his own head when he is about to attack the policemen with it. He steams and burns and in the appalling agony falls off the cliff into the sea.

2.6.1 With the publication of *Brighton Rock* Greene's preoccupation finds a frame of reference that is explicitly religious. Roman Catholicism gives meaning and coherence to the narrative for the first time in this novel. The religious dimension of the novel makes manifest a perfect balance of the two sets of antinomies: Right and Wrong to which Ida Arnold commits herself, and Good and Evil represented by Rose and Pinkie. The richest spiritual experience might be possible even through experience of Hell and Greene finds a perfect objective correlative in the hellish aspects of Brighton. Human existence becomes meaningful not in the insignificant day to day living but in a total commitment.

2.6.2 *Brighton Rock* is a tragedy showing the progressive deterioration of Pinkie ultimately resulting in his damnation. Greene himself told an interviewer that Pinkie is a man who goes to Hell.[22] The incidents are so cleverly manipulated the setting so carefully laid and the atmosphere so convincingly evoked that one tends to believe that the book makes for a set of conditions contrived to make out a case for the possibility of grace even under extreme circumstances besides asserting the validity of free will.

2.6.3 Pinkie is deeply evil. In his case the ordinary human categories no longer describe what he is and he is a link between

21. R.W.B. Lewis, "The Trilogy of Graham Greene", *M.F.S.* Vol. 3, No. 3.
22. *The Times*, October 29, 1951, p. 103.

human and the cosmic or ontological evil. His grey eyes, we are told, are "ageless" and that they had an effect of heartlessness like those of old women in whom human feeling had died. They are touched with "the annihilating eternity from which he had come and to which he went." Pinkie's eyes and face are described with significant care. His young-ancient poker-face told nothing. It is unhappy childhood, as in Andrews's case, that vitiates the boys' existence and poisons his being though childhood is not the only factor in his case. The school dividers condition his cruelty and he wonders "What would be the fun if people don't squeal?" He is always haunted by the nauseating memories of his parents' sex-act and the act repels him. Hate is the element in which he lives. He hates music. He is ruthless in his cruelty and he is dreaded by the members of the gang. He brushes aside the possibility of Heaven with a 'Maybe'. 'Hell lay about him in his infancy', is the author's comment besides the remark that he couldn't picture any eternity except in terms of pain. The key to Pinkie's mental conditioning lies in his horror of the sex act:

> It was Saturday night. His father panted like a man at the end of a race and his mother made a horrifying sound of pleasurable pain. He was filled with hatred, disgust, loneliness; he was completely abandoned; he had no share in their thoughts -- for the space of a few minutes he was dead -- he was like a soul in purgatory watching the shameless act of a beloved person. (p. 189)[23]

Experience of sex comes to him as a horror very early for him. He tells the assembled wedding party waiting for his bride at the registry office:

> "You wouldn't have known Annie Collins, would you? ...She went to the same school I did," the boy said. He took a look down the grey street and then the glass before *Married Love* reflected his young and hopeless face. "She put her head on the line", he said, "up, towards Hassocks. She had to wait ten minutes for the seven-five. Fog made it late from Victoria. Cut off her head. She was fifteen. She was going to have a baby and she knew what it was like. She'd had one two years before, and they could 'have pinned it on twelve boys." (p. 167)

Everyday Pinkie encounters the passion of Judy and Dallow which is scarcely concealed from the blind husband. To add to this the actual

23. Page numbers of *Brighton Rock* refer to the Penguin edition, 1968.

act always haunted him with nausea. Sylvie, her skirt drawn up in the Lancia, repels him. When a prick of sexual desire disturbed him he wonders: "Was there no escape - anywhere - for anyone? It was worth murdering a world." After the humiliation of being beaten by Colleoni's men he takes refuge in a garage and when he comes out he finds: "The new raw street cut in the chalk was empty except for a couple pressed against each other out of the lamplight by a wooden fence. The sight pricked him with nausea and cruelty." (p. 110) Pinkie finds grossness everywhere: in the news agent's shop, in the glass shelter, in the note left by Judy, in the wedding presents Cubitt gives him; in short, everywhere. This is in turn Greene's view of the seedy world, his special vision of a wasteland, without values, without hope and without God. The most significant symbol of evil is the principal character, Pinkie. He boastfully rationalizes his propensity to self-willed evil: "Perhaps when they christened me the holy water didn't take. I never howled the devil out." The evil of Pinkie is more than just the result of his childhood and his upbringing, both matters pertaining to social environment. It is psychological. The choice made by Rose is also deliberate. The choices are irrevocable. While Pinkie chooses Evil and damnation, Rose chooses to be with him and be damned rather than follow Ida's advice and be right with her. When Ida pleads with her to leave Pinkie, Rose does not answer. We are told: "The two words [Right and Wrong] meant nothing to her. Their taste was extinguished by stronger foods - Good and Evil. The women could tell her nothing she didn't know about these - she knew by tests as clear as mathematics that Pinkie was evil - what did it matter in that case whether he was right or wrong".(p. 201) When she sees people coming back from the Mass, she does not envy them for if they had had their salvation she had Pinkie and damnation. When Ida finally asks her to take precautions against pregnancy she thinks: "A child ... the child would have a child ... it was like raising an army of friends for Pinkie. If they damned him and her, they'd have to damn them too. She'd see to that there was no end to what the two of them had done last night upon the bed: it was an eternal act." (p. 202)

2.6.4 Set against the eternal absolutes are the ephemeral values of Ida - Right and wrong. At one level the novel is a theses on commitment. Rose and Pinkie are committed to one set of norms, Good and Evil, while Ida is committed to Right. For Ida 'an eye for an eye' and justice are more important than anything else and hence her pursuit of Pinkie. Greene presents in this novel the gaping schism between the two sets of values. Good and Evil are eternal absolutes while Right and Wrong derive from the matrix of social justice and decorum. Pinkie is a malefactor and he is - if at all a man is capable of being damned - damned. But Greene believes that he has existence in terms of eternity. Accepting Evil and embracing it amounts to a belief in ultimate things, since the belief in the devil presupposes the belief in God. But Ida's complacent attitude towards the adequacy of human beings belongs to the lower order of mankind's thinking. As Anthony Burgess writes[24] "In a sense, it is better for one's soul to pursue evil rather than right. It is a dangerous paradox, but it produced a superb novel." The principals in the previous novels, Andrews, Dr. Czinner and Anthony Farrant are failures but Pinkie being a Roman Catholic gave Greene the opportunity to equate his guilt and anxiety with the consciousness of sin. His angst is a sign of his self-willed estrangement from Grace. Pinkie is a tragic character whose fall is not from a mundane eminence but from Grace.

2.6.5 Greene seems to hate lukewarm, spineless creatures who are not alive to the ultimate values. For him Heaven and Hell are facts of moral theology and of man's moral experience. Human beings have to validate their existence by a clear-cut unambiguous choice. Ida Arnold is treated with evident irony and deep-seated contempt. She is like one of those creatures in Dante's Vestibule of the Futile whom "mercy and justice scorn both". Eliot, who shares this view with Dante that people who do not have positives are as good as dead, embodies this truth perhaps in the women of Canterbury, 'Partly living and partly dying', in *The Murder in the Cathedral* and also the crowd over London Bridge. "Sin is behovely", says St. Juliana of Norwich. That is to say that a life of indifference is as good as death and we can even say, even a life of evil is better than a life of indiffference. The spiritually asleep do not wish to wake up. Hence the poet calls April the cruellest month. Greene hardly hides his contempt for Ida; the old vulgarized Grecian name, her blousiness and her flair for 'good living' are for him destestable. "Death shocked her," we are told, "life was so important. She was not religious. She did not believe in heaven hell, only ghosts and ouija boards." (p. 36) Her verve for life is purely carnal: "It's going to be exciting, it's foing to be fun, it's goint to be a bit of life." (p 45) she tells herself about the hunt. The razor sharp sentences cut out her figure unmistakably: 'Camaraderie, good nature, cheeriness, hell like

24. Antony Burgess, *The Novel Now* (London: Faber, 1967, p. 61.

shutters before a plate glass window.' (p. 78) "She liked a good time, her big breasts bore their carnality down frankly", (p. 81) "Her big breasts, which had never suckled a child of her own, felt a merciless compassion." (p. 122) Barnacled with pieces of popular wisdom her words and actions are in tune with her blousiness: "You're young (she pleads with Rose) you'll have plenty of fun - if you don't let them get a grip on you. It's natural. Like breathing. Don't take away the notion that I'am against love." (p. 124) She reminds us of Anthony Farrant who consoles himself saying that God does not mind a bit of indulgence, 'human nature', now and then. But Ida's complacency amounts to spiritual pride which is really shallowness. She argues with Rose that people do not change and with a characteristic note of omniscience advances a theory regarding human nature in a phrase which actually provides the title of the novel: "Oh no, they don't. Look at me. I've never changed. It's like those sticks of rock: bite it all the way down, you'll still read Brighton. That's human nature." (p. 200) Greene makes a sharp distinction between the socio-ethical plane of Right and Wrong symbolized by Ida and the religious - spiritual plane of Good and Evil symbolized by Rose and Pinkie. The religious categories of Good and Evil are the transcendent ones. Ida takes upon herself the responsibility to see justice done. "If you believed in God, you might leave vengeance to Him, but you couldn't trust the one. Vengeance was Ida's." (p. 37) It is her instincts which guide her, not God. Greene makes fun of Ida when he tells the reader: "She carried her air of compassion and comprehension about her like a rank cheap perfume." When she tells Rose that she doesn't want to let the innocents suffer Greene comments: "the aphorism came clicking out like a ticket from a slot machine." Greene is ironical of her middle-class morality: "... no one could call her really bad -- a bit free and easy perhaps, a bit Bohemian. ... She knew what was Right and what was Wrong. God didn't mind a bit of human nature". When Rose whispers to her "Confession ... repentence" she tells her "That's just religion. Believe me. It's the world we got to deal with." (p. 200) But for all we know Ida's moral world is filled with transparent vulgarity and shallowness. It is in contrast with the heroic world of Rose where the latter does not hesitate to bear the burden of both Good and Evil.

2.6.6 Pinkie's damnation is self-chosen. He is committed to evil both by temperament and deliberate choice. The cement play ground and his home condition his being. He trailed the clouds of his own glory after him. Hell lay about him in his infancy. He has been brought up a Roman Catholic and he has been in the choir. Once he even vowed to be a priest. But then cruelty is his habit and nature. Even with this, the idea of confession nags at his mind now and then: "A moth wounded against one of the lamps crawled across a piece of driftwood and he crushed it out of existence under his chalky shoe. One day, one day, ... One confession when he was safe to wipe out everything." (p. 110) Snatches of liturgy come up to his mind: Dona Nobis pacem. When they come to his mind he feels a faint nostalgia "as if for something he had lost or forgotten or rejected." The phrases are meaningful. Pinkie has lost his childhood, forgotten good and rejected Grace. He is not quite dead to the goodness in Rose but he is more aware of his own Evil and he thinks that they are made for each other. He sees himself at a particular stage in the book as a full grown man for whom the angels wept. In his cunning union with Good he is moved by a kind of sensuality. But the sex-act scares him. He wonders: "Like cats. It was the commonest game under the sun -- why be scared at what the dogs did in the streets." (P. 181) He wants to be attracted to eternity by commiting himself to Evil. He says "Credo in unum Satanum". We are told: "the ribs of his body were like steel bands which held him down to eternal repentence." (p. 182) He knows that Rose loves him but whatever love meant, he feels that it is not an eternal thing like hatred. He is fascinated with damnation and there is a crucial passage where we find him looking for it in the most unlikely place and getting disappointed. After the marriage and the consummation, in the morning he goes out for a walk. "In an alley between two shops, the old woman sat upon the ground; he could just see the rotting discoloured face: it was like the face of damnation. Then he heard the whispers: 'Blessed art thou among women', saw the grey fingers fumbling at the beads. This was not one of the damned; he watched with horrified fascination: this was one of the saved." (p. 190) The distinguishing mark of Pinke's evil is his demonic pride. He tells Dallo with "dreary pride": "I suppose I'm real Brighton -- as if the single heart contained all the cheap entertainments, the Pullman cars, the unloving weekends in gaudy hotels, and the sadness of coition." (p. 222) There is pride again in what he tells Rose: "Perhaps when they christened me the holy water didn't take. I never howled the devil out." Though he is conditioned by his childhood he is not merely a symbol of corrupted innocence. It is his pride which makes him the leader though he is the youngest of the gang. To him the word 'murder' conveyed no more than the words 'box' 'giraffe' 'collar'. His zealously guarded virginity has something arrogantly ascetic about it. When at last he gives way to the last human weakness and 'graduates' in it an infernal pride overtakes him. In the context of his Catholic faith it makes him live in utter disregard of the forces of Good. With pride goes a habitual, brutal cruelty. "A leather jacket buzzed up the pane and the Boy caught it in his hand. It vibrated like a tiny watch spring in his palm. He began to pull off the legs and wings one by one. 'She loves me,' he said, 'she loves me not. I've been out with my girl, Spicer.'" By clever juxtaposition Greene makes clear Pinkie's contemplated treatment of Rose. But their union is significant. Without Rose Pinkie is just a silly, proud, cruel brat. With his union with Rose begins a terrible drama of the religious experience of Hell. It is only with her at his mercy -- an object of his inbred hatred of Good -- that he is capable of real damnation. Pinkie is nothing without her, bringing to our mind "For without me, you can do nothing" (St John XV, 5). Pinkie's great certainty of Hell comes in direct confrontation with Rose's faith in Heaven which he brushes aside as a mere possibility: "Oh, maybe, maybe." (p. 54) Rose tells him that she would not get sleep if she did not attend the Mass he tells her arrogantly: "I don't care what you do ... I don't go to Mass". There are several moments in the book where the two stand as eternal opposites tempting each other. On the chalkbank, before their marriage Rose tells him that she is a Roman Catholic and in a cavalier fashion he brushes aside her remark:

> 'I don't take any stock in religion. Hell -- it's just there. You don't need to think of it -- not before you die.'
> 'You might die sudden.'
> He closed his eyes under the bright empty arch, and a memory floated up imperfectly into speech. 'You know what they say -- "Between the stirrup and the ground, he something sought and something found."
> 'Mercy.'
> 'That's right: mercy'. (p. 92)

Reference has already been made to Pinkie's confidence that a single confession when he is safe would wipe away everything. But prayer eludes him at the time of the direst need. He knows that repentence is necessary and he does not have the energy to repent. He dies without God, burnt with the vitriol of his own hatred.

2.6.7 From a choir boy and an intended priest to a juvenile delinquent and a murderer, from Hale's murder to the final death by burning, Pinkie's tale has the swift pace and inevitability of tragedy, if not the culminating perception of the tragic hero. Whether one would agree that Pinkie is a tragic hero or not is only an academic question but Greene's vision of life as it emerges from the book is tragic. The horror of hell is studiously depicted by Greene. The climate of evil pervades the book. The Brighton and Pinke of the book are a region and a state of mind. So are the other characters. Ida, Sylvie and Judy are enough to illustrate the point. Nelson Place is a hole and in the hole, we are told, were murder, copulation, extreme poverty. There is crude passion everywhere. Out of the lamplight by a wooden fence Pinkie finds lovers pressed against each other. Judy wishes good luck to Pinkie while washing her brassiere. A match an old man strikes in a glass shelter lights a man and a girl cramped in a corner. The newspapers announce sordid news: "Assault on a school girl in Epping Forest". The lawyer Prewitt with his horrible indigestion and twisted mind is an imbecile inhabitant of the lust ridden wasteland; 'I watch the little typists go by carrying their little cases. I'm quite harmless. A man may watch. My God, how neat and trim." (p. 212) He tells Pinkie: 'The worst that can happen to you is you'll hang. But I can rot." (p. 211) He it is who brings out the Hell theme explicitly with patent poignancy. He amazes the Boy who watches him with fascination and fear by saying: "You know what Mephistopheles said to Faustus when he asked where Hell was? He said: "Why this is Hell, nor am I out of it.'"

2.6.8 In retrospect Greene himself appears to notice the growth of unsuspected dimensions in the book. He writes in his introduction to the new Collected Edition in 1970 "*Brighton Rock* began as a detective story and continued, I am sometimes tempted to think, as an error of judgement" and further "probably emotion has been astir before that, or how was it that a book which I had intended to be a simple detective story should have involved a discussion, far too obvious and open for a novel for the distinction between good and evil and right and wrong and the mystery of the appalling strangeness of the mercy of God .." The book is labelled an 'entertainment' at first but later it becomes a 'novel' since it has aspired towards the condition of tragedy. If the entertainment is Ida's and the tragedy is Pinkie's, Rose too must become a tragic figure. Her love for Pinkie is an exemplification of Greene's obsession with tragic love. The waiflike heroine is a favourite type with Greene and there is an intense pathos and irony built around Rose's devotion. Her innocence, though theologically it does not amount to virtue, it being a passive quality, has something angelic about it. She agrees to take the leap suggested by Pinkie in the cleverly explained suicide-pack but then it is her cowardice that saves her. Death scares her: "The evil act was the honest act, the bold and the faithful -- it was only lack of courage, it seemed to her, that spoke so virtuously .. She hadn't been afraid to commit mortal sin -- it was death not damnation which was scaring her." (p. 244) By a curious inversion the act of "cowardice" saves Rose from the act of endless despair and ultimate damnation; but in so far as it does so, Rose is miraculously saved from being a monster that Pinkie turns out to be.

2.6.9 If the tragic hero's fall in classical tragedy is from worldly eminence, Pinkie's in this novel is from Grace. In the final analysis Brighton Rock is the vehicle for Greene's exposition of the problem of evil in a world that has strayed into regions of godlessness. It is a remarkable achievment for sheer delineation of the artist's vision of the tragic aspects of the 'terror of life'. The vision is one of violence, brutality, squalor and evil. The imagery aids the impression and keywords like 'hell', 'poison', 'war', 'soured virginity' contribute to the total effect of the picture. The central metaphor is that of the battlefield. "It was like the map of a campaign marked with flags". (p. 201) "She was like a chariot in triumph -- behind were all the battalions -- right is right, an eye for an eye." (p. 233) "The woman's laughter was like defeat." (p. 227) "She was like a figure-head of victory." (p. 247) Pinkie tells Rose what he feels about life: "I'll tell you what it is. It's a jail, it's not knowing where to get some money. Worms and cataract, cancer. You hear'em shrieking from the upper windows -- children being born. It's dying slowly." (p. 229) The girl with the severed head on the railway line, adultery, violence and grossness everywhere, that is human life. We recall Greene's remarks in his travel book:[25]

> To-day our world seems peculiarly susceptible to brutality., There is a touch of nostalgia in the pleasure we take in gangster novels in characters who have so agreeably simplfied their emotions that they have begun living again at a level below the cerebral ... It is not, of course, that one wishes to stay for ever at that level, but when one sees to what unhappiness, to what peril of extinction centuries of cerebration have brought us, one sometimes has curiosity to discover if one can from what we have come to recall at which point we went astray.

2.6.10 *Brighton Rock* marks the end of the first phase of Greene's work as a novelist. The Catholic belief, the ineradicable sense of sin,

25. Graham Greene, *Journey Without Maps* (London, Heinemann, 1936), p. 10.

seems to give Greene the necesary formula to build up the tragic sense. A Catholic, with his rigid code, cannot find excuses for escape; he moves between two clear polarities: salvation and damnation. Besides the Catholic overtones becoming explicity and prominent, Greene's fiction from this point onwards gathers momentum in successfully mingling the comic with the tragic. Exaggeration is a device in comedy and the exaggerated insistance on the creed of Satan, the megalomania which totally controls Pinkie, his obsessive preoccupation with sex-aversion and his criminality make him a grotesque monster. Any amount of concession cannot succeed in making him human. The monstrosity is carried to the limit of absurdity and the final impression that Pinkie leaves is that of a grotesque creature. His professions to the vocation of the evil give rise to an ambiguity and one feels whether such a monstrosity which has strangulated all pulsations of Good can succeed at all and lend itself to transfiguration. In so far as Pinkie becomes a grotesque figure, he inevitably belongs to the world of farce. The exaggeration, the farciality and the absurdity in Pinkie get him closer to the Vice of comedy. There is also the surrounding comedy of Ida and her ways. There is a blurring, as though deliberate, of the tragic focus by a constant exaggeration and melodrama. If Ida is treated ironically, Pinkie is almost given a cynical treatment. The two orders are heterogeneously juxtaposed as comic extremes as it were. The unconscious comic sense of Greene seems to play havoc with a situation which would have been almost a perfect tragedy. The novel seems to fail aesthetically because it seems to fall between two stools: it seems to slip between the Scylla of sombre tragedy and the Charybdis of exaggerated comedy. Though this was originally classed as an 'entertainment', the tragic develops such an intense polarity that it almost breeds its own opposite, it becomes a grotesque tragedy and spills into the comic.

Chapter 3

The Novels of the Second Phase

> *The truth is seldom tragic, for human beings are not made in that grand way. The truth may be sad but truth is nearly always grotesque as well.*
>
> *Graham Greene*

3.1 The comic vein which surfaces in *Brighton Rock* becomes dominant in *The Confidential Agent* and mingles with the tragic sense. The intermingling is artistically subtle and effective. *The Confidential Agent* deals with a melodramatic plot. There is a hunt in which the hunter and the hunted reverse their parts. The subject is the machinations of two rival political gangs in an unnamed country to secure coal from England for the civil war at home. The agents are called simply D. and L. In this melodrama of Kafkaish psychological realism, the focus is on D. He is a victim of shell-shock and the whole action is seen through his eyes. His psychological state is authenticated with frequent reminders of his past, his traumatic experiences and his delicate flair for literature. He is a lecturer in Romance Languages. He has discovered Berne MS of the Song of Roland which reestablishes Oliver and makes the story a tragedy.

3.1.1 The war leaves D. a psychological wreck. We are told: "He carried the war with him" and "bombing planes took flight from between his eyes, and in his brain the mountains shook with shell-bursts." (p. 10)[1] The war conditions his mind. "You couldn't live six months in prison expecting everyday to be shot and come out at the end of it anything else but a coward." (p. 22) "... You Couldn't be buried in a bombed house for fifty-six hours and emerge incredulous of violence." (p. 32) Next to the war, it is his academic life that makes him what he is. "Years of academic life might make one a good judge: it didn't make one a good executioner." (p. 140) "He might be a good judge, but he would never make an executioner. War toughened you but not to that extent: he carried around his neck like a dead albatross the lectures in Romance, the Song of Roland; the Berne MS." (p. 142) A piece of wreckage in the fractured surface of a war-ravaged world, D. thinks that he carries war in his heart and that he ought to wear a bell like the old lepers

1. Page numbers refer to *The Confidential Agent*, Penguin edn. 1971.

3.1.2 Rose, the peer's daughter, says that she hates melodrama again and again. She calls D. a quixote. When he tells her that he is afraid she retorts: "Don't be melodramatic, I can't stand melodrama" (p. 19) She finds his behaviour funnily mysterious and tells him: "If only you wouldn't be funny. You say these melodramatic things. I've told you — I don't like melodrama." (p. 25) D. muses over his situation and thinks that he is not made for melodrama: "In melodrama a secret agent was never tired or uninterested or in love with a dead woman." (p. 53) Rose comes to apologise for the incident of the car and when D. tells her that he did not really expect to find her there after the incident of the previous evening, she tells him: "I never thought they meant to smash you as they did . It was that fool Currie. But if you start being melodramatic again ... Is it a new kind of confidence trick? Is it meant to appeal to the romantic female heart? Because you'd better know, it doesn't work."(p. 58) Inspite of all her detestation of melodrama it is she who is both romantic and melodramatic. She rings up D. having taken his diary from Currie, arranges a solicitor for him when he is arrested and finally leaves England with him. She and Else are of a piece — victims of the terror that modern life is. As D. realizes, it is not just a question of there being a civil war on. Things are not any finer or better in England. It is the two penny novelette and the cinema that shape both the imagination and phrase of Else as well as Rose. Rose talks fluently about father-fixation and nothing shocks her.

3.1.3 *The Confidential Agent* marks the beginning of the second phase of Greene's writing. In it the comic seeps through the melodramatic in the guise of the absurd. The word 'absurd' itself recurs several times and the sentence from Santayana could well be the epigraph for this book, 'Everything in nature is lyrical in its ideal essence, tragic in its fate and comic in its existence". The situations in the book are absurdly comic. When D. tells Rose that the place where they wish to have dinner is crowded he realizes: "It was absurd, of course, to feel afraid..."(p. 22) He suspects Rose of being an agent and then realizes that the doubt is absurd. He has a premonition when he takes the papers from Else that he is leaving behind something else which needed his care but then he feels that it is absurd. What he thinks absurd fear comes true and becomes a horrible fact. The author sums up the situation in the middle of the book:

> He suddenly realized how absurd it all was. He was a confidential agent employed in an important coal deal on which the fate of a country might depend: she was a young

> woman, the daughter of a peer whose coal he wanted;... a child had been murdered by the manageress of Mr. K. — acting, presumably on behalf of the rebels, although they were employed by his own people. That was the situation: a strategical and political and criminal one. (pp. 130-131)

For D., whose heart is full of pity for Else, the absurdly old girl of fourteen, the newspaper phrase 'Bloomsbury Tragedy Sensation' is absurd. Disastrously it is not a sensation but a tragedy. Lying in Mr Forbes's hotel on being released on bail and wondering whether Forbes is going to Rose or his mistress Sally he feels: "This at last was the end: the sooner he was back now the better: he could begin to forget the absurd comic image which remained fixed in his mind of a girl tossing a bun into the fog." (p. 197) The absurd characterizes several incidents in the book. The assault on D. in the roadhouse a few hours after arrival in Dover and later on the way to London, the Enternationo scene with K. biting his fingers, D.'s journey to Lord Benditch's place in the company of a pasty child of seven and its mother in the underground, the negotiations with Lord Benditch and his colleagues with one of them snoring in the chair and the scene in the embassy, to name a few, have the touch of absurdity. Towards the end of the book, soon after his release from prison, when he finds himself trapped by another enemy, D. is baffled: "God, he thought, could only really be pictured as a joker — it was absurd to have come all this way only to encounter Captain Currie at the end of it." (p. 198)

3.1.4 The tragic sense is evident in the form of the terror of life. Else is a typical product of the twentieth century world of horror and corruption. She is a symbol of corrupted innocence, another incarnation of Annie Collins, of whom Pinkie tells the guests at the registry office. Brought up on the penny dreadfuls and having encountered the rawness of human passion prematurely, she is the fault of the society which has banished innocence. It is not merely a question of poverty. Even the young girl, Rose, the Peer's daughter, has an astounding knowledge of the world. When she tells D. about the Jew who wants to marry her and about his mistress in Shepherd's Market whom she has had aetectives to cover, we are told:

> For the second time that day D. was shocked. He remembered the child in the hotel. You learned too much in these days before you came of age. His own people knew death before they could walk — they got used to desire early-- but this savage knowledge, that ought to come slowly, the gradual fruit of experience ... It was as if the

> whole world lay in the shadows of abandonment. Perhaps it was still propped up by ten just men — that was a pity. Better, scrap it and begin again with newts. (p. 64)

3.1.5 In spite of the violence and the horror that pervades the book it is comedy via the absurd that gets the prominent place. The book has the generic happy ending of a comedy with the confidential agent regaining his trust in the world. The tragic sense of the terror of life is mingled with the comedic overtone and nothing really matters ultimately. This is evidenced in D.'s realization while seeing the blonde heroine weeping more tears: "If we lived in a world, he thought, which guaranteed a happy ending, should we be as long discovering it? Perhaps that's what the saints were at with their incomprehensible happiness — they had seen the end of the story when they came in and couldn't take the agonies seriously." (pp. 65-66) As the saints, perhaps, so the creative artist. The author too can see the end of the story. There is a clinical detachment of the psychoanalyst with which the creative artist probes the personalities of the characters. Viewed in the context of the realization that everything in life is comic in its existence, suffering does not appear a very serious thing.

3.2 *The Power and the Glory* (1940 attains a new height in the intermingling of the tragic and the comic strains. The tragic aspect is projected through the portraiture of the abandonment and desolation that characterize the Mexican state, the background of the novel. Violence, corruption and seediness which have always formed the texture of Greene's tragic vision are very much here. But like the mysterious grace which appears to irradiate the priest's pathetic plight in the novel, the comic strain mingles with the tragic. At a point in the novel the priest speaks of love to the lieutenant of police: "...God is love. I don't say the heart doesn't feel a taste of it, but what a taste. The smallest glass of love mixed with a pint pot of ditch water. We wouldn't recognize that love." An intermingling to a similar extent of the comic and the tragic appears in this novel. The reader feels the author's power reflecting the mysterious operation of Grace and His glory. The comic manifests itself in the portraiture of the chief protagonists in different degrees as well as in the juxtaposition of incident and character.

3.2.1 The tragic sense in *The Power and the Glory* consists in the main in the horror of abandonment. *Brighton Rock* pictures horror but the exaggeration becomes absurd and for that reason comic and the novel does not go higher than an expedition into horror. In *The Power and the Glory* the essential horror of existence is irradiated by the mystery of mysteries, Divine Grace. Greene's awareness of Evil gains a deeper insight and Evil here is symbolically presented in the godless Mexican state where abandonment pervades the climate. 'Abandonment' seems to be one of the key-words in the novel. The dentist, Mr Tench, realizes the extent of his abandonment. His hopes of returning home to England come to nothing with the peso dropping in value. A man in the process of drift (his wife has not agreed even to divorce him), perpetual indigestion and hidden pain in the stomach are his lot. Scorched by the heat of the merciless Mexican sun for fifteen years and trapped in mere vacancy he remembers the watercans in the snapshot he preserves better than his children; his wife's bonnets better than her face. Conditioned by the pain which is his profession he realizes when he had failed to collect the cylinder of ether from the *General Obregon*: "It didn't matter so much after all: a little additional pain was hardly noticeable in the huge abandonment." (p. 18)[2] The priest on the run feels abandoned when the boat which he expects to carry him to safety sails without him. The Mexican father whose wife reads the life of a saint to her children, too, is aware of the abandonment: he tells his wife: "We have been abandoned here. We must get along as best we can. (p. 28) Viewed with the insight given by him by his own sin, the world appears for Padre José an abandoned vessel: "The glittering worlds lay there in space like a promise — the world was not the universe. Somewhere Christ might not have died. He could not believe that to a watcher there *this* world could shine with such brilliance; it would roll heavily in space under its fog like a burning and abandoned ship" (p. 29) An object of insufferable mockery, listening to the derisive voices of the children in the patio 'Come to bed, José' he feels: "there was no respect anywhere left for him in his home, in the town, in the whole abandoned star."(p. 30) To his little son of fourteen the Mexican father explains: "You don't remember the time when the Church was there. I was a bad Catholic, but it meant — well, music, lights, a place where you could sit out of this heat — and for your mother, well, there was always something for her to do. If we had a theatre, anything at all instead, we should not feel so — *left*"(p. 51) In the context of this pervasive abandonment the priest is aware of an 'immense load of responsibility'. He thinks that it is indistinguishable from love. When he comes to the woman who bears his child he entreats her to let him stay there for a few days thinking that if he left the state, "he would be having her too abandoned." (p. 67) The priest feels the

2. Page numbers of *The Power and the Glory* refer to the Penguin edn. 1967

sense of abandonment in the hut where he shelters with the yellow-fanged mestizo. The same feeling comes to him when he is not recognised when arrested for possessing liquor: "In an odd way he felt abandonment because here was no sign of recognition."(p. 136) Back in the banana station, where a girl sheltered him once, but now mysteriously deserted, the priest finds another creature totally abandoned: "And it came: a mongrel bitch dragged herself across the yard: an ugly creature with bent ears, trailing a wounded or a broken leg, whimpering. There was something wrong with her back. She came very slowly: he could see her ribs like an exhibit in a natural history museum. It was obvious that she hadn't had food for days: she had been abandoned."(p. 141) The bitch makes him thoughtful of his own condition: "It was the oddest thing that ever since that hot and crowded night in the cell he had passed into a region of abandonment — almost as if he had died there with the old man's head on his shoulder and now wandered in a kind of limbo, because he wasn't good or bad enough ... Life didn't exist anymore: it wasn't merely a matter of the banana station. Now as the storm broke and he scurried for shelter he knew quite well what he would find — nothing." (pp. 147-48) In the scene where the Mexican woman leaves her dead child with a lump of sugar the priest feels the sense of abandonment all the more sharply. The priest's desolation is underscored by the presence of the dead child: "Shivering and sweating and soaked with rain he came up over the edge of the plateau. There was nobody there — a dead child was not someone, just a useless object abandoned at the foot of one of the crosses: the mother had gone home."(p. 157) The storm transforms the land itself to a state of abandonment; "he was moving alone across that blank white sheet, going deeper every moment into the abandoned land." (p. 157) Padre José's refusal to see him makes the priest feel very unhappy: "His head dropped between his knees; he looked as if he had abandoned everything and been abandoned." (p. 205) With the execution of the priest Mr Tench feels deserted.

3.2.2 Against the background of this vast abandonment an intense spiritual drama takes place. The action entails the priest's self-realization overlaid with a conflict between Catholicism and Marxist secularism. In this state Catholicism is forbidden and priests who do not conform to the new law are persecuted and hunted down. In this land of blazing heat languid vultures always lie in wait for carrion. "A few vultures looked down from the roof with shabby indifference" (p. 7), "the vultures on the roofs looked contented, like domestic fowls, they searched under wide dusty wings for parasites." (p. 12) There are beetles and mosquitoes and the mosquitoes are like people: "In the hot marshy land people bred as readily as mosquitoes." Worms swell the bellies of the children — they eat dirt from the bank. There are snakes too which are both physical and figurative. There is sin, the horror of poverty and their inevitable result, violence, everywhere. The lieutenant of police takes it as a challenge to hunt down the fleeing priest and shoots a few hostages. Abject poverty and misery claim the characters as their own. Mr Tench, the Mexican father, Mrs Fellows, the police chief, known as the jefe — each lives in a world of pain.

3.2.3 Dental decay is used as a suggestive image to underscore the corruption which characterizes the life in the book.[3] Mr Tench looks into the stranger's mouth and says: "Your teeth." One canine had gone, and the front teeth were yellow with tartar and carious.' (p. 14) The mestizo, the Judas figure, has only two teeth left: "canines which struck yellowly out at either end of his mouth like the teeth you find enclosed in clay which have belonged to long-extinct animals."(p. 84) Here is primordial evil indeed. His "yellow canines jut out of the open mouth." The chief of police wails: "My tooth. It poisons the whole of life." (p. 23) Professor Theodore Ziolkowski[4] points out that "it would be possible to set up an elaborate scale of tooth decay in this novel, for virtually every figure is characterized by the state of his dental health." After documenting all the significant references to odontology Professor Ziolkowski concludes: "It needs to be stressed again that the elaborate rhetoric of dental images is meaningful in the larger context of the novel: for Greene is portraying a society that is falling apart with corruption and decay."

3.2.4 Abandonment, squalor and corruption are part of the larger aspect of Evil in Greene's tragic vision. Corruption is as rampant as violence. The more painful aspect of corruption is its presence in the very young. It is not merely the sinful priest and his foil, the lapsed Padre Jose, who are symbols of corruption. Coral and Brigitta are victims of the ubiquitous corruption which is part of the general condition of life. Coral is thirteen; "she was of an age when Mexican girls were ready for their first man." (p. 37) Like Annie Collins mentioned in *Brighton Rock* and Else in *The Confidential Agent*, she too had been corrupted quite early. She tells the fleeing

3. Elizabeth Sewell ("The Imagination of Graham Greene", *Thought*, 29, 1954) points out an 'immoderate' interest in disease and putrefaction in Greene's work, and particularly, an obsession with dental decay.

4. "The Telltale Teeth: Phychodontia to Sociodontia" *PMLA*, Jan. 1976.

priest that she has lost her faith at ten and confronts her mother with the question whether she believed in the Virgin Birth. John Atkins thinks that Coral is pregnant and the following passages might suggest that. When her mother tells her she has got a headache, the little girl says "Of course, I have a little one too." (p. 52) "After half an hour she began to feel tired — she wasn't used to weariness so early in the day: she leant against the wall ... An awful pain took her suddenly in the stomach — she missed a load (counting the bunches taken out to be loaded) and tried to catch up in her calculations: the sense of responsibility for the first time felt like a load borne for many years ... It was a new pain (not worms this time), but it didn't scare her." (p. 54) "The child stood in her woman's pain ... a horrible novelty enclosed her whole morning, it was as if today everything was memorable." (pp. 54-55) We are told,: "she had a false air of impregnability" (p. 33) and the 'false' turns out to be true in an ironical way. Brigitta, below ten, is in the same plight. Her maturity is appalling. She shocks the priest saying: "Pedro says you aren't a man. You aren't any good for women" (p. 81) and the priest feels: "The world was in her heart already, like the small spot of decay in a fruit." (p. 81) It is the decay which makes him pray: "Oh God, help her. Damn me, I deserve it, but let her live for ever" (p. 82) and sharply realize towards the end of the book: "This was the love he should have felt for every soul in the world." (p. 207)

3.2.5 The central dialectic of the novel turns on spiritual faith and Christianity represented by the feckless and aidless priest, himself an abject specimen of the weaknesses of the flesh, and the Godless Marxism which aims at total elimination of poverty. The conflict is made poignant by the extreme devotion of the protagonist, the priest's sense of duty and the lieutenant's zeal for eliminating God. But, of the two, it is the priest who can delve deeper into the mystery that is existence. With a saint's eye he can discover the beauty in the worst evil. In the prison cell, in a corner copulation goes on. A pious woman is horrified and the priest speaks like a saint:

> The pious woman said aloud with fury, "Why won't they stop it? The brutes, the animals!"
>
> "What is the good of your saying an Act of Contrition now in this state of mind?"
>
> "But the ugliness ...".
>
> "Don't believe that. It's dangerous. Because suddenly we discover that our sins have so much beauty."

> "Beauty," she said with disgust. "Here. In this cell. With strangers all round."
>
> "Such a lot of beauty. Saints talk about the beauty of suffering. Well, we are not saints, you and I. Suffering to us is just ugly. Stench and crowding and pain. *That* is beautiful in that corner — to them. It needs a lot of training to see things with a saint's eye: a saint gets a subtle taste for beauty and can look down on poor ignorant palates like theirs. But we can't afford to."
>
> "It's mortal sin."
>
> "We don't know. It may be. But I'm a bad priest, you see. I know — from experience — how much beauty Satan carried down with him when he fell. Nobody ever said the fallen angels were the ugly ones. Oh no, they were just as quick and light and ..." (pp. 130-131)

It is this saintly charity and insight into the nature of things that forms the sum and substance of the ultimate message of the book suggested by the title taken from the Lord's prayer: "And lead us not into temptation, but deliver us from evil. For thine is the kingdom, and the power, and glory, forever." The suggestion can be made that Greene sees in the world of faith and of men this divorce between power and glory to the detriment and erosion of both. Power and glory seem to be in happy unison in the biblical sentence from which the title is taken. In the novel we find a rigid and unyielding dialogue between power and glory as roughly embodied in the police lieutenant and the priest. Without this confrontation and rigidity a union between the two could be envisaged. As it is, in the novel, they are bitterly opposed to each other: Power opposed to glory; glory opposed to power. The power of the state tries to wipe out or even annihilate the glory of the spirit paving the way for the Godless world that Greene shudders to see.

3.2.6 Greene sees in the division of power and glory paradox, irony and cruel absurdity. He sees the world without theological blinkers and elusive paradox and makes the whiskey-priest a mock-heroic figure. The comedy is in his success being a failure. He is deliberately made to look like a clown. These strands of the comic introduced through the characters as well as the incidents make the novel a combination of the tragic and the comic in a complex manner. The priest has a 'tramp's face' and we are told, "he is a little man dressed in a shabby dark city suit." He carries under his arm a novel: 'bits of an amorous scene stuck out.' But when Mr

Tench opens it, he finds Latin which does not appear to belong. In the photograph, the only one the lieutenant has for purposes of identification, the priest is a youngish man. "He sat there, plump, with protuberant eyes, bubbling with harmless feminine jokes." (p. 22) His head has been encircled with ink as if to suggest the mock-halo of a mock-saint. There is something clownish in his tipsiness as when we are told: "He began to pray, bouncing up and down to the lurching slithering mule stride, with his brandied tongue: Let me be caught soon. ... Let me be caught." He had tried to escape, but he was like the King of a West African tribe, "the slave of his people, who may not even lie down in case the winds should fail."(p. 19) The way in which he answers Coral when she says that he does not sound afraid cannot be taken seriously: "A little drink will work wonders in a cowardly man. With a little brandy, why, I'd defy the devil." So saying, we are told, he 'stumbled in the doorway.' (p. 42) Having agreed to hear the confessions in the village he reaches after leaving the banana station, he breaks down from sheer physical exhaustion and once again we discern the comic vein in the villagers' devotion to the priest: "What do you think he has come here for? He is a very holy father. There he is in my hut weeping for our sins." (p. 45) However imperfect he is as a man, he is a priest devoted to his duty in a most unswerving manner. Padre José too is a comic figure in that he sees the absurdity underlying things, pointing them out in his interior monologues. He realizes the absurdity of the situation with the child's coffin in the graveyard. "He knew it was absurd: a life time of self-analysis enabled him to see himself as he was, fat and ugly and old and humiliated." (p. 49) The anonymous priest deliberately unnamed is said to have a buffoon's face. He *is* a buffoon in the sense that with his humility he knows what he is as against what he is expected to be and realizes that he cannot live up to the spiritual heights his vocation expects him to rise to. The humility of the priest depends upon his comic dimension which also keeps him at the human level. He giggles again and again. When Coral asks him to tap three times, two long taps and a short one, he giggles like a child and asks how a long tap is tapped. When he wants to show her a card trick and she tells him that she does not have any cards he giggles again. These are attempts at taking things lightly and the sad comedy consists in their being totally inadequate. When the lieutenant comes and tells him that Padre José's wife would not allow her husband to hear his confession, the priest giggles. "But no sound could have been more miserable than the half-hearted attempt." (p. 205) There is grotesqueness in the disparity between what he aspires to be and what he actually is. The priest himself is not unaware of it. "a damned man putting God into the mouths of men; an odd sort of servant, that for the devil." He is shown as a mysteriously paradoxical compound of the lapsed priest and a vehicle of the mysterious Grace. He knows that only the childless man has the right to call strangers his children. "Someone had inked round the priest's head to detach him from the girls' and women's faces: the unbearable grin peeked out of a halo." (p. 58) The priest wishes to become an actor deliberately and cultivates being an actor: "In the old days he often practiced a gesture a long while in front of a glass so that he had come to know his own face as well as an actor does. It was a form of humility — his own natural face hadn't seemed the right one. It was a buffoon's face, good enough for mild jokes to women, but unsuitable at the altar rail."(p. 59) When the mule suddenly sits under him he scrambles off and begins to laugh. He has a shame-faced lightness of heart when he realizes how five years ago he gave way to the unforgivable sin of despair. The comic mode in operation in the novel lies in the juxtaposition of incident and strokes of characterization like these. While the whisky-priest is committed to his duty with an intense awareness of his fleshly limitations, the police lieutenant is grandiose and humourless. He has the dignity of an idea and he has the makings of an ascetic who subordinates everything to the realization of his goal. He issues orders to search the huts himself standing in the middle of the clearing. "... a turkey cock paced with evil dignity into the centre of the circle, puffing out its dusty feathers and tossing the long pink membrane from its beak."(p. 74) But the whisky-priest has great humility. When his woman turns him out saying that he is no longer wanted by anyone, he tells her that is not what she wants or he wants implying that it is His will. She tells him that a martyr like him would make people mock. The word 'martyr' stings him into further thought. He replies: "It's difficult. Very difficult. I'll think about it. I wouldn't want the Church to be mocked at." The two scenes juxtaposed after one another bring into a sharp focus the comic contrast between the humourless ambition of the lieutenant and the humility of the priest. The moment his case is thrown on the rubbish dump, he becomes susceptible to mockery than ever before, and, as if to prove this, Brigitta accosts him. He prays silently: "O God, give me any kind of death — without contrition, in a state of sin — only save this child."(p. 82) He knows that the mestizo would betray him. Then he thinks of Judas himself and how he is made a comic figure. "... it seemed to him a good thing that the world's traitor should be made a figure of fun. It was too easy otherwise to idealize him as a man who fought with God — a Prometheus, a noble victim in a hopeless war."(p. 91) He is not cut out to be a heroic figure but a comic one. Padre José is another foil to the priest. The priest considers him to be superior to him. "Perhaps Padre José was the better man — he was so humble that he was ready to accept any amount of mockery: at the best of times he has never considered himself worthy of priesthood." In this context the priest analyses his own motives and he thinks that it is only pride. "Even his attempts at escape had been half-hearted because of his pride." Again and again, we find the priest in self-confession making himself more and more humble. And then pity wells up in him. He is reminded of an oilgusher abandoned by some prospectors. Is it God who is the prospector? Is it his own soul that is prospected and left abandoned?"... it wasn't a good enough field apparently to justify further operations, but there it stood for forty-eight hours against the sky, a black fountain spouting out of the marshy useless soil and flowing away to waste - fifty thousand gallons an hour. It was like religious sense in man, cracking suddenly upwards, a black pillar of fumes and impurity, running to waste."(pp 96-97) And then he is forced to hear the mestizo's confession. This leads him to a greater understanding of God; "Man was so limited: he hadn't even the ingenuity to invent a new vice: the animals knew as much. It was for this world that Christ had died: ... — it needed a God to die for the half hearted and the corrupt."(p. 97) With the mestizo's intention of betrayal becoming cruelly evident, he finds God's image in everything: "But at the centre of his own faith there always stood the convincing mystery - that we were made in God's image. God was the parent, but He was also the policeman, the criminal, the priest, the maniac and the judge. Something resembling God dangled from the gibbet or went into odd attitudes before the bullets in a prison yard or contorted itself like a camel in the attitude of sex."(p. 101) Seeing God in the lowliest of the low is the apogee of spiritual evolution. The Bhagavadgita characterizes the spiritually evolved man in a similar vein:"The learned hold as equal in their sight a Brahmana gifted with wisdom and humility, a cow, an elephant and even a dog and a dog-eater too."[5]

3.2.7 The priest's self-realization entails a progress not only through fornication and dipsomania — the path to absolute humility, the most valuable of human acquisitions, paradoxically, entails a shedding of everything — to the point of spiritual nudity. Before his

5. W. Douglas, P. Hill, *The Bhagavadgita* (Fifth Reading, 18) (London: Oxford University Press, 1953), p. 115.

case is thrown on the rubbish dump (p. 79) he is first divested of his clothes. He exchanges his 'dark shabby city suit' for the clothes the peasant wears (p. 44) and then the papers of his ordination crumpled into a ball are dropped by Padre José's wall: "... It was like the final surrender of a whole past."(p. 118) Comic irony is present in the fact that the priest is caught but not caught for what he is wanted for. The end is not to be and the priest is divested of yet another thing, not merely external like the suit, or the case, or the papers. "He began to say silently an act of contrition, while they picked the brandy bottle out of his pocket, but he couldn't give his mind to it. That was the fallacy of death-bed repentence - penitence was the fruit of long training and discipline: fear wasn't enough."(p. 118) At this stage in his quest for spiritual realization the priest says: "I don't know how to repent." He thinks that he has lost the faculty to repent. "Repentence needed a confessor to draw the sinner's mind slowly down the drab passages which led to horror and grief." In the midst of the herd of criminals he feels an odd sense of companionship. The end may be there but then one never knew. "If God intended him to escape He would snatch him away from in front of a firing squad."(p. 129) The change in the pious woman's attitude towards him underlines the irony of existence. Her complacency is irritating and he tries to break it down telling her about his child. But this, instead of inculcating a degree of humility in her, makes her angry: "The sooner you are dead the better."(p. 131) Fear having been overcome, after the night in the cell, he feels only regret. Seeing the mestizo in the morning he thinks,: "God had decided. He had to go on with life, go on making decisions, acting on his own advice, making plans."(p. 13) He suffers the appalling agony of a man caught in the octopus arms of what he deems his own free will. Then again there is hope. The lieutenant offers him a five peso piece — the price of a Mass. Paradoxically enough, if we equate the task of emptying pails in the cell with a Mass, while the others get the benefit of the task having been accomplished, it is the priest who gets the benefit of the Mass in terms of spiritual illumination. His further progress now entails a complete loss of human dignity. He quarrels with a dying mongrel bitch for a bone and realizes what human dignity amounts to. "Then he suddenly laughed, this was human dignity disputing with a bitch over a bone."(p. 143) In an ironical way becoming rich entails renunciation. After gnawing at the bone snatched away from the dying bitch the priest eats a lump of sugar meant for the Mexican child killed with three bullets consoling himself with: "If God chose to give back life, couldn't He give food as well?"(p. 157) It is after these stages of self-realization, by shedding physical vestments as well as acquiring a new humility that the priest finds himself in the bungalow of the Lehrs. It has been five years since the last priest came there and he thinks that he need not go to Las Casas as a beggar. The comic strain comes into noticeable operation once again in the haggling of the people over the price of a baptism. Then, again, when the shopkeeper offers him liquor on credit and treats him to a drink, the memory of the police chief drinking his liquor comes back to him vividly. "The memory was like a hand, pulling away the case, exposing him." He finds the brandy musty on the tongue and then "he drank his brandy like damnation."(p. 169) With even brandy turning musty for him, the priest gets a greater degree of enlightenment. But then he suddenly finds no point in not drinking. Only with drink does he brace himself to the priestly task and begins preaching and consoling: "Lust is not the worst thing. It is because any day, any time, lust may turn into love that we have to avoid it. And when we love our sin then we are damned indeed."(p. 172) Then he realizes that he loves his child, the fruit of his sin. After thinking that he has lost his faculty of repentence he thinks that he has lost another. Seeing the man in the cantina with a chain of beads falling between his fingers the priest thinks that he has lost the faculty of judging. Thus acquiring more humility he finds himself in the Hamletian dilemma scribbled in a childish hand on the back of the slip of paper which the mestizo brings to him from the Yankee. He finds the trap close irrevocably. However imperfect, he still clings to his duty with relentlessness. The Yankee's death leaves him distraught and he prays: "O Merciful God, after all he was thinking of me, it was for my sake" and then he feels that here appears to be no contrition in his prayer. Taken by the lieutenant who says that he never believed he would return, he says: "Even a coward has a sense of duty."(p. 190) In the long dialogue, waiting for the rain to subside, he tells the police lieutenant why he stayed. "The fact is, a man isn't presented suddenly with two courses to follow: one good and one bad. He gets caught up."(p. 195) He attributes his fall to pride. "... It was all pride. Just because I'd stayed. I wasn't any use, but I stayed."(p. 196) There does not appear to be any pride in the way he forgives the mestizo at the end. Instead there is a Christlike charity. "You think my blessing will be a blinker over God's eyes. I can't stop him knowing all about it. Much better to go home and pray. Then if he gives you grace to feel sorry, give away the money" and finally says "I'll pray for you."(p. 197) Talking of love, when the lieutenant says that he wants to let his heart speak: "Oh," the priest said, "that's another thing altogether. God *is* love. I don't say the heart doesn't feel a taste of it, but what a taste. The smallest glass of love mixed with a pint pot of ditch water. We wouldn't recognize *that* love."(p. 199) Locked in the prison and never to escape again, the priest drinks brandy the lieutenant gives him as a generous gesture. As the liquid touches his tongue, he remembers his child. One thing leads to the other as it did earlier. He prays: "Oh God, help her. Damn me, I deserve it, but let her live for ever." Then he becomes aware of his futility and failure. He has done nothing for anybody. He is not even Hell-worthy. "Tears poured down his face: ... He felt an immense disappointment because he had to go to God empty-handed, with nothing done at all. It seemed to him, at the moment, that it would have been quite easy to have been a saint. It would only have needed a little self-restraint and a little courage. He felt like someone who has missed happiness by seconds at an appointed place. He knew now that at the end there was only one thing that counted — to be a saint." (p. 210) The conflict is talked about retrospectively in terms of a bullfight (an entertainment, though cruel) after the priest is executed. "... the little man was a routine heap beside the wall something unimportant which had to be cleared away. Two knock-kneed men approached quickly. This was an arena, and the bull was dead and there was nothing more to wait for anymore.'

3.2.8 Greene has a capacity to discern the comic even in the most serious of situations and characters. As Henry Fielding writes:[6] "life everywhere furnishes an accurate observer with the ridiculous." The tropes in which the protagonists are described are intended to be comic. If it seemed to the whisky priest that 'it would have been easy to have been a saint' the lieutenant has the 'dignity of the idea'. His hatred of the priest springs as much from his Marxist zeal as from his hatred of the sleekness, the comfort and the happiness of the priests. The good things of life come to them very early and without much effort. Even from the photograph, the priest is capable of rousing the lieutenant's hatred which is only jealousy at bottom. "A natural hatred as between dog and dog stirred in the lieutenant's bowels."(p. 22) School is for him an unhappy memory and he had helped to wipe it out. "There was something disinterested in his ambition: a kind of virtue in his desire to catch the sleek respected guest of the first communion party." (p. 23) The author tells us that "there is something of a priest in his intent observant walk — a

6. Author's Preface to *Joseph Andrews*.

theologian going back over the errors of the past to destroy them again." He is a mystic too, and what he experiences is not God directly but an infinite vacancy. He does not believe in the sacrifice of the priests and he does not have any sympathy at all with the weakness of the flesh. With the task of hunting down the priest accomplished he tears down the pictures of both the gunman and the priest from the wall. He falls asleep with utter weariness and hears laughter, laughter all the time, and sees a long passage in which he could find no door. Here is derision at the futility and endlessness of his mission and the final disillusionment. There is as much 'ridiculous' ambition in him as there is in the priest: both have a great deal of 'vanity' from which affectation proceeds according to Fielding, in that both wish to 'purchase applause' both of themselves and that of others. The priest is aware of it in the holiness derived from the commitment to religious duty and convicts himself of pride and cowardice. To the extent that he laughs at himself and his vanity he becomes a less comic figure than the lieutenant. The political zeal of the lieutenant touches the mark of absurdity: "He would eliminate from their childhood everything which had made him miserable, all that was poor, superstitious, and corrupt. They (the children in the patio) deserved nothing less than the truth — a vacant universe and a cooling world, the right to be happy in any way they chose. He was quite prepared to make a massacre for their sakes — first the Church and then the foreigner and then the politician — even his own chief would one day have to go. He wanted to begin the world again with them, in a desert."(p. 58)

3.2.9 At one level, hilarious comedy reigns in the scene where the whisky-priest stands host to the chief of police. During this 'party' the governor's cousin tells him about the first thing he can remember:

> "The first thing I can remember with any distinction is my first communion. Ah, the thrill of the soul, my parents round me ..."
> "How many parents have you got?"
> "Two, of course."
> "They couldn't have been around you — you would have needed at least four - ha, ha."
> "Salud!"
> "Salud!"
> "No, but I was saying — life has such irony. It was my painful duty to watch the priest who gave me that communion shot — an old man."(pp. 112-113)

But the irony of life is present in the little scene itself. The fugitive is with the police chief and the police chief says incidentally: "If it was me, I'd let the poor devil alone." This is what he does too, of course, without knowing that the quarry is right in his presence.

3.2.10 Greene's talent is evident in the balance in which the tragic and comic elements are held. In the intermingling of the two the tragedy of the hunted priest reaches unsuspected heights. The quality of the comedy lies in the ironical dimension invested powerfully in the lieutenant and suggestively in the priest. The two strands are artistically interwoven. As the story progresses we find the graph of humility, charity and an awareness of the weaknesses of human beings rising to the height of saintliness in the persecuted priest. He appears at moments as a scapegrace and an embodiment of incongruity while the lieutenant is a comic paradox. The priest can also be seen as a study in anti-heroism and failure, like all Greene's heros so far. He is painted as a 'picaro' and he persists in priesthood for even very fleshly reasons. But for occasional streaks of his true vocation he would have been a buffoon. Notwithstanding the fact that the comic strain is present in the novel, Greene makes statements about the ultimate things: regarding sin nobody can be a judge; suffering has sanctity; humility is endless; at the end there is only one thing that counts — to be a saint. Love for the Divine emerges from human love, even carnal love. The skill of the novelist is such that we feel convinced about the dramatic effectiveness of the statements illustrated in the novel. In fiction the success of the attempts at carrying conviction is determined by the presentation of a tenable view of the world making it emerge from artistically plausible conditions. A baleful vulture of doom, as the blurb on the Penguin edition points out, hovers over this modern crucifixion story but above the vulture soars an eagle — the inevitability of the Church's triumph. The gravity of the these is successfully translated into art through a unique tragicomic vision. Padre José is in a special kind of contrast to the whisky-priest. He is a figure of pure fun, an island of pure ludicrousness in the vast desolation. He is not subject to the tension of the central theme of the preservation of vocation. He is a spoiled priest but his range lies lower since he does not go any close to sharing the central tragedy. "Come to bed, Padre José," which is the routine refrain of the mocking children is like a chorus of frogs and limits his personality within the confines of broad farce. He seems to lie just beyond the spectrum of tragedy-comedy complex. The gravitation of the commitment to the vocation of priesthood in the whisky-priest pulls him, on the other hand, into the range of the spectrum of the tragedy-comedy blend. He draws his strength from his vocation. Consciously or unconsciously Greene creates the technique which he liberally uses in his subsequent work: it is a technique in which tragedy preserves comedy from bathos and comedy saves tragedy from a highbrow and unconvincing solemnity. One simple instance of Greene's contrapuntal mechanism should serve to illustrate the point. Eventhough Greene clothes the lieutenant in unequivocal dignity, the bob of spittle that the boy aims at his revolver holster is just the comic touch which rightly deflates his dogmatic importance and preserves the unassailable continuity of the living church.

3.3 *The Ministry of Fear* (1943) is an 'entertainment' cast in the mould of a melodrama consisting of a series of thrills. The war-ravaged London provides the background of this tense thriller. At a point in the ramifications of the plot, the principal character is asked: "You don't have a taste, sir, for the Sublime - or the Ridiculous?" "Perhaps," he replies, "I prefer human nature plain." (p. 99)[7] The distinguishing quality of Greene's vision manifests itself as a picture of this 'human nature' in this book. Greene's interest has been to fathom the motives for human behaviour, a complex affair, a journey without maps. In a world that is primarily odd, people are comic. Mr. Rennit, the seedy detective specializing in divorce cases, is optimistic of peace coming bringing him a crop of divorces, and breaches of promises, and he looks forward to getting that 'gold mine.' Thus we are told:

> Listening, Rowe thought, as he so often did, that you couldn't take such an odd world seriously: though all the time he did, in fact, take it with a mortal seriousness. The grand names stood permanently like statues in his mind: names like Justice and Retribution, though what they both boiled down to was simply Mr. Rennit, hundreds and hundreds of Mr. Rennits. But, of course, if you believed in God - and the Devil - the thing wasn't quite so comic. Because the devil - and God too - had always used comic people, futile people, little suburban natures and the maimed and warped to serve his purposes. When God used them you talked emptily of nobility and when the Devil used them of Wickedness, but the material was only dull shabby human mediocrity in either case. (p. 34)

7. Page numbers refer to *The Ministry of Fear*, Penguin edition, 1965.

3.3.1 Abandonment continues to be the lot of people and it is a fundamental aspect of existence in war-torn London, the offices of Orthotex, as well as the operator, Mr. Rennit. Experience has given the Austrian, Willi Hilfe, an 'amusing nihilistic abandon.' (p. 51) With Rennit's desertion Rowe 'felt a degree more abandoned.' (p. 79) When reporting to the Scotland Yard Rowe feels again 'abandoned'. (p. 166) Lust goes with abandonment. "An old man moves across the aisle and at the end of the shelter two lovers lay on a mattress with their hands and knees touching." (p. 68) Regal Court, the place for clandestine lovers, is full of it:

> A door in the passage was ajar and odd sounds came through it as though someone were alternately whistling and sighing, but nothing to the page seemed strange. He just went on: he was a child of this building. People of every kind came in for a night with or without luggage and then went away again; a few died here and the bodies were removed unobtrusively by the service lift. Divorce suits bloomed at certain seasons; co-respondents gave tips and detective out-trumped them with larger tips - because their tips went on the expense account. (p. 103)

On Mrs. Bellair's bedtable there 'was a little lubricious book called Love in the Orient: (p. 187) Dental Decay, an important symbol and obsession in Greene, figures in the book along with reference to painful dentists. The dentist with 'his blue chin and his look of experience' appears in Rowe's dream and the reason for Rowe's tension and unhappiness is a man with carious teeth whom he cannot help pity. "... When he opened his mouth you saw his teeth were in a shocking condition, black stumps like the remains of something destroyed by fire." (p. 97) He blows "the stale smell of carious teeth enthusiastically" in Rowe's direction. Pain, with which dentistry is always associated, leaves a scar on Rowe's young mind and he remembers the dentist of his boyhood days, "he suffered agonies from an inefficient dentist he knew as Mr. Briggs." (p. 95)

3.3.1 While the main elements of abandonment, lust, dental decay and pain continue to figure prominently in this 'entertainment', there is something superimposed on these. *The Ministry of Fear* shows a distinct progress in the treatment of pity. Greene has always portrayed pity/love as an ambivalent feeling. If in *The Confidential Agent* D. 's love for Rose is more pity than love; Rowe's love for his wife is only pity. Pity is the driving force of Rowe in *The Ministry of Fear*. The word itself occurs about twenty times in the book. Rowe is susceptible to pity, the worst of all emotions. Pity can destroy. Out of pity he asks his landlady to have a piece of cake, and looking at the crippled visitor Rowe "felt his dangerous pity stirring in his bowels." (p. 27) Rowe persists to be Mr. Rennit's client. "... he might have left it if he had known any other address, and if it had not been for that sense of pity which is so much more promiscuous than lust." (p. 33) It is pity, he thinks, the jury had for him when they acquitted him of the charge of killing his wife. The papers called it mercy-killing. "Mercy to her or mercy to me. They didn't say. And I don't know even now." (p. 39) The sense of pity haunts Rowe. 'A voice would whisper, "You said you killed for pity, why don't you have pity on yourself? Why not indeed? except that it is easier to kill someone you love than to kill yourself." (p. 42) This leads on to the next proposition: "One doesn't necessarily kill because one hates: one kills because one loves." (p. 139) The sense of danger conveyed down the telephone line ignites his pity. Anna tells him that they would get him in the dark. He senses danger and is immediately reminded of something. "... this suspense was what somebody else had experienced, watching from day to day his pity grow to the monstrous proportions necessary to action." (p. 61) The monstrous act of his childhood, striking the rat with his cricket bat again and again, is owing to his pity. He could not bear the sight of the rat's pain "Not one of them guessed that what had come over him was the horrible and horrifying emotion of pity." (p. 70) The poster, "Let not man prevail", in the book-stall makes Rowe muse: "For in all the world outside that room man had indeed prevailed; he had himself prevailed. It wasn't only evil man who did these things. Courage smashes a cathedral, endurance lets a city starve, pity kills..." (p. 79) Rowe is made and conditioned by pity. He used to pity his friend (he has very few friends indeed) Wilcox for his domineering and hockey-playing wife. It is because of his pity that he agrees to carry the load of books up the stairs of Regal Court. Even a stranger like the Austrian girl Anna Hilfe knows what makes Rowe what he is: "You had a great sense of pity. You didn't like people to suffer." (p. 136) His adventurous visit to the 'sick bay' is also an act motivated by pity. He promises Stone to come back since "A terrible sense of pity moved him: he felt capable of murder for the release of that gentle tormented creature." (p. 150) Mr. Prentice of the Scotland Yard tells Rowe: "Pity is a terrible thing. People talk about the passion of love. Pity is the worst passion of all: we don't outlive it like sex." (p. 184) It is, once again, 'the awful stirring of pity' that stings Rowe into action after seeing at Dr. Forester's killing 'on an Elizabethan scale'. In the end when he is sent away by

Hilfe with bitterness (reminding him of his past as a murderer) Rowe recapitulates the pity he saw and knew and felt:

> He thought of a dead rat and a policeman, and then he looked everywhere and saw reflected in the crowded court the awful expression of pity: the judge's face was bent, but he could read pity in the old fingers which fidgeted with an Eversharp. He wanted to warn them - "Don't pity me. Pity is cruel. Pity destroys. Love isn't safe when pity's prowling round." (p. 233)

3.3.3 The influence of childhood in forming character and even a single memory conditioning the whole of future is once again stressed here. Raven's bitter childhood is a horrible memory of his mother bleeding across the table, and Pinkie's of the Saturday nocturnal exercise of his parents and the cement play-ground. Rowe's childhood conditions him permanently:

> He was playing in a haystack with the vicar's son and a strange boy with a foreign accent and a dog called Spot. The dog caught a rat and tossed it, and the rat tried to crawl away with a broken back, and the dog made little playful excited rushes. Suddenly he couldn't bear the sight of the rat's pain any more: he picked up a cricket bat and struck the rat on the head over and over again; he wouldn't stop for fear it was still alive." (p. 70)

3.3.4 The view of life as explicitly expressed in the book is one which is conditioned by war, violence and treachery. The atmosphere of distrust which goes along with this kind of life is subtly deepened with quotations from the romantic tale of Charlotte Yonge's *The Little Duke* for which the principal character, Rowe, never loses his admiration. On the one hand the book is a reflection of the excellent character of the little Duke, a compound of the best virtues; courage, humility and love of God; on the other it is a picture of distrust and violence. Greene cleverly epigraphs the chapters with quotations which deepen the mood. Rowe tells his mother in the dream: "This isn't real life any more. Tea on the lawn, even-song, croquet, the old ladies calling, the gentle malicious gossip, the gardener turning the wheelbarrow full of leaves and grass. People write about it as if it still went on; lady novelists describe it over and over again in books of the month, but it is not there any more." (p. 69) He tells her further about his hiding and the war and the blitz:

> It sounds like a thriller, doesn't it, but the thrillers are like life - more like life than you are, this lawn, your sandwiches, that pine. You used to laugh at the books Miss Savage

> read— about spies, and murderers, and violence, and wild motor-car chases, but dear, that's real life: it's what we've all made of the world since you died. I'm your little Arthur who wouldn't hurt a beetle and I'm a murderer too. The world has been re-made by William le Queux. (p. 69)

The thriller and the crime story not only reflect life but also condition it. He tells his mother in his dream: "Let me lend you the History of Contemporary Society. It's in hundreds of volumes, but most of them are sold in cheap editions: *Death in Piccadilly, The Ambassador's Diamonds, Diplomacy, Seven Days' Leave, The Four Just Men.*" (p. 70) We are told that Rowe, before his shell-shock and the adventure of the cake, has been a journalist and his imagination works like that of a writer who is primarily interested in human nature. While Rowe guesses what he must have been before the shock: "You weren't a detective," Johns exclaimed, "you were a detective writer." (p. 129) Mr. Rennit, carried away out of his depth by murder, tells Rowe: "Life, you know, isn't like a detective story. Murderers are rare people to meet. They belong to a class of their own." But Rowe's training as a journalist makes him aware that there is something more in life than the clue for the mystery of the missing diamond or the clue relating to the murder. The mystery is more in the murderer as a human being and an investigation into the motives of human behaviour is more in his line than anything else. Happiness, he realizes regaining his memory via Tolstoy, should always be qualified by the knowledge of misery: "Knowledge was the great thing... detailed passionate trivial knowledge." (p. 196) It is this which appears to interest Greene also. This 'passionate trivial human knowledge' is Greene's forte as a creative artist. With it goes a sense of seeing play-acting around everywhere and seeing absurdity and comedy which reign supreme even over inexplicable sorrow and suffering. Rowe, like his creator, is aware of mummery and playacting. At the seance "Why all the mummery" he thought. (p. 61) Anna's act of taking a candle-stick as a weapon makes him think of a player: "It was like watching a small girl play Lady Macbeth." (p. 217) The oddity of existence is observed in a moment of insight. Mr. Prentice says: "Life can be very odd. Oh, very odd. You should read more history." (p. 171) When Mr. Prentice closes his eyes at a stage in interrogating Rowe, Greene's authorial voice rings: "it was perhaps affectation, but who could live without affectation?" (p. 175)

3.3.5 The comic appears in the juxtaposition of events here as elsewhere in Greene's fiction. The ungregarious Rowe has very few friends. We are told about his comic meeting with Boojie (p. 79) and then the hockey-playing wife of his friend Wilcox. When he goes to see Wilcox a middle aged woman welcomes him and tells him "I'm Mrs. Wilcox" and exclaims, "Henry's mother." (p. 87) The scene where Greene describes Rowe's efforts to get a cheque cashed by Wilcox juxtaposed with the arrival of the mourners and the forming of the procession is farcical. Rowe goes to Prentice the detective from Graves, another officer of the Scotland Yard, and there he gets a sympathetic hearing. The professional rivalry between the two is comic as evident in Prentice's sympathy: "Poor Graves - the passionate crimes of railway porters are his spiritual province. In this branch our interests are more bizarre. And so he distrusts - really distrusts us." Absurdity is evident in the seance at Mrs. Bellairs' and it amuses Rowe. Willi Hilfe too is aware of the absurdity in life though he belongs to the fifth column. "He treats murder as a joke with a tang to it." Rowe meets with absurdity in the fact that the photograph, which Dr. Forester shows him as his, does not appear to be his at all. Towards the end of the book when Jones's buttons are dug out on the island, the author reflects: "So is a poor human creature joined respectably together like a doll: take him apart and you are left with a grocery-box full of assorted catches and buckles and buttons." (p. 199) Here is a blend of the tragic and the comic in an illuminating clarity.

3.4 *The Heart of the Matter* (1948) shows Greene's tragic vision in its most intense focus. It deals with a just man's gradual corruption, decay and finally his hopeless death. Like Greene's Liberian exploration the novel is a symbolic exploration of the human heart. The disintegration of the principal character is at the heart of the book.

3.4.1 Though laid in a far-off West African colony, the essence of the background in this novel is of a piece with what went before. The place is chosen because like the principal character, Scobie, Greene believes that human nature has not had enough time to disguise itself there. There are, even figuratively speaking, vultures (in one place Greene calls them scavenger birds) lizards, moths, cockroaches, chigoes, mosquitoes, rats and pyedogs. As O'Brien writes:[8]

> Zoological metaphor, akin to the symbolism of the medieval bestiaries, is congenial to Catholic writers: Bloy's anger swells into bisons, hippopotami, and thirsty lions: Peguy

8. Conor C.O'Brien, *Maria Cross* (London: Burns and Oates, 1963) pp. 62-63.

> praises the visceral in terms of a herd of four-stomached ruminants; Mauriac's Mediterranean insects rear stiffly and hieratically, displaying their wing-cases in some arid and fatal sexuality. Mr. Greene's carrion birds and beasts are normally conventional symbols of the corruption that waits upon the flesh and the horror of a world without God. But here, in *The Heart of the Matter,* they are something more; they have moved, as it were, closer to an organism whose impending dissolution is more apparent.

There is the smell of the Zoo and the scent of a monkey-house. The climate alternates from suffocating heat to insufferable rain. Malaria and blackwater ravage the population irrespective of their nationality. Corruption reigns supreme and the principal character is aware of it. The world around him as he sees it is his own private world and he thinks that he has a mission to understand it, pity it, love it. It is against this sort of background that the spiritual drama in the novel take place. The novel is divided into three books with three parts each stringing together the various scenes which the chapters hold together. The slow disintegration of Scobie's personality and its final crumbling can be seen from three focal points: "It seemed to Scobie that life was immeasureably long. Couldn't the test of man have been carried out in fewer years? Couldn't we have committed our first major sin at seven, have ruined ourselves for low or hate at ten, have clutched at redemption on a fifteen-year-old death-bed?"(p. 51);[9] "What an absurd thing it was to expect happiness in a world so full of misery. ... Point me out the happy man and I will point you either egotism, evil - or else an absolute ignorance."(p. 117) and "His hilarity was like a scream from a crevasse."(p. 200) The three points occur in the three books. The first occurs in the middle of the first and the others at fairly initial scenes in the second and the third books. The first is occasioned by the feeling of responsibility; the second by an illumination consequent on a miserable and pathetic suicide; and the third by a sense of pitiful exhilaration.

3.4.2. A Deputy Commissioner of Police in a West African colony, Scobie is middle-aged and has been married to the poetry-loving and intellectual Louise for about fifteen years. The Commissioner calls him Scobie the Just, as the Athenians called Aristides. At the Ealing altar, he vowed to be the guardian of her happiness. There is something of the ascetic in him; "Other men slowly build up the

9. Page numbers refer to *The Heart of the Matter*, Penguin ed., 1966.

sense of home by accumulation ... Scobie built his home by a process of reduction."(p. 15) He loves Africa and, asked why, he tells the Commissioner vaguely: "It's pretty in the evening." The memory of his dead child has been the conditioning influence on his personality. The ugliness of his wife is another influence. We are told: "He watched her through the muslin net. Her face had the yellow ivory tinge of atabrine; her hair which had once been the colour of bottled honey was dark and stringy with sweat. These were the times of ugliness when he loved her, when pity and responsibility reached the intensity of a passion."(p. 21) It is his pity which makes him think that she is a 'joint under the meat cover'. The intellectual Louise realizes how he pities her and once she asks him: "Do you love anyone, Ticki, except yourself?"(p. 24) A social failure and a wet blanket as she is, the very fact that a stranger, Wilson, gives her his attention makes Scobie happy. An exile in his own house, the only place he likes for being alone and happily at peace with himself is the bathroom with the rat at the edge of the bath. His being passed over for promotion does not bother him except for the pain that Louise should be disappointed. When she asks him miserably to find a way of sending her to South Africa and thus unloads her burden, he promises to manage her passage-money somehow. The next minute she is happily asleep: "she was like a tired carrier who has slipped her load." Now the burden is all Scobie's. His request for an overdraft turned down by the bank manager, Robinson, Scobie begins to feel desperate. In the routine search of the ship the EsperanÇa, receiving a trip from a steward, Scobie looks for a concealed letter and finds it. Scobie sees in the captain a fat boy of the school __ an inescapable object of pity. Listening to his painful story of the suspicious wife and the loving daughter Scobie puts the letter in his pocket. The burden of another man's offence is added to his own: "he could feel the millstone weighing on his own breast."(p. 50) Here comes the crucial passage about the 'test'. (p. 51 quoted earlier). He is utterly weary. He writes the report but then reading the smuggled letter changes his mind and he tears the letter and goes home towards Louise's misery. He walks with more courage than a man 'walking to the place of is execution.' At home Louise begs him "Tell me one idea. Just one." The author describes a lizard on the wall which Scobie has been observing all the wile. "His eyes followed the lizard as it pounced." Scobie feels that "In human relations kindness and lies are worth a thousand truths." When Louise tells him that she has got nothing except him, his pity stirs in him again. "The lizard flicked across the wall and came to rest again, the wings of a moth in his crocodile jaws." He prays for peace and Louise senses his feelings and asks with tenderness: "Poor dear, you wish I were dead like Catherine. You want to be alone." and he replies obstinately: "I want to keep you happy."(p. 58) We hear the author's voice again: "Despair is the price one pays for setting oneself an impossible aim" and "only the man for goodwill carries always in his heart the capacity for damnation." (p. 59) When Louise tells him that she would never forgive Pemberton for making him go on a long trek (without evidently knowing about Pemberton's suicide) he replies: "Don't talk nonsense dear. We'd forgive most things if we knew the facts."(p. 75) In a fever while he is away he thinks only of arranging her happiness forgetting the while "what experience had taught him__ that no human being can really understand another, and no one can arrange another's happiness."(p. 81) It is the look on Pemberton's face, just like the fat boy's appearance of the Captain which makes him an offender for the first time, that moves Scobie. Pemberton looks like a child in a night-shirt quietly asleep: "the pimples were the pimples of puberty and the dead face seemed to bear the trace of no experience beyond the class room and the football field."(p. 83) When Father Rank tells him that suicide is terrible in that it puts one beyond mercy he retorts: "Even the Church can't teach me that God doesn't pity the young."(p. 84) Limp as a rag with the fever having run its course in him, he comes back home. For a moment he is apprehensive that Louise may follow Pemberton's method. He rushes downstairs and tells her that the passage will be arranged. With the passage arranged (with money borrowed from the Syrian against his better judgement), Scobie becomes more and more alienated from his true self. His loneliness intensifies: "hand in hand they watched their separation anchor in the bay".(p. 83) "They seemed to be sitting miles apart separated by a waste of dishes." Although they are near enough to be able to touch each other "it was as if the whole coast-line of a continent was already between them." (p. 96) Thus by the end of the first book Scobie has lost his personal integrity by borrowing money from one whom his judgement told him to keep away from, and professional integrity by not reporting against the offending captain. But this is only the first stage. The 'test' of which he is aware is not fully taken and he has not yet committed the major sin and the redemption is yet to become manifest.

3.4.3 Book Two takes his pity to greater heights and leads him to further violations. The passengers who survived forty days in an open boat arrive and Scobie begins to see "the enormous breach pity has blasted through his integrity." (p. 108) Prayer does not give him the solace he needs and it becomes a useless formality; "He felt himself free from serious sin because it had never occurred to him that his life was important enough one way or another." (p. 103) A kind of spiritual ennui already begins to prey on him and he becomes a victim of utter weariness: "He didn't drink, he didn't fornicate, he didn't even lie, but he never regarded this absence of sin as a virtue". (p. 109) With the 'responsibility' sent away he becomes more lonely and the shipwrecked passengers attract him as a light attracts the moths. The feelings of responsibility and pity grow to monstrous size in the hospital scene. He sees the shipwrecked girl: "Her arm as thin as a child's lay outside the blanket, and her fingers clasped a book firmly. Scobie could see the wedding-ring loose on the dried up finger." Later he always remembers "How she was carried into his life on a stretcher grasping a stamp-album with her eyes fast shut."(p. 115) There, in the hospital, he remembers Pemberton and tells himself that it is absurd to expect happiness in a world full of misery. His pity rises to the zenith. "If one knew, he wondered, the facts, would one have to feel pity even for the planets? If one reached that they called the heart of the matter?"(p. 117) Seeing the dying child whom he has been asked to look after for a short while, he remembers his own child who died thousands of miles away: "When he looked at the child, he saw a white communion veil over her head: it was trick of light on the pillow and a trick of his own mind." He closes his eyes with his hands: "Looking bet ween his fingers he could see the six year old face convulsed like a navvy's with labour." He prays ardently: "Father, give her peace. Take away my peace for ever, but give her peace." The prayer seems to have been answered and peace (the most beautiful word in the language and the feeling he valued most) now eludes him forever. When he is asked to read to another shipwrecked child he takes upon himself to read a story of his own making to make the boy happy. Pity makes him barter away his own peace for the peace of the child. The rains set in, falling "in interminable tears." (p. 127) The scene is set for his further fall. Seeing the shipwrecked and widowed Helen, in the Nissan but he wonders "How could a child like that act the part of a woman whose husband has been drowned more or less before her eyes?" (p. 131) After some 'silly aimless talk' he walks home with an extraordinary happiness. Pemberton's letter signed 'Dicky' comes back to him in his dreams. He is wanted by the Commissioner and the Colonial Secretary comes to satisfy himself about the case of the diamonds found in the crop of a parrot. He becomes aggressive and lies that he has an appointment with Yusef. Then he visits the Syrian and the quarrel which issues is 'like a lovers' quarrel.' He finds that Yusef has put him in a nasty position taking advantage of his having lent him money. On the way home he enters the Catholic church and in the confessional pours forth his ennui: "I don't know how to put it, Father, but I feel — tired of my religion. It seems to mean nothing to me. I've tried to love God - but -" he made a gesture which the priest could not see, turned sideways through the grill. "I'm not sure that I even believe." The priest's routine words bring him no relief. In the next scene he takes some stamps to Helen and tells her how the telegrams about his daughter Catherine's illness and death reached him in the wrong order. When she tells him about Bagster stroking her leg on the beach Scobie feels "sadly like an evening tide responsibility bearing him up the shore."(p. 149) Her childish immaturity stirs him and he is worried that Bagster is not the man to accept responsibility. He tells himself that with more than thirty years between them they are safe with each other. When she tells him, "It's good to talk to you. I say anything I like. I'm not afraid of hurting you. You don't want anything out of me. I'm safe." he tells her "We are both safe." The drunken Bagster howls to her from outside to be a sport and let him in. When he goes away after some time, they kiss. The author comments: "What they had both thought was safety proved to have been the camouflage of an enemy who works on terms of friendship, trust and pity."(p. 153) With the damage of adultery done"she lay in the odd cramped attitude of someone who has been shot in escaping." Seeing the future clearly he thinks of its sadness: "Was it the butterfly that died in the act of love? But human beings were condemned to consequences. The responsibility as well as the guilt was his — he was not a Bagster: he knew what he was about. He had sworn to preserve Louise's happiness, and now he had accepted another and contradictory responsibility." At this stage he is poignantly aware of yet another wrong and another victim, not either Louise or Helen but God. With adultery instilled into his veins Scobie's fall is rapid. When she begins to nag him saying: "I don't want your pity" he is aware of its being not a question of her wanting it: "Pity smouldered like decay at his heart. He would never rid himself of it. He knew from experience how passion died away and how love went, but pity always stayed. Nothing ever diminished pity. The conditions of life nurtured it. There was only one person in the world who was unpitiable — himself."(p. 170) With his self-pity grows the meanness of Helen's taunting. When he tells her that he is a Catholic and he cannot have two wives she sniggeringly retorts: "It's a wonderful excuse. It doesn't stop you from sleeping with me — it only stops you marrying me." (p. 171) He feels appallingly tired and disappointed and then promises to do anything for her; he wants only her happiness. Going home he composes a letter on Government paper (perhaps he wants to make it irrevocable that way): "I love you more than myself, more than my wife, more than God I think..." Having thrust the letter under her door he wonders why he has written that he loves her 'more than God.' In the next scene Father Rank comes in for a drink and tries to attract him with his self-revelations. Scobie toys with the idea of shifting his burden and then gives it up thinking that he knows the answers as well as the priest does. The magic feeling of comfort is nowhere to be found. He goes once again to the Nissen hut at midnight. The drunken voice is heard in the distance and he thinks of going to bed at home and confessing the next morning. "Virtue, the good life, tempted him in the dark like sin."(p. 178) But he resists the 'temptation' and knocks. The door opens immediately and the quarrel is quickly made up. When she entreats him never to go away from her no matter what she says, he replies "I promise" with a sense of despair "as though he were signing away the whole future." (p. 179) He becomes another Faustus for not quite the same reason. He mentions to her his letter which she has never seen. Urged by Helen that he should go home for they might be watched, he comes back home and remembers: "I'll always be here if you need me as long as I'm alive" and feels that it constituted an oath as ineffaceable as the vow by the Ealing altar. The agony in him begins. The Lord's prayer lies dead on his tongue. "I don't want to plan any more ... They wouldn't need me if I were dead. No one needs the dead. The dead can be forgotten. O God, give me death before I give them unhappiness."(p. 181) When these words sound melodramatic to his own ears, he thinks of suicide. "The priests told you it was the unforgivable sin, the final expression of an unrepentent despair, and of course one accepted the Church's teaching. But they taught also that God had sometimes broken his own laws, and was it more impossible for him to put out a hand of forgiveness into the suicidal darkness and chaos than to have woken himself in the tomb, behind the stone? Christ had not been murdered: you couldn't murder God: Christ killed himself: he had hung himself on the cross as surely as Pemberton from the picture-rail." (pp. 181-82) Upto this point the process of imitating Christ is confined to Scobie's exercising of pity. In the next scene the telegram from Louise about her arrival comes. At the dinner party (with the real Argentine beef Dr. Sykes talks of Pemberton's suicide. She light-heartedly talks about the safest way of killing oneself. With Pemberton's suicide in the background, Louise's letter in his pocket and Dr. Sykes's banter, Scobie's mind is almost made up. Back from the party, he receives Helen's note and there is Yusef waiting for him. Yusef promises to return him the letter he has written to Helen on condition that he give a small packet to the ships captain. He threatens Scobie that in case he does not accept the terms he would have the tell-tale letter handed to Louise as soon as she lands. With his personal integrity compromised by the act of borrowing from Yusef and the human by accepting contradictory responsibilities of preserving the happiness of two women, his professional dignity is compromised by accepting to smuggle the contraband package. The snares around him begin to close upon him. During the routine search of the ship, pausing by a mirror he sees 'poised over his own shoulders a stranger's face, a fat sweating face." He wonders who it can be and realizes that "it was only this new unfamiliar look of pity that made it strange to him." He ponders over the question whether he is really one of those whom people pity. From pitying others he deteriorates into becoming an object of pity.

3.4.4 Book Three shows a further degeneration. Scobie finds himself on the horns of a dilemma when Louise importunes him to go to communion with her. If he went he,would he taking God in mortal sin and if he did not, he would be making Louise suspicious. However much and however ardently he wished to avoid giving pain, it is only pain that he thinks he is capable of giving. He begins to doubt himself and wonders whether he loves either of the two women or it is only that his "automatic terrible pity goes out of any human need— and makes it worse." (p. 198) When Louise persuades him to go to Mass with her he says that he has not done anything terrible. Told that missing Mass on Sunday is mortal sin just as much as committing adultery, he says with attempted lightness "Adultery's more fun."(p. 199) He talks with hollow jocularity and Louise does not fail to notice the change in him: "Dear Henry, I've never known you so cheerful." This is a decisive blow. "The ground has given way beneath his feet. ...His hilarity was like a scream from a crevasse."(p. 200) A police officer though he is, Scobie pitifully fails to see that his wife's sudden return might have been necessitated by rumours reaching her in West Africa. At least her reference to adultery must have warned him of the possibility. The scream from the crevasse occurring almost at the beginning of the third book marks the swift fall. Like his hilarity his further actions are reckless and disastrous. His whole personality crumbles with the slow disintegration of his lies. He takes his problem to Helen who cannot even understand it. "But I simply don't understand. If you believe in Hell, why are you with me now?" Scobie's spiritual dilemma with theological proportions surfaces here when she taunts him with the words: "A death-bed repentence." Kissing the sweat off her hand he says: "I can regret the lies, the mess, the unhappiness, but if I were dying now I wouldn't know how to repent the love."(p. 202) The spiritual scruples and the *impasse* are beyond Helen's understanding. It is all 'hooey' to her. With the octopus arms of circumstances (most of them self-made) closing in upon him Scobie's personality crumbles miserably. His awareness of the fact that he set himself an impossible task does not give him an idea as to how to accomplish it. He begins to playact — pretending pain in the chest. He remembers how in childhood he played Hotspur in the school play and recalls Lousie and others at the altar rail. Excusing himself from going to communion with the brandy he drinks (supposedly to alleviate the pain), he feels the sense of exile. The sense of love stirs in him once again: "the love one always feels for what one has lost, whether a child, a woman, or even pain." He feels that he knows the answers— no one can really comfort or console him. "We Catholics are damned by our knowledge."(p. 211) He realizes that adultery is an abstraction: "the woman, the occasion, no longer the bewildered child clutching the stamp-album, listening to Bagster howling outside the door: that moment of peace and darkness and tenderness and pity 'adultery'." In this frame of mind he goes to confession and is refused absolution. Hearing the priest's words that there is nothing automatic in absolution and that it depends on his state of mind and that he must know the wrong he has done before coming there, he realizes that his footsteps have taken him "out of sight of hope" "for his exploration of the territory of despair."(p. 214) The next day he disregards Louise trap and goes to Mass decisively. He knows that he is desecrating God because he loves a woman and wonders: "was it even love, or was it just a feeling of pity and responsibility?" (p. 215) The miracle for which he hopes all along never occurs and Father Rank comes down the steps bearing God. Scobie opens his mouth and makes one last attempt to pray: "O God, I offer my damnation up to you. Take it. Use it for them." and then he is aware of the 'pale papery taste of his eternal sentence on the tongue'. After this the vacillation is gone. He looks up the symptoms of *angina* he has to feign. The Commissioner tells Scobie that he is going to succeed him after all. Leaving a note to Louise he goes to Helen who taunts him again: "'If there's one thing I hate it's your Catholicism. I suppose it comes of having a pious wife. It's no bogus. If you really believed, you wouldn't be here." Anger drains out of him. Feeling hysteria mount again he says: "I can't bear to see the suffering, and I cause it all the time. I want to get out, get out."(p. 224) Then he finds Ali spying on him and says miserably 'I've lost the trick of trust.' His personal quality of begetting trust irretrievably lost, he becomes more acutely aware of the sense of exile. He talks deliberately of the coming Christmas conjuring up before his eyes the picture of 'a bleeding face, of eyes closed by the continuous shower of blows: the punch-drunk head of God reeling sideways.'(p. 228) He goes to Yusef and tells him of Ali and Yusef promises to sort out the trouble. Scobie parts with his broken rosary to show Ali as a token of his summons and Ali is killed. Ali's death has an effect on Helen and she offers to go away from his life. He tells her again: "I want to stop giving pain." After planning the details of a sad parting Helen suddenly says: "I don't mind going on as we are. I don't mind the lies. Anything." Then Scobie makes the irrevocable decision. "When he was young, he had thought love had something to do with understanding, but with age he knew that no human being understood another."(p. 235) He begins concocting his diary with entries about sleeplessness. The doctor tells him that he is not at all sure it is *angina* but prescribes sleeping pills. Scobie realizes that human love has robbed him of love for eternity. Clutching the packet of the pills he cries out in anguish; "You see it's an *impasse*, God, an impasse."(p. 251) Touching Louise's fingers for the last time he muses and prays: "I can't give her pain, and I can't go on giving you pain. Oh god, if you love me as I know you do, help me to leave you." Louise gone to bed, he sits down and hears the voice of solitude: "Throw away those tables. You'll never be able to collect enough again. You'll be saved. Give up playacting." He is determined already and with two draughts of whisky he drowns the dozen tablets. He falls down with the words: "Dear God, I love ..." With Scobie dead, the life of the by-standers does not come to standstill. Wilson comes to see Louise and points out the difference in ink in the entries relating to sleeplessness in the diary. She refuses to believe in the suicide theory saying: "After all, in spite of everything, he was a Catholic."(p. 261) Helen sluts unenthusiastically with Bagster and Father Rank offers consolation to Louise. "For goodness' sake, Mrs Scobie, don't imagine you — or I — know a thing about God's mercy."(p. 263) He tells her that the Church knows all the rules but it does not know what goes on in a single human heart. "It may seem an odd thing to say — when a man's as wrong as he was — but I think from what I saw of him, that he really loved God."(p. 264)

3.4.5 The private universe of Greene, at this stage, is permeated by gloom. The tragic is more prominent here than in anything that Greene has written so far. *Brighton Rock*, *The Power and the Glory* and the *The Heart of the Matter* form a trilogy in projecting the dark personal vision of the creative artist. As R.W.B. Lewis remarks:[10]

> In so far as they (*Brighton Rock, The Power and the Glory* and *The Heart of the Matter*) constitute a trilogy, Greene's three novels reverse the direction of the great religious trilogy, *The Divine Comedy*. Dante's poem moves from ignorance to knowledge, from discord to harmony, from unspeakable darkness to overwhelming light. Greene's trilogy moves stealthily, deepens into the darkness, moves through the annihilation of our confidence in human knowledge to an awareness of impenetrable mystery, moves from the deceptive light to the queerly nourishing obscurity.

This underscores the fact that the book is a tragedy. But a 'Christian tragedy' is considered a contradiction in terms and it has been asked if it is possible for a Christian novelist to render a human story that is both tragic and Christian at the same time. The deep wound of tragedy would no longer be deep if God is the Lord of life and history. The term is self-contradictory in the sense that tragic art must be purely tragic while Christian faith is beyond the dimension of tragedy. But, quoting Preston Roberts,[11] Nathan A. Scott (Jr)[12] says that a Christian tragedy is possible, since, "the events and meanings of which Christian theology consists ... are not simply and purely 'beyond tragedy' and literary tragedy is not simply and purely tragic.' He writes that *The Heart of the Matter* is "something closely approaching tragedy":

> "Scobie is Greene's exemplum of the Christian hero in a tragic situation: here is the branch that grows out of the 'stony rubbish' of our world - the man, who being caught up and possessed by the example of Christ's charity, discovers, as Christ discovered in Gethsemane, that goodness involves suffering, but who does not refuse that suffering, so profound is his compassion for his fellow creatures, his compassion being nurtured by the 'conditions of life'. And

10. R.W.B. Lewis, *The Picaresque Saint* (London: Gollancz, 1960), p. 263.
11. Preston Roberts, "A Christian Theory of Dramatic Tragedy" *The Journal of Religion* XXXI (Jan. 1951), p. 8.
12. "The Christian Tragedian" in R.O. Evans (ed), *Graham Greene*, (Lexington, Kentucky Univ. Press, 1967), pp. 40-41.

> the fact that his attempt to reenact our Lord's passion proves unsuccessful leaves us not with the pity and terror of Greek tragedy but rather with something like the judgement and forgiveness of the gospels. For, though Scobie betrays God, the last words on his lips, as he falls to the floor after taking the poison are 'Dear God, I love...' and the resonances of meaning and implication that have been stirred within us by the total action persuade us that he is himself loved and shall be forgiven in some "brave new world."

The tragedy of Scobie is that stated by Leon Bloy: "the only tragedy in the world is the tragedy of not being a saint." When one does not look from the point of the conventional generic ending in death and if one goes through the novel and beyond into the artist's vision, Scobie's is an unmixed tragedy. The author is never in doubt about the principal's destiny. He is one who 'goes to purgatory'. Though it is true that the novel takes one to the very problem of charity in an uncharitable world showing apparently the sense of tears in things, the intellectual-theological mess created by Scobie proceeds from his own hypersensitivity to spiritual scruples. Greene himself notes the fact. The pity of Scobie forms the subject of a stimulating discussion in the perceptive analysis in O'Brien's *Maria Cross*:[13]

> Pity is an equivocal and often impure disposition. It descends from piety, is inspired by charity, and is said to mean *compassion*, the ability to suffer a fellow-creature's hurt. Yet the verb betrays the cloven hoof; a pitying glance, a pitying tone, assaults from above the personality. "Something implying contempt," says a standard dictionary definition. It is perhaps a form of love, but not a form of which anyone wishes to be the object. Charity is not puffed up, but he who is addicted to pitying others may be exalting himself above them. Were one - monstrous operation - to remove the element of love from pity, one would be left with a hybrid vampire emotion, compound of pride and parasitic insecurity and looking singularly like cruelty.

Scobie appears to have exalted himself not only above the two women he undertakes to protect under the wing of his responsibility, he goes a step further and tries to imitate Christ. As Kenneth Allott and Miriam Farris write, in him we see "the paradox of the creature

---

13. Conor C. O'Brien, 'The Anatomy of Pity', *Maria Cross* (London: Burns and Oates, 1963), p. 57.

more compassionate than its creator."[14] The pity which should reflect human charity debases Scobie and reduces the people whom he pities to pitiability. His charity does not have the marks of disinterestedness, tranquility and humility which are said to be its essential attributes. His love is not a liberating force. If his love is motivated by pity and inspired by the love of God, how can the love of God lead to his alienation from Him? Scobie himself seems to be aware of the impurity: pity is called the "terrible promiscuous passion." It is only a fevered sensibility that sees crucifixion as deliberate suicide. When he tells Father Rank that he seems to be tired of his religion what he implies, perhaps, is that he is tired of his scruples. Had he said 'scruples' in the place of 'religion' it would have been nearer the truth. Scobie commits a series of indiscretions and mistakes inspired by his inadequate grasp of theology. His final act of despair (the price one pays for setting oneself an impossible aim, by his definition) proceeds from excessive emotionalism and sentimentality going under the guise of pity. His morality, like his theology, is shaky.

3.4.6 *The Heart of the Matter* is an unbalanced mixture of the tragic and the inadequate comic strands. The gloom of tragedy is punctuated with patches of the comic. Scobie's exaggerated sensibility and sensitivity to religious scruples and his aggressive and at times presumptuous religiosity appear to be an exercise in the darkest tragedy. Critics feel that Scobie is a man fighting with illusory windmills of spiritual scruples. His suicide is incomprehensible. If he believes in the scruples really, he could not have braved purgatory merely for the sake of two neurotic women. It is George Orwell who, reviewing the novel in *The New Yorker* (17th July, 1948), points out that "by trying to clothe theological speculations in flesh and blood, it [the novel] produces psychological absurdities." Zabel[15] considers the novel a piece of tendentious fiction. He quotes Philip Toynbee:[16] "A stern theological dogma [is] grossly degraded into melodrama, to an extent which allows a non-believer to speak blasphemy. It is intolerable." Walter Allen[17] finds the novel the least satisfactory of Greene's major novels - Scobie is conceived in sentimentality. Zabel finds that it is not Greene's most convincing book and says: "Its excessive manipulation keeps it from

14. Kenneth Allott and Miriam Farris, *The Art of Graham Greene* (London: Hamish Hamilton, 1951), p. 217.

15. Morton D. Zabel, *Craft and Character* (London: Gollancz, 1957), p. 384.

16. *The Observer*, December 5, 1955.

17. Walter Allen, *Tradition and Dream* (London, Phoenix, 1964)

being that." Greene himself realizes that the "scales [have been] too heavily weighted, the plot overloaded, the religious scruples of Scobie too extreme."[18] These judgements of the critics point out to one fact: Scobie's scruples and his final act appear to be contrivances to prove a thesis. There is another cause for the failure which can be traced to imbalance. The tragedy is heavy and the comic strain in the book is ineffective. The comic scenes do not relieve the gloom. Rather, they make the darkness visible. Scobie undertakes to read something to the shipwrecked boy and the story he concocts, though Kai Laitenen[19] sees it as one of the few comic passages in the novel, adds to the pathos of Scobie when the reader realizes that it serves only to intensify the gloom of Scobie's insufferable situation. The Wilson - Harris scenes as well as the Wilson - Louise scenes do not provide the comic relief the reader might expect. While Harris giggles at what the fortune-teller tells Wilson, Wilson himself is apprehensive. The cockroach hunt which could have only been comic deepens Harris's sense of loneliness in the wilderness that Africa is for him. His rules are the 'Queensberry rules' but he is a sad figure with inconsequent feelings of self-importance. Wilson's love affair with the 'literary Louise' misses the mark of being a comic interlude. As there is pathos in his visit to the tin-roofed brothel, there is pathos again in the love-scene where he lies uncontrollably bleeding on the floor between the table and the meat safe with Louise standing over him "as though he were a corpse." Dr. Sykes's garrulity and the way she suggests the easiest and the safest way to end oneself fails to be the comedy it purports to be. Helen cries out: "What a beastly talk this is. You've got no business to tell..." It is one of the grimmest scenes of the grimmest dramatic irony.

3.4.7 *The Heart of the Matter* shows the tears in things and comedy is hard to find in it. It is severely divorced from comedy. To be a true tragedy it is too heavily laden with sentimentality, and for that reason it is less convincing. If only the comic buffer were there the absurdities of the spiritual tight corners created by the principal character would have been less suffocating. Because of the near absence of the usual Greene comedy the novel seems to dip into a depression unknown either in *Brighton Rock* or *The Power and the Glory*. This only serves to prove that tragedy proper in Greene's fiction is doomed to the macabre as in *Brighton Rock* or the

18. *Introduction to Three Novels* (Stockholm, Norstedts, 1962)

19. "The Heart of the Novel" in R.O. Evans (ed.), *Graham Greene*, op. cit.

melodramatic in *The Heart of the Matter*. The strength of *The Power and the Glory* lies in its balance of tensions between the tragic and the comic: the interplay adds to the power of both the strands. By the omission of a scene in *The Heart of the Matter* (restored for the first time in the recent Collected Edition), Greene writes, "I thought I had gained intensity and impetus, but I had sacrificed tone." The point appears to be applicable to the whole novel with justification since the usual comedy does not irradiate it with the livingness retaining the contact with reality. Greene himself is not unaware of it. He explains at length why the book did not satisfy him and clinches his argument with the conclusion: "Perhaps Scobie should have been a subject for cruel comedy rather than for tragedy..."[20] (Ellipsis Greene's)

3.5 Greene's 'entertainments' with the rich comic sense in them are the full-dress rehearsals of the comic vision to appear in its full glory. The 'entertainments' accommodate his growing comic sense and progressively coalesce into the 'novels' enriching them as comedies. *The Third Man* (1949), a short novel meant to be a film, is a case in point. The story of a pencillin racketeer with the innumerable deaths he causes before the investigation with a couple more afterwards is a sad one. But as Greene writes: "Reality in fact was to be only the background of a fairy tale."[21] Concluding the review of *The Heart of the Matter* in *The Times Literary Supplement*[22], the reviewer writes of Greene: "He is a writer whom it is not easy to classify, but one whose power of development, in style and attitude of mind, seems to show an ever-renewed vitality." The vitality lies in the rich comedy that goes with the fairy-tale in this novel.

3.5.1 The background against which the fairy-tale is laid is the literally war-torn four-powered Vienna:

> ... the smashed dreary city of Vienna divided up in zones among the four powers; the Russian, the British, the American, the French zones, regions marked only by a notice board, and in the centre of the city, surrounded by the Ring with its heavy public buildings and its prancing statuary, the Inner Stadt under the control of all four powers. (p. 2)[23]

20. Introduction to *The Heart of the Matter*, Collected edn., 1971.
21. Introduction to *The Third Man*, Collected edn., 1976.
22. May 29, 1948, p. 302.
23. Page numbers refer to *The Third Man*, Bantam Books, 1968.

The 'I' of the book is a police officer, a Colonel Calloway of Scotland Yard, who meets Rollo Martins, an English visitor, in Vienna. By the time Martins reaches Vienna, his friend Harry Lime's body is being lowered into the grave. The hero-worshipping and friendship-loving Martins is slowly convinced of his friend's role of a monstrous racketeer. Martins agrees to be a decoy after knowing that the man is still alive. Shot by the police and in pain, Lime is shot again by his friend and dies. The stock themes of childhood, pursuit and betrayal are here but what makes the book very interesting is the personality of Rollo Martins. He is a writer of Westerns and an odd combination of the careful and the reckless: "There was always a conflict in Rollo Martins - between the absurd Christian name and the sturdy Dutch (four generations back) surname. Rollo looked at every woman that passed and Martins renounced them forever. I don't know which of them wrote the Westerns." (p. 6) Rollo and Martins sway between conservatism and liberalism, calculation and recklessness, scepticism and hero-worship. In the first few pages the character comes out alive and before the tension of the thriller becomes intense, we get the absurdly sweet portrait of Rollo Martins. The sadness of the raw material of the racketeer in the background is completely transformed in the finished product of the final impression the novel leaves. Rollo Martins writes Westerns under the pseudonym B. Dexter. The British Cultural Relations Society representative mistakes him for *the* Dexter, the novelist, whom they are expecting. Crabbin, the agent of the society, arranges a literary discussion which Rollo is to initiate and wind up later answering the questions of the listeners. The scene is the point where the strands of the plot concerning Martins's visit to Vienna to see his friend and the writer's visit to his fans intersect. The rich comedy of the scene makes us forget the racketeer and the search for him: Martins tries to escape from the police trial and gets caught by the literary society man and a hilarious scene follows:

> Crabbin interposed quickly for the sake of the Austrians:
>
> "That is a little joke of Mr. Dexter's. He meant the poet Gray - a gentle, mild subtle genius - one can see the affinity."
>
> "And he is called Zane Grey?"
>
> "That was Mr. Dexter's Joke. Zane Grey wrote what we call Westerns - cheap popular novelettes about bandits and cowboys."
>
> "He is not a great writer?"

> "No, no, Far from it," Mr. Crabbin said. "In the strict sense I would not call him a writer at all. Martins told me that he felt the first stirrings of revolt at that statement. He had never regarded himself before as a writer, but Crabbin's self-confidence irritated him — even the way the light flashed back from Crabbin's spectacles seemed an added cause of vexation. Crabbin said, "He was just a popular entertainer."
>
> "Why the hell not?" Martins said fiercely.
>
> "Oh well, I merely meant..."
>
> "What was Shakespeare?" (p. 65)

The comedy lies also in the fact that Dexter's callousness and even ignorance pass for his originality. The comic goes in the form of fun. But the important question is still there. Cannot an entertainer be a great writer? Shakespeare is a poet, but more important than his poetry for his success is his capacity to entertain. Greene is impatient with academic formalism and he asserts that a popular novelist could be a great one too.

3.5.2 Religion does not become a matter of morbid sentiment or incomprehensible dilemma for Lime, the racketeer. He is a Catholic but one with a difference from Catholics like Scobie and the whisky-priest. He is a Catholic without scruples - with a vengeance as it were. We are told that if Martins earned a thousand taxed, Lime without scruples earned thirty-thousand without taxes. In his discussion with Martins he says:

> "In these days, old man, nobody thinks in terms of human being, Governments don't, so why should we? They talk of the people and proletariat, and I talk of the mugs. It's the same thing. They have their five-year plans and so have I."
>
> "You used to be a Catholic."
>
> "Oh, I still *believe*, old man. In god and Mercy and all that. I'm not hurting anybody's soul by what I do. The dead are happier dead. They don't miss much here, poor devils," ... (p. 102)

3.5.3 The final impression that the book leaves is one of light comedy. Rollo Martins tells the Scotland Yard man, "I'm a buffoon. I like playing the silly fool ..." (p. 14) and he does play the fool - not only in the British Cultural Society meeting but throughout his visit to Vienna. What he wants to discover - Lime's possible murderer -

turns out to be a discovery of his friend's being alive and his guilt. He liked to make people in the image of what he thought of them. Anne tells him angrily once: "For God's sake stop making people in your image. Harry was real. He wasn't just your hero and my lover." He undertakes like the fool that he is to make the officer "look the biggest bloody fool" and in the end has to accept defeat like a buffoon falling off the trapeze in the circus show: "I haven't won. I've lost." (p. 116) As the author himself says with his deep insight: "There is a lot of comedy in these situations if you are not directly concerned." (p. 88) With the fear that just flashes on the screen (the book is meant to be a film), it is the comedy that remains.

3.6 "Writing is a form of therapy;" Greene writes,[24] "sometimes I wonder how all those who do not write, compose, or paint can manage to escape the madness, the melancholia, the panic fear which is inherent in the human situation." Maurice Bendrix, the 'I' of the novel *The End of the Affair* (1951), is a novelist whose profession is the chartering of the human situation. The writing of this novel could be viewed as a form of self-designed therapy for the obsessive hatred which during the course of his narration "gets curiously mislaid." Greene himself writes:[25] "the slow discovery by a novelist of his individual method is exciting, but a moment comes in middle-age when he feels he no longer controls his method, he has become its prisoner." The novelist-hero is conscious of this problem and expresses (etymologically the word means pressing out) his difficulty: "If this book of mine fails to take a straight course, it is because I am lost in strange region. I have no map."(p. 49)[26] The difficulty is far from being one of technique. It is there in the more important subject and attitude: "When I began to write the story down, I thought I was writing a record of hate, but somehow the hate has got mislaid." (p. 128) At one level the central antinomy is in the power of the artist and the power of God.

3.6.1 Greene tells us[27] that in a passage of Baron Von Hugel he underlined the following: "the purification and slow constitution of the Individual into a Person, by means of the thing element, the apparently blind Determinism of Natural Law and Natural Happenings ... Nothing can be more certain than that we must admit

24. Introduction to *The Collected Stories*, Collected edn., 1972.
25. Introduction to *The End of the Affair*, Collected edn., 1974.
26. Page numbers refer to *The End of the Affair*, Penguin edn., 1960.
27. Introduction to *The End of the Affair*, Collected edn., 1974.

and place this undeniable, increasingly obtrusive, element and power *somewhere* in our lives: if we will not own it as a means, it will grip us as our end." Bendrix experiences problems at two levels: at the level of cultivating art and the level of being human. In both he ends as a grotesque figure. As an artist he suffers from insufferable intellectual pride and as a man from obsessive egotism. Since he never prepares for owning the Superior power it grips him as his end. Greene's intention seems to be to show the inexplicable, unknowable and gratuitous working of Grace. At the highest level Grace is the subject of the novel.

3.6.2 If *The Power and the Glory* traces the evolution of a saint through a human conflict between the well-defined polarities of the State and the Church, *The End of the Affair* deals with the mysterious power of sanctity directing and shaping human existence. Greene transcends the moral order and shows the operation of Grace even in - by worldly standards - a 'fallen woman'. While the sacramental view of Christianity leads to the apocalypse of the divine within the imperfections of the human, Greene shows that the divine offers a stark alternative to the total corruption of the human. What matters is faith though its arrival is gratuitous and inexplicable. As a creative artist he makes manifest his saintly sympathy and treats corrupt human love with understanding. He is influenced by French Catholic writers like Leon Bloy and Mauriac. While Bloy held "I could have been a saint, a worker of wonders. I have become a man of letters", and Mauriac: "One would have to be a saint. But then one would not write novels"[28], Greene asserts about the central character in *The Confidential Agent*: "He was damned like a creative writer to sympathy." Saintly sympathy is the characteristic feature of Greene's outlook. For his sinners he has a more than Christian sympathy - a creative writer's compassion. He does not believe in a literature which does not anatomize and expose the raw flesh of sin.[29] His view of literature and the vocation of the artist are evident in the passage he admiringly quotes from Newman:[30]

> I say from the nature of the case, if literature is to be a study of human nature, you cannot have a Christian literature. It is contradiction in terms to attempt a sinless literature of sinful man.

28. as quoted by Martain in *The Responsibility of the Artist*, New York, 1960.

29. With great perceptiveness Greene makes the whisky-priest say: "It needs a lot of learning to see things with a saint's eye."

30. Graham Greene, *Who do I write*? (London: Percival Marshall, 1948), p. 32.

The suffering of a jealous lover is at the heart of this novel where the mistress is sanctified at the end in spite of her carnality. Both his suffering (which emanates from his love-in-hate feeling and that of Sarah, the result of love), discover and bring into being an unknown region of his heart as suggested by the epigraph from Bloy:

> Man has places in his heart which do not yet exist, and into them enters suffering in order that they may have existence.

Oddly enough Bendrix is a curious mouthpiece without 'responsibility' or sympathy. His obsessive hatred culminates in his self-realization and marks a step in his spiritual progress towards faith.

3.6.3 Bendrix is proud of his professional skill. He begins the story in the middle saying: "A story has no beginning or end ..." If the affair is the beginning and the prayer at the close of the novel the end, the event of Bendrix's meeting Henry is the middle. Had Bendrix believed then (in the middle) in God, he would have believed in the moment which chooses the novelist by a superior ordinance. But he did not believe. The conceit of the novelist begins to break: "If this book of mine fails to take a straight course, it is because I am lost in a strange region. I have no map."(p. 49) After the death of Sarah, Bendrix gets a further insight when his conceit is shed: "If I were writing a novel I would end it here: a novel, I used to think, has to end somewhere, but I am beginning to believe my realism has been at fault all these years, for nothing in life now ever seems to end."(p. 144) The shedding of conceit marks the beginning of his real inward-looking stance. He wonders how he can love Sarah if he hates her so much. "Can one really hate and love? Or is it only myself that I hate? I hate the books I write with their trivial unimportant skill, I hate the craftsman's mind in me..."(p. 178) It is at this point that Bendrix's self-realization as a man and as an artist coincide. As an artist he starts in conceit and ends up in humility. As a man he is obsessed with hatred. Through vengefulness he realises that the lover who ousted him from Sarah's love is God and fills himself with God-hatred. Then the miracles badger him with doubt and, endowed as he is with the artist's insight, he knows the origin of a sanctity of which the miracles are an evidence. Urticaria may be susceptible to faith-cure and so is perhaps the tummy ache of Parkis's boy. But how about the conversion in himself? That at least should be a miracle to convince himself. The comedy here is too deep for words. The cuckold confides his trouble to his wife's lover who in turn employs a detective to find out truth for his own reasons. Both have been fooled by Sarah's real lover. The man whom he mocks and teases first becomes his friend and he consents to share his house with him and look after him like an affectionate friend.

3.6.4 In Sarah the process of self-realization and self-integration has a shorter journey. Starting with unflinching adultery she falls in love in a real sense and prays, without even believing, to 'whatever might exist'. In a few minutes she is convinced of His being and the painful conflict begins. She hates Him but cannot escape Him. At first it is the desert only which she dreads. She wonders: "If one would believe in God, would He fill the desert?" She shares not only the happiness but also the unhappiness of her lover. Here is her realization: "It's as if we were working together on the same statue, cutting it out of each other's misery. But I don't even know the design." (p. 90) Her pain intensifies her doubt: "You can't have a merciful God and this despair."(p. 91) She tries to come out of the restrictions of the vow telling herself that it has just been hysteria. Out of revenge she tries to stir up her lechery with a man called Dunstan but without success. She painfully puts it down: "You let me sin, but you take away the fruits of my sin. You let me try to escape with D., but you don't allow me to enjoy it. You make me drive love out, and then you say there's no lust for you either. What do you expect me to do now, God? Where do I go from here?"(p. 98) With the realization that she is a bitch and a fake she wonders what He has seen in her. In this frame of mind she understands: "Henry is gentle and patient. You can find it in Maurice who thinks he hates, and loves, loves all the time."(p. 99) Understanding is the first step to saintliness and she cannot hurt Him with lust gone from her and more so if she does not get any pleasure from adultery. She racks herself: "I want to do something that I enjoy and that will hurt you. Otherwise it is but mortification and that's an expression of belief. And believe me, God, I don't believe in you yet, I don't believe in you yet." She can think of only one way of hurting Him. She wants to run away with Bendrix. But even that she cannot accomplish. Reflecting on Smythe's strawberry mark she gets another revelation: "We can love with our minds, but can we love only with our minds? Love extends itself all the time, so that we can even love with our senseless nails: we love even with our clothes, so that a sleeve can feel a sleeve."(p. 108) Then in a rage at the thought that the body seems necessary for feeling and that it makes one coarse, beastly and materialist she dips her finger in the "so-called holy water" and makes "a kind of cross" on her forehead. With this the way to self-realization is assured. From the rationalist's arguments against God she begins getting a sense of "inverted belief." She knows pain and knows that it goes into her lover's writing: "Maurice's pain goes into his writing: you can hear the nerves twitch through his sentences. Well, if pain can make a writer, I'm learning, Maurice, too."(p. 117) She wants to stop giving them pain and prays: "Dear God, if only you could come down from your cross for a while and let me get up there instead. If I could suffer like you, I could heal like You."(p. 118) Greene tells us that pain teaches quickly. Sarah learns to imitate Him: "I shut my eyes and put my mouth against the mark. I felt sick for a moment because I fear deformity, and he sat quiet and let me kiss him, and I thought I am kissing pain and pain belongs to You as happiness never does ... You might have killed us with happiness, but you let us be with you in pain." But the human weakness is too powerful to be overcome. Even at the last moment before faith finally settles down in her she tells herself: "I want Maurice, I want ordinary corrupt human love."(p. 121)

3.6.5 Greene writes in his preface to *Three Plays*:[31]

> The strain of writing a novel, which keeps the author confined for a period of years with his depressive self, is extreme, and I have always sought relief in 'entertainments'— for melodrama as much as farce is an expression of the manic mood.

His 'entertainments' serve more or less as spring boards for the leap into the novels and the fusion of the strains of comedy and tragedy. After *The Third Man*, an entertainment, *The End of the Affair* soars high with a blend of the comic and the tragic from the depression left by *The Heart of the Matter.* Basically, the story is that of a sensual woman discovering in a terrifically personal way that her lecheries are but a form of divine love. The book is deliberately fraught with absurdities and ambiguities. The miracles introduced at the end are almost matters counter-productive of laughter and the heroine's death also makes for comedy. The conception that a novelist should find his material in such a way as Maurice Bendrix does is comic and so is the pursuit — by now a stock theme in Greene. Henry is the comic figure of an Elizabethan cuckold wearing horns. In this novel comedy and tragedy are almost on a par with each other. From the constricted atmosphere of *The Heart of the Matter* there is a significant point of departure in the career of Greene as a creative artist. The new direction, unmistakably, is towards the preponderance of the comic. *The Heart of the Matter*

31. Quoted by David Pryce-Jones, *Graham Greene, op. cit.*

takes a plunge into tragedy and in *The End of the Affair* Greene gives up the predominantly tragic mode. One valid proof of this is that Bendrix tries to be absolutely unsentimental. The artist realizes on the one hand that the solemnity of tragedy is not enough, on the other, the frivolity of comedy, unleavened by tragedy, would not take him to the heart of the matter. The tragic intention in the novel is evident from the epigraph. But the interpenetration of the tragic by the comic takes the artist's vision to a new clarity. Here, in this novel, the comic and the tragic are blended as in the conversion of Smythe, or in the death of Sarah of a cold. The treacherously light tone of this high-strung spiritual drama is deliberately maintained and sustained in order to save the novel from the upsurge of a disastrous sentimentality that mars *The Heart of the Matter.* The result is that while the earlier novel almost falsifies life, this one gives the reader a new insight. Things begin to fall into their places. Existence is shown through a more lucid perspective.

3.6.6 Conflict which is central to a tragedy is here as the tragic element. The 'Jealous God' is confronted by a jealous lover. A purely personal evil confronts God face to face. Sarah almost steps out of her evil and accepts God while Bendrix, obstinate in evil, persists in his egotistic claim on Sarah's love. The problem of evil is seen in the perspective of a personal relationship between man and his God and the only available solution to it is in the approximation to sainthood. 'Abandonment' occurs again as a key word though in a different sense from which it appears in *The Power and the Glory.* The source of Sarah's sanctity lies in her capacity to lose herself in love with perfect abandon in moments of love. ".. her abandonment touched the strange mathematical point of endlessness, a point with no width, occupying no space." Sarah gives up her love for the sake of His love since she has established a line of communication with God. Pain is the medium for the Christian eradication of evil. She evaluates her experiences of pain in terms of creative suffering. Bendrix drifts into the wild flux, "the love of hatred and the hatred of love." He tries with all his agonizing fury to pursue his rival beyond his beloved's grave and becomes the tragicomic figure of a fallen man. As a writer he has been wrong in not recognizing his rival - so as a man he denies His existence. His agnosticism follows from his professional pride, intellectual arrogance and conceit. The surrender (of memory, intellect and intelligence) has not been complete.

3.6.7 Although physical deformity is an aspect of tragedy, it could not be in itself a source of true tragic feeling. An emphasis on it belongs to the domain of the grotesque or the comic. In Greene's principal characters physical deformities are signs to show a symbolic failure to adjust to environment and a failure to triumph. The deformities announce their failure in a society which judges by externals. Anthony Farrant has a scar, Raven a hare-lip, and Pinkie a pigeon-chest. Two of the characters in *The End of the Affair* have deformities. Bendrix is lame (he has one leg a little shorter than the other, the result of an accident in childhood) and the rationalist Smythe has an ugly strawberry mark on his cheek. Perhaps these explain their sense of failure and alienation. The obsessed hero with his intellectual pride is cured to some extent of his conceit through a process of suffering. The story has a joyous ending for Smythe and Parkis and a beatific close for Sarah It has an illuminating comic close for Bendrix in the sense that he affectionately shares digs with the man whom he cuckolded. The epigraph makes sure as do the events in the novel that the secret places in Bendrix's heart are brought into existence by pain which enters it through a divine design.

3.6.8 Ursula Spier[32] quotes the Allots who have been told by Greene that he made a positive attempt to exclude melodrama from the novel then being written and argues: "Greene did not succeed in avoiding melodrama in *The End of the Affair.*" She begins saying: "Catholicism, which he chose for himself, is itself melodramatic, in that faith is the only explanation for its basic concepts, since they cannot be explained intellectually. And faith, however one defines it, has aspects of melodrama." From this she proceeds to show that the recurrent plot formula — pursuit — is an ingredient of melodrama while admitting that the pursuit in the novel is at different levels. "Sublimated, refined to a corollary, but still very much there." The boy Lance, though a minor figure, supplies here a Gothic element of melodrama. Spier writes that the interjection as a whole of the concept of God is an example of melodramatic writing. She makes the comment that critics made before: God is allowed to become a character. "Bendrix and Smythe, not only Sarah, address Him before we are through and He is allowed to do everything but answer." Finally the information about Sarah's Baptism in her childhood smacks of the manipulation in a detective story. Greene's creation of suspense followed in the strategy of marginal comments is a literary device ('cliff-hanging') to heighten the melodramatic effectiveness. Having thus traced all these elements which she calls

32. "Melodrama in Graham Greene's 'The End of the Affair'," *MFS*, (Autumn, 1957).

melodramatic she concludes: "Greene has used some of the oldest, most commercial and hackneyed devices and situations that, I imagine, can be found. Yet, though he has used melodramatic devices widely, he has not written a cheap melodramatic story" since "all is fair if the means produce a beautifully turned-out book that speaks its piece clearly." Greene once told his interviewers:[33] "...melodrama is one of my working tools and it enables me to obtain effects that would be unobtainable otherwise, but on the other hand I am not deliberately melodramatic; don't get too annoyed if I say that I write in the way I do because I am what I am." Though the melodramatic devices are apparent, the purpose of using them points to the harnessing of the comic spirit. This remark applies to Spier's analysis point by point. If faith has aspects of melodrama, it also has aspects of comedy in its larger definition of being a step higher than joy. Pursuit here belongs to the domain of comedy since it follows from a basically funny presumption. It becomes acutely so in the act of Parkis pursuing the man who pays him. Lancelot, Parkis's boy, we learn, is named mistakenly so for Parkis confused Lancelot for Galahad. He is really a Gothic element which raises a good laugh. The spirit of comedy is enhanced by the deliberate introduction of God as an unseen but omnipresent character, making fools of everyone for His is the power and the glory for all that happens. The manipulation of Sarah's Catholic birth also is an element necessary for the dominance of the spirit of comedy which is the real force of the novel. Taken in consonance with statements like: "I've caught belief like a disease"(p. 43) and in consonance with the word 'infection' used in statements relating to faith, Sarah's Baptism revealed at the end is provided as an antidote to mockery. Greene shows that nothing can make a mockery of God. The mocker gets converted and mockery could be a first step towards faith. God is the priest and those who came to scoff remain to pray. The mockers are mocked: therein lies the joy of comedy.

3.6.9 The comic is at work right from the beginning of the novel. The novelist-hero starts with mocking himself. Comedy is seen best when there is the full play of irony. The ironic mode is in operation for Bendrix ridicules himself for his insight which is blurred by his professional pride. A typical Greene hero as he is, Bendrix is cynical to the point of being obsessive as when he says: "To me comfort is like the wrong memory at the wrong place". (p. 7) Nevertheless he recognizes the element of grotesque in life. Having employed Parkis

33. Martin Shuttleworth and Simon Rowen, "The Art of Fiction: Graham Greene", *The Paris Review*, No. 3 (Autumn 1953), pp. 24-41.

he realizes; "We are not hurt only by tragedy: the grotesque too carries weapons, undignified, ridiculous weapons." (p. 51) It is the painful grotesque that marks the beginning of the third phase in Greene's writing. Having failed in keeping on to his hatred he mocks at everything, his professional talent not excepted: "Henry James once, in a discussion with Walter Besant, said that a young woman with sufficient talent need only pass the mess-room windows of a Guards' barracks and look inside in order to check on the details, *I think at some stage of her book she would have found it necessary to go to bed with a Guardsman if only to check on the details*." (emphasis mine) Bendrix finds Henry a comic figure. He belongs to a department "hopelessly damned to unseriousness." The comedy is sustained in the meeting with Henry. Bendrix hates and teases him and teases himself: I could pretend to be a jealous lover" and then tells him further : "betrayed lovers are tragic, never comic". Henry himself is conscious of the grotesque: "But this is fantastic, I don't know what I've been thinking about. First to tell you and then to ask you. One can't spy on one's wife through a friend - and that friend pretend to be her lover". To the reader the comic irony is evident. Bendrix need not *pretend*. His reply is a mockery of himself: "oh, it's not done, but neither is adultery or theft or running away from the enemy's fire. The not done things are done every day, Henry. It's part of modern life. I've done most of them myself." (p. 17) In retrospect, the ambivalence of love and hatred becomes strikingly evident to him: "Hatred seems to operate the same glands as love; it even produces the same actions. If we had not been taught how to interpret the story of the Passion, would we have been able to say from their actions alone whether it was the jealous Judas or the cowardly Peter who loved Christ?" (p. 27) But the demon in him is terrible. Hearing Sarah cough, he tells us "I wished I had been able to whistle a tune, something jaunty, adventurous, happy; but I have no ear for music." (p. 33) Parkis, the humourous figure, says wherein comedy lies: "If you look at it from the outside, it's really quite funny." (p. 40)

3.6.10 Love in The End of the Affair is frank and realistic. "Sometimes she would come in between two queues, and we used to make love between the greengrocer's and the butcher's." (p. 34) Sarah is unabashed and guiltless. "We can hear him," she said, and added with horrifying lucidity "there's one stair which always creaks." (p. 45) Comically enough, the code word the lovers use for love-making is 'onions'. But it is this love that sharpens Bendrix's awareness and rouses his spirituality in an odd way: "The words of human love have been used by the saints to describe the vision of God; and so, I suppose, we might use the terms of prayer, meditation, contemplation to explain the intensity of the love we feel for a woman. We too surrender memory, intellect, intelligence, and we too experience the deprivation, the *noche oscura*, and sometimes as a reward a kind of peace. The act of love itself has been described as the little death, and lovers sometimes experience too the little peace." (p. 46) This insight leads to a further one, "I have never understood why people who can swallow the enormous improbability of a personal God boggle at a personal devil. I have known so intimately the way that demon works in my imagination. ... I can imagine if there existed a God who loved, the devil would be driven to destroy even the weakest, the most faulty imitation of that love." (p. 58)

3.6.11 The horns along the walls in the lounge of Henry's club bring to Bendrix's mind their suitability for symbolizing a cuckold. The comic spirit reaches the highest point in the interview there where the egotistic novelist's venomousness and the sedately tender thoughtfulness of the wronged husband come into sharp focus:

"Sit down," Henry commanded with the authority of his tears, and I obeyed him. He said, "I've been thinking. Were you two lovers, Bendrix?"

> "Why should you imagine...?"
>
> "It's the only explanation."
>
> "I don't know what you are talking about."
>
> "It's the only excuse too, Bendrix, Can't you see that what you've done is - monstrous?"
>
> As he spoke he turned his hat over and checked the maker's name.
>
> "I suppose you think I'm an awful fool, Bendrix, not to have guessed. Why didn't she leave me"? Had I got to instruct him about the character of his own wife? The poison was beginning to work in me again. I said, "You have a good safe income. You're a habit she's formed. You're security." He listened seriously and attentively as though I were a witness before the Commission giving evidence on oath. I went sourly on, "You were no more trouble to us than you'd been to the others."
>
> "There were others too?"

"Sometimes I thought you knew all about it and didn't care. Sometimes I longed to have it out with you- like we are doing now when it's too late. I wanted to tell you what I thought of you."

"What did you think?"

"That you were her pimp. You pimped for me and you pimped for them, and now you are pimping for the latest one. The eternal pimp. Why don't you get angry, Henry?"

"I never knew."

"You pimped with your ignorance. You pimped by never learning how to make love with her, so she had to look elsewhere. You pimped by giving opportunities ... You pimped by being a bore and a fool, so now somebody who isn't a bore and a fool is playing about with her in Cedar Road."

"Why did she leave you?"

"Because I became a bore and a fool too. But I wasn't born one, Henry. You created me. She wouldn't leave you so I became a bore. Boring her with complaints and jealousy." He said, "people have a great opinion of your books." "And they say you're a first-class chairman. What the hell does our work matter?"(p. 65)

Another example of the high point of comedy manoeuvred through irony is evident in the scene where Bendrix tell Parkis: "That was Galahad. Lancelot was found in bed with guinevere."(p. 75) Another example of 'lamentable comedy; is in Smythe's entreating Bendrix to let Sarah have a Catholic funeral.

'And what have I to do with it?" (Bendrix asks)

"She always said that her husband had a great respect for you."

He was turning the screw of absurdity too far ... Once in the blitz I saw a man laughing outside his house where his wife and child were buried.(p. 140)

The comic rises very high in the novel in Bendrix's exclamations and gibes:

"It was I who penetrated her, not you.,"(p. 162)

"Don't give me your professional pity, father. Keep it for your penitents."(p. 177)

> "you are a devil, God, tempting us to leap."(p. 186)
>
> "I hate you, God, I hate You as though You existed."(p. 181)

3.6.12 Bendrix's certainty in his powers and insight, again, is comic. Reading the scrap of letter rifled from Sarah's waste-paper basket he jumps to a conclusion regarding the other who ousted him from Sarah's love and having read it in full thinks that he can elope with her. Even the reading of the journal does not make him realize the truth. On the very first page he boasts about his "professional pride to prefer the near truth, even to the expression of near-hate." But this is his understanding of truth: "Now I know the whole absurd story of the vow, now I was certain of her love, I was assured of her. If two people loved, they slept together; it was a mathematical formula, tested and proved by human experience." (p. 125) Till the very end he vacillates between love and hate and here is a passage which cancels out his earlier assertion: "When I began to write our story down, I thought I was writing a record of hate, but somehow the hate has got mislaid and all I know is that in spite of her mistakes and her unreliability, she was better than most."(p. 128)

3.6.13 Within the framework of the writing, in terms of explaining themselves and their introspection the contrast between Bendrix and Sarah is fraught with comic undertones. As pieces of self-revelation the following passages, the first set from Bendrix and the second from Sarah, can be seen as embodying the contrast:

> "...a novelist (has) to amass his trivial material before picking the right clue." (p. 25)
>
> The reviewers said it was the work of a craftsman; that was all was left of me of what had been a passion. I thought perhaps with the next novel the passion would return ... (p. 35)
>
> I had wanted to convey the sense of passion through some common simple episode without any rhetoric in words or action, and it worked.(p. 43)
>
> "I remember the trivial details very well; the manageress asked ..." (p. 44)

The following are from Sarah

> His love is like a medieval chastity belt: only when he is there with me, in me, does he feel safe. ... If one could believe in God, would he fill the desert? (p. 89)

> It is as if we are working together on the same statute cutting it out of each other's misery. But I don't even know the design. (p. 90)
>
> You let me sin, but you take away the fruits of my sin. ... God, where do I go from here? (p. 98)
>
> I don't mind my pain. It's their pain I can't stand. Let my pain go on and on, but stop theirs. (p. 118)
>
> Henry took a day off work. I don't know why. He gave me lunch and we went to the National Gallery. ... He was like a parent coming down to school and taking the child out. But he's the child.(p. 118)

While Bendrix's writing appears fraught with the consciousness of writing in spite of the persona being a novelist, Sarah's writing strikes the reader as genuinely spontaneous.

3.6.14 The tragic mode taken in isolation leads to a constraint which a creative writer like Greene cannot withstand for long. The genius of self-expression is such that it constantly craves to find an outlet which particularly suits it. Comedy is the one for Greene. In *The End of the Affair* the comic spirit comingles with the tragic in the right measure and communicates a rich sense of life. The tragic and the comic rhythms, to use once again the terms of Susanne K. Langer, intertwine themselves and make *The End of the Affair* a successful work of art. The strength of a work of creative imagination depends upon the interpenetration of comedy and tragedy. But for the pervasion of the comic spirit *The End of the Affair* would not have taken the artist from the oppressive gloom of *The Heart of the Matter*. It must however be borne in mind that the triumph of the comic mode in Greene does not denote the negation of the tragic; it only means that the tragic has been fully subsumed under the inclusive comic mode. George Santayana's words, "Everything in nature is lyrical in its ideal essence, tragic in its fate and comic in its existence", comes to our mind when we come across a passage like this in *The End of the Affair*:

> I wished to shatter the deadness of this buried room with laughter. I sat down on a sofa and began to shake with it. I thought of Sarah dead upstairs and Henry asleep with a silly smile on his face, and the lover with the strawberry mark discussing the funeral with the lover who had employed Mr Parkis to sprinkle his door-bell with powder. The tears ran down my cheeks as I laughed.(p. 140)

3.7 If a fantasy has to be judged by its power of invention, a 'frivolity' like the 'little story' *Loser Takes All* (1955) should be judged by the strength of being light-hearted. In a dedicatory letter, Greene writes that the entertainment is a 'frivolity' and makes his intention in writing it clear: "... this tale has not been written for the purposes of encouraging adultery, the use of pyjama tops, or registry office marriages. Nor is it meant to discourage gambling." The work is refreshingly light-hearted after the thick-laid seriousness in *The Heart of the Matter.* Greene does entertain in abundance here and the comic spirit pervades as pure and amusing frivolity.

3.7.1 The frivolity consists in the day-dream-like quality of the inaccessible and until then unknown employer Gom (the good old man) fixing the wedding of his assistant accountant at Monte Carlo promising a cruise later on his yacht, "*Luxe, calme et volupté.*" The 'I' of the tale is the assistant accountant, the middle-aged Bertram, in love with Cary. The lovers go to Monte Carlo and wait there for the *Seagull.* They go through the wedding without their host, who fails to turn up at the appointed time. Bertram plays at the Casino and wins a lot of money but in the process loses the girl who falls in love with a young man. Dreuther (the Gom) arrives at last and suggests a plan to Bertram to win his wife back. The incidents in the book, the tight-lipped waiting, the money worry, the young man losing money and winning the girl, Bertram winning money and losing her, the despairing acts of the wife and the husband, and finally the clever idea of the man who married four times are all comic. The title itself is a funny reversal of Hemingway's *Winner Takes Nothing.*

3.7.2 The successful accountant Bertram is a comic figure without himself being aware of it. He is eager to sleep with the young woman with whom he falls in love after being separated from his wife for fifteen years. But it is about all he fails to accomplish until Dreuther tells him of a plan. In his professional pride in competence he invents a 'system' which leads him to reflect:

> I watched them playing their systems, losing a little, gaining a little, and I thought it was strange how the belief persis-ted— that somehow you could beat the bank. They were like theologians, patiently trying to rationalise a mystery. I suppose in all lives a moment comes when we wonder — suppose after all there is God, suppose the theologians are right. Pascal was a gambler - who staked his money on a divine system. I thought, I am a far better mathematician than of these - is that why I don't believe in their mystery, and yet if this mystery exists, isn't it possible that I might

> solve it where they have failed? It was almost like a prayer when I thought; it's not for the sake of money — I don't want a fortune — just a few days with Cary free from anxiety. (pp. 51-52)[34]

But his very success with the system makes him a failure. Fifteen thousand pounds, in value, is an inadequate compensation for what he lost after having started playing his system. There is a comic twist when, like Conrad in *It's a Battlefield*, he expects a dismissal and gets a promotion.

3.7.3 If the seasoned realist Bertram is comic, so is the romantic young woman Cary. While one professes to have no superstitions (I am not superstitious, but it is impossible when you have reached forty and are conspicuously unsuccessful not sometimes to half-believe in a malign providence."(p. 8), the other is steeped in them. While the one never forgets his profession, the other is all for fun in an unconventional ways. Cary often makes such statements "I'd love to live in sin."(p. 24) "It would rather be fun wouldn't it, if he were a bit late."(p. 34) "We could always run up bills,"she says and adds, "not so much fun really as living in sin, I suppose."(p. 35) "Nobody will really believe we are married and that'll be fun."(p. 25) "I don't feel married, it's fun not feeling married."(p. 48) Having a romantic soft corner for the poor and the downfallen she wants to pity Bertram for his loss but when he says that he has won, she shambles back under the bed clothes. She admits as much to him herself. She married a man she met at the bar of the Volunteer, someone who liked cold sausages and travelled by bus because taxis were too expensive. As he was very lucky and won a lot of money, she did not like him any longer. Dreuther, though he has never seen her (there lies the comic aspect, the light-hearted frivolity), finely sums her up and says she is romantic.

3.7.4 Dreuther is human and a pleasant antithesis to the millionaire Krogh in *England Made Me*. While Krogh understood nothing better than a graph of production and while human relationships baffled him, Dreuther, said to have married four times, placidly old and above sex, (Gom!) is skilled in solving problems men like Bertram face. He has a musician's head and a mane of white hair. "Where other men collected pictures to escape death duties, he collected for pleasure."(p. 10) The comic in him reaches a new height when he says: "An O.M. (or probably a C.H.) are the only honours that remain respectable."(p. 11) He has a refined literary

34. Page numbers refer to the *Loser Takes All*, Heinemann, 1966.

taste, a reflection of natural benevolence and gentility: "Don't depend too much on his Classicism. There are moments in Racine, Mr Bertrand (sic), when the abyss opens."(p. 17)

3.7.5 Bertram is comically, refreshingly, free from religion. "... everyone before me had accepted the perfection of the machine and no machine is perfect; in every joint, rivet, screw lies original sin."(p. 18) He is aware to the very bone that existence is comic, himself being a comic person. He sees in Dreuther the "part of a Haroun who could raise a man from obscurity and make him the ruler of provinces."(p. 21) He sees himself as an actor and blames the writer for writing him such a part. In that funny scene in the Orphée where he takes the fantastic woman and gets seen by Cary whom the hungry young man also brings there, Bertram is tempted to say to her: "This isn't me. I didn't write this. It's my part. Blame the author." (p. 108)

3.7.6 In all novels of Greene very often the comic reaches the highest point in a particular scene. In *Loser Takes All* the highest comedy is here:

> "I wish you'd forget him."
> "Oh, I'm not a bit interested in him, darling. I don't like young men. I expect I've got a father fixation."
> "Damn it, Cary, I'm not old enough to be your father."
> "Oh yes, you are," she said, "puberty begins at fourteen".
> "Then in fifteen and a half years from tonight you may be grandmother."
> "Tonight?" she said nervously, and then fell silent. The fireworks exploded in the sky. I said, "There's your catherine wheel."(p. 35)

3.7.7 *Loser Takes All* bears evidence to the shift in Greene's artistic centre of gravity. Written with "the hope that it would prove an amusing, agreeable *nouvelle*" and deliberately intended "to smash the mask"[35] ("A reputation is like a death mask") and called a 'frivolity', it shows the sustained pervasion by the comic which has unmistakably dominated the more serious novel, *The End of the Affair*. The spirit of the slender book is well reflected in the lines from Baudelaire the Gom recites:

> *"Vois sur ces canaux*
> *Dormir ces vaisseaux*
> *Dont l'humeur est vagabonde;*

35. Greene's introduction to *Loser Takes All*, Collected edn., 1976.

C'est pour assouvir
Ton moindre desir
Qu'ils viennent du bout du monde."[36]

There is a strength in the 'frivolity' since Greene is not so much concerned with theological speculations here as the recovery of a sweetness of temper conducive to a larger awareness of life's little ironies. Though tragedy and theological terminology have gone hand in hand in the earlier phase of Greene's fiction, the "entertainments" make an increasing use of comedy to find a fresh objective correlative for his vision. A work like *Loser Takes All* is a regular step of the imagination towards truth

3.8 Greene writes that *The Quiet American* (1955). "technically at least"[37] is a more successful book than *The End of the Affair*. Technical considerations apart, *The Quiet American* is a more successful book in the intermingling of the comic and the tragic strands.

3.8.1 Robert O. Evans[38] traces the intellectual milieu of the novel to France and the existentialist thinking of Sartre and calls Greene's thinking as reflected in *The Quiet American* aesthetic existentialism. Even without God, everything is by no means permissible. Greene does not take so much interest in the actual here as in the psychological motives of his principal character. Fowler, the chief character in the novel, believes in free choice and thinks that he himself makes what he is. In doing so he has to accept the full responsibility for what he has done as well as for what he has become. Greene, being a champion of the individual, makes Fowler believe in the implications of the choice and the resultant action which would lead to an endless chain of consequences. One cannot throw a stone into a pond and prevent ripples. With this problem in mind Fowler actively, vociferously, refuses to be involved. But one cannot start with a set belief and refuse to encounter reality. Despite his elaborate precautions Fowler finds himself unable to refrain from getting involved. He makes a courageous choice acquiescing with the dictum: "One has to take sides, if one has to stay human." He knows too "You cannot exist, unless you have the power to alter the future." But having set the wheels of consequence

36. Francis Scarfe (*Baudelaire*, Penguin, 1967) translates these lines: "See how the craft, nomads by bent, are slumbering in the canals: It's to gratify your slightest desire that they come from the world's end."

37. Introduction to *The End of the Affair*, Collected edn., 1974.

38. "Existentialism in Graham Greene's The Quiet American," MFS, Vol. 3. No. 3 (Autumn 1957).

in motion by the action of his choice, he causes the death of a young man whom in a way he has always wanted to protect. He knows he has to take the responsibility but then as a human being he tries to warn him of the action and hands the decision to a power not directly called God. The psychological motive for Fowler's action is complex. It would not have been so if Fowler's desire to get Phuong back bears a causal relationship to the death of Pyle. The 'quietism' is an untenable stance, and action is dangerous. The epigraphs to the book clarify that quietism will not do:

> *I do not like being moved: for the will if excited; and action*
>
> *Is a most dangerous thing; I tremble for something factitious,*
>
> *Some malpractice of heart and illegitimate process; We're so prone to these things, with our terrible notions of duty."*
>
> (*Amours de voyage* Canto II, xi) — Clough

Quite in keeping with Clough's feelings Fowler does not like 'being moved' and he actively dislikes Pyle's actions with his "terrible notions of duty". But Fowler's moral sense is too powerful for him to enable him to resign himself into quietism. As Miriam Allott writes:[39]

> The tragicomic temper of this writing sees to it that Fowler's decision to act, which is founded on a sense of moral outrage and the desire to prevent further violence and suffering, should nevertheless result in betrayal, murder and - as the result of yet another ironical twist to the plot - considerable material advantage to himself. As we pursue the windings of the story it also becomes apparent that the author's tragicomic method acts as a necessary distancing device for certain strongly obsessive emotions.

Allott also links up the lines from Byron provided by Greene as a second epigraph[40] as an instance of irony. She points out Byron's

---

39. "The Moral Situation in The Quiet American", R.O. Evans (ed.) *Graham Greene* op. cit.

40. This is the patent age of new inventions
    For killings bodies, and for saving souls,
    All propagated with the best intentions.
    Don Juan, Canto I, CXXXII

frequent emphasis in his satirical verse on the connection between 'good intention' and, so to speak, the road to hell and concludes:[41]

> The epigraph from Byron thus underlines Greene's sardonic commentary on a combination of qualities now distressingly prevalent, i.e, the high development of moral intelligence, so that the skill too often gets used for 'killing bodies' instead of helping to make them good and happy.

If the title is an ironical way of assessing the distress caused by the well-intentioned American, it is also by implication a comment on the central English character in the novel. He is committed to be *degage*, by profession as well as by temperament but ironically, once again, the stance that he has to take is not a question of either his profession or his temperament - it is a matter of his moral perceptiveness. This much of comic irony is evident in the book. This irony runs as a strong undercurrent contributing to the spirit of comedy, notwithstanding the sad death of the 'innocent' American.

3.8.2 The backdrop and the political action are meant to accentuate convincingly the human situation which takes the central focus in the novel. The political struggle in Indo-China during the '50s between the Colonialist France and the nationalistic Vietminh acting under the banner of Communists made it necessary for the US to interfere with a view to saving the world from what they thought expanding Communism posing a threat to their own democratic ideals. Political thinkers think up a magnificent Third Force which would prevent Communist expansion. Alden Pyle, the Harvard graduate, places implicit faith in theories. He is a serious-minded dogooder acting on ideological impulses. Fowler sums him up with the economy characteristic of the journalist: "He's a good chap in his way. Serious. Not one of those noisy bastards at the Continental. A Quiet American." (p. 15)[42] His little library in Saigon bears testimony to his seriousness. Asked why he was killed, Fowler breaks out furiously:

> 'They killed him because he was too innocent to live. He was young and ignorant and silly and he got involved. He had no more of a notion than any one of you what the whole affair's about, and you gave him money and York Harding's books on the East and said, "Go ahead. Win the East for

41. "The Moral Situation in The Quiet American", R.O. Evans (ed.): *Graham Greene* op. cit.

42. Page numbers of *The Quiet American* refer to the Penguin edn. 1967.

> democracy." He never saw anything he hadn't heard in a lecture-hall, and his writers and his lecturers made a fool of him. When he saw a dead body he couldn't even see the wounds. A Red menace, a soldier of democracy'. (p. 31)

Pyle carries the classroom about him wherever he goes. The human situation never elucidated in the books of political theory he is made to read, he remains a curiously innocent child in a world which has strayed away into ugly experience. Fowler tells us: "He was incapable of imagining pain or danger to himself as he was incapable of conceiving the pain he might cause others." (p. 61) The mature cynic Fowler sees a schoolboy's adventure story. The reference is quite a recurring one. Allan Quatermain's *King Solomon's Mines* has always been a favourite for Greene right from his childhood. In the heroic act of saving Fowler's life amidst dangerous circumstances Pyle come out as a hero:

> Before I could reply he was out of whisper's range - he was moving as quietly as he knew how, with frequent pauses. I could see him in the light of the burning car, but no shot came; soon he passed beyond the flames and very soon the silence filled the footprints. Oh yes, he was being careful as he had been careful boating down the river into Phat Diem, with the caution of a hero in a boy's adventure story, proud of his caution like a Scout's badge and quite unaware of the absurdity and the improbability of his adventure. (pp. 111-112)

His shoes besmeared with blood split by the bomb, Pyle looks white and beaten and ready to faint. Fowler tells him: "Go home to Phuong and tell her about your heroic deed - there are a few dozen less of her country people to think about" and tells himself: "What's the good? he'll always be innocent; you can't blame the innocent, they are always guiltless. All you can do is to control them or eliminate them. Innocence is a kind of insanity." (p. 162)

3.8.3 Miriam Allott argues that for a reader interpreting the book in existentialist terms it is naturally hard to believe that Fowler loves Phuong. "Through her, and through the reactions which she arouses in Fowler, the author succeeds in making us see how inevitable Fowler's ultimate commitment really is."[43] Fowler is intended to be a sardonic figure mocking at the young man's love warning him

43. "the Moral Situation in *The Quiet American*", R.O. Evans (ed.) Graham Greene op. cit.

saying: "Love's a Western word. We use it for sentimental reasons or to cover up an obsession with one woman. You're going to be hurt, Pyle, if you aren't careful." (p. 132) But it is not the commitment to general good alone which makes him interfere as he does. His cynicism is mature to the extent of saying that he is simply a journalist and not even a leader-writer. Pyle's innocence and Fowler's cynicism are in ironical contrast, again a device to focus sharply on the comic aspect of existence.

3.8.4 Fowler is middle-aged and older than Maurice Bendrix in The End of the Affair. Like Bendrix again he is a non-believer. He does not look beyond his nose and the detachment he tries to cultivate is only a reflection of his desire to be *degage*. He has a shade more hard-dyed egotism shading off into disquieting uninterestedness which is the mark of a mature cynic. Greene has a particular liking for Baudelaire's "*L'invitation au Voyage*." Fowler has the poem in mind and he loves the line about the good humour of the vagabond and he wishes to be one without being tied down. Like Bendrix Fowler has an urge to tease the innocent and he mocks Pyle at first mentally: "Well, he was in his element now with the whole universe to improve." (p. 17) When Vigot tells him of Pyle's death and how he was doing a lot of harm he comments: "God save us always from the innocent and the good." (p. 18) A journalist as he is, Fowler tries to look at himself with a reporter's eye. Having identified Pyle's body he walks back with Phuong to his flat with an illumination. "I was no longer on my dignity. Death takes away vanity - even the vanity of the cuckold who mustn't show his pain."(p. 19) While Bendrix tried to live the life of a natural man without God, Fowler wants to live the unnatural life of a man whose creed would be not to be *engage*. He emphatically tells Vigot, the police officer, that he is not involved and tells himself: "It had been an article of my creed. The human condition being what it was, let them fight, let them love, let them murder, I would not be involved. My fellow journalists called themselves correspondents; I preferred the title of reporter, I wrote what I saw; I took no action - even an opinion is a kind of action." (p. 27) This is not simply an assertion, he tries hard to live up to it. His statement "I'm tired of flying four hours for a press conference" makes the Economic Attache look at him with disapproval. But there is something basically human in his impulse to protect Pyle. "That was my first instinct - to protect him. It never occurred to me that there was greater need to protect myself. Innocence always calls mutely for protection when we would be so much wiser to guard ourselves against it: innocence is like a dumb leper who has lost his bell, wandering the world, meaning no harm." (p. 36) But Pyle's innocent wandering does infect Fowler who is driven to act. The determination, "Let them fight, let them love, let them murder, I would not be involved", is broken. If Pyle's innocence calls out mutely for his protection and stings Fowler into action, it is the consequences of the young man's innocence that lead him deliberately to fight, to love, to murder. Once he looks at himself as Pyle would perhaps see him: Suddenly I saw myself as he saw me, a man of middle-age, with eyes a little bloodshot, beginning to put on weight, ungraceful in love, less noisy than Granger perhaps but more cynical, less innocent. ..."(p. 39) His attitude towards Phuong is not love in the sense one normally associates with it, nor is it lust. This makes matters more complicated. "From childhood I had never believed in permanence, and yet I had longed for it. Always I was afraid of losing happiness. This month, next year, Phuong would leave me. If not next year, in three years. Death was the only absolute value in my world. I envied those who could believe in a God and I distrusted them." (p. 43) But he fails to realize that when one loses life there is nothing to have again for ever. As he does not believe in God, so he does not believe in confession either. He tells the priest "If I believed in any God at all, I should still hate the idea of confession. Kneeling in one of your boxes. Exposing myself to another man. You must excuse me, Father, but to me it seems morbid-unmanly even." (p. 49) In Phat Diem, in the thick of the battle, he is afraid of death: "Even though my reason wanted the state of death, I was afraid like the virgin of the act." (p. 51) Human understanding, by definition, is deficient according to Greene and with regard to Scobie in *The Heart of the Matter* he says: "When he was young, he had thought love had something to do with understanding, but with age he knew that no human being understood another." (pp. 244-5) Thinking of Pyle, walking one morning months after his death with Phuong by his side, he reflects that he did not understand her either. "Time has its revenges, but revenges seem often sour. Wouldn't we all do better not trying to understand, accepting the fact that no human being will ever understand another, not a wife a husband, a lover a mistress, not a parent a child? Perhaps that's why men have invented a God a being capable of understanding. Perhaps if I wanted to be understood or to understand I would bamboozle myself into belief, but I am a reporter; God exists only for leader-writers." (pp. 59-60) In Fowler's belief man makes a cage of his religion with holes: "with doubts left open to the weather and creeds opening on innumerable interpretations. My wife had found her cage with holes and sometimes I envied her. There is a conflict between sun and air: I lived too much in the sun." (p. 86) Acting finally according to his choice, he tries to relegate the responsibility of taking care of the consequences to a superior power: "I handed back the decision to that somebody in whom I did not believe: you can intervene if you want to ..." (p. 179) He aspired only for one thing - peace of mind. Though he tells himself that Phuong is just a matter of comfort, he cannot feel unhurt nevertheless at the thought that he has been cuckolded by Pyle. Reading his wife's letter which conveyed her dissent to the divorce he wanted, he comes upon an insight: "I hadn't realized how open the sexual wounds remain over the years."(p. 117) He is proud of having an insight into human character as revealed in his outburst against Pyle: "I hope to God you know what you are doing here. I wish sometimes you had a few bad motives, you might understand a little more about human beings." (p. 132) Taunted by Pyle that he has been unjust to Phuong by keeping her "as a comfortable lay" until he left, Fowler interposes: "She's a human being, Pyle. She's capable of deciding." Then he reflects: "One never knows another human being." (p. 133) Almost symbolically he does not find the card of his profession on him after the bomb incident. He is no longer *dégagé*. Fowler tells Heng about Pyle and Heng's invisible friends shift like rats behind the wall. He is reminded of Captain Trouin when Heng tells him: "Sooner or later, one has to take sides. If one is to remain human."(p.172) Fowler regrets his unbelief even at the end of the narration: "Everything had gone right with me since he (Pyle) had died, but how I wished there existed someone to whom I could say that I was sorry."(p. 187)

3.8.5 Innocence and involvement are both terms which it is difficult to identify as absolutes in an individual. The tragic seeps into the comic leaving the impression of tragicomedy. Fowler is correct in his estimate of Pyle who does not really belong in the scene of Indo-China: "He looked more than ever out of place: he should have stayed at home. I saw him in a family snapshot album, riding on a dude ranch, bathing on Long Island, photographed with his colleagues in some apartment on the twenty-third floor. He belonged to the skyscraper and the express elevator, the ice-cream and the dry Martinis, milk at lunch, and chicken sandwiches on the Merchant limited."(p. 19) This is as much as to say that Pyle's role is ambiguous and absurd. Fowler thinks of himself in terms of an actor in several places in the novel. In the battlefield near Phat Diem he could see himself as a player. "The wind was up again, prowling for an entry. The Canvas curtain sagged (I was reminded of

Polonius stabbed behind the arras) and the candle wavered. The shadows were theatrical. We might have been a company of barn-stormers."(p. 54) After Pyle's death which she does not know about, Phuong asks Fowler if he would like another pipe. He says he would like one and narrator records: "I took off my tie and shoes; the interlude was over." Then he breaks the news and the reader is told: "She put the needle down and sat back on her heels, looking at me. There was no scene, no tears, just thought — the long private thought of somebody who has to alter a whole course of life." The whole thing could look as a tragedy only if it were seen through Phuong's eyes and then the writer takes the fullest precautions to keep her as the blissfully ignorant woman who does not think at all. Here is a picture of Phuong drawn by the journalist:

> She's no child. She's tougher than you'll ever be. Do you know the kind of polish that doesn't take scratches? That's Phuong. She can survive a dozen of us. She'll get old, that's all. She will never suffer like we do from thoughts, obsessions — she won't scratch, she'll only decay. (p. 133)

The persons however would like to retain the objectivity that should make him a reporter and adds: "I knew I was inventing a character just as much as Pyle was." (p. 133) Though allowance has to be made for the imposition of Fowler's idea of an oriental woman aspiring for a comfortable marriage, Phuong still remains a waif-like woman, all of a piece with Greene's bevy of the pathetically self-effacing females. Here is an example of tragedy seeping into what would otherwise have been comic:

> 'It would be very uncomfortable for you if we were not married.'
>
> 'But perhaps your wife will divorce you.'
>
> 'Perhaps.'
>
> 'I will come with you anyway,' she said. She meant it, but I could see in her eyes the long train of thought begin, as she lifted the pipe again and began to warm the pellet of opium. She said, 'are there skyscrapers in London?' and I loved her for the innocence of her question. She might lie from politeness, from fear, even for profit, but she would never have the cunning to keep her lie concealed.
>
> 'No,' I said, 'You have to go to America for them.' She gave me a quick look over the needle and registered her mistake. Then as she kneaded the opium she began to talk at random of what clothes she would wear in London, where we should

> live, of the Tube-trains she had read about in a novel, and the double-decker buses: would we fly or go by sea. 'And the Statue of Liberty ...' she said.
>
> 'No, Phuong, that's American too."(p. 80)

The tragic operates not only in the complexly involved human relations with the major characters coming into juxtaposition from three corners of the world resulting in the pathetic death of the American Pyle but also in the form of horrible and inexplicable deaths of innocents in the war and bombing. The realistic picture of war observed at close quarters contributes to the pathos. In Phat Diem Fowler sees deaths which begin to shake him from his complacent attitude of *dégagé*:

> The canal was full of bodies; I am reminded now of an Irish stew containing too much meat. The bodies overlapped: one head, seal-gray, and anonymous as a convict with a shaven scalp, stuck up out of the water like a buoy. There was no blood: I suppose it had flowed away a long time ago. (p. 52)

There are the mother and the child in a ditch near a farm building:

> They were clearly dead: a small neat clot of blood on the woman's forehead, and the child might have been sleeping. He was about six years old and he lay like an embryo in the womb with his little bony knees drawn up.(p. 52)

The two soldiers with the unused sten in the watch-tower are objects of abject pathos. Fowler hears a low cry from what is left of the bombed tower and realizes that at least one of the two is alive. He reflects:

> I was responsible for that voice crying in the dark: I had prided myself on detachment, on not belonging to this war, but those wounds had been inflicted by me just as though I had used the sten, as Pyle had wanted to do.(p. 112)

The tragic is conveyed with poignancy when Fowler sees airborne the fate of the victims of war: "The cannon gave a single burst of tracer, and the sampan blew apart in a shower of sparks. We did not wait to see our victims." After the bicycle-bomb incident the thing takes a grotesque (p. 148) look. Fowler remembers the bicycle wheel gaily spinning like a top. It is not tragic any longer: it becomes absurd:

> A woman sat on the ground with what was left of her baby in the lap; with a kind of modesty she had covered it with her straw peasant hat ... The legless torso at the edge of the

> garden still twitched like a chicken which has lost its head.(p. 161)

3.8.6 The restoration of the balance in favour of the comic is affected through a scene where the police chief Vigot and Fowler play Quatre Vingt-et-un, a fortnight after Pyle's death:

> When he (Vigot) had got rid of his last match he said, '*Capitaine*', and I called the waiter for drinks. 'Does anybody ever beat you?' I asked.
>
> 'Not often. Do you want revenge?'
>
> 'Another time. What a gambler you could be, Vigot. Do you play any other game of chance?'
>
> He smiled miserably, and for some reason I thought of that blonde wife of his who was said to betray him with his junior officers.
>
> "Oh well," he said, "there's always the biggest of all."
>
> "The biggest?"
>
> "Let us weigh the gain and loss," he quoted, "in wagering that God is, let us estimate these two chances. If you gain, you gain all; if you lose you lose nothing.'"
>
> I quoted Pascal back at him — it was the only passage I remembered. "Both he who chooses heads and he who chooses tails are equally at fault. They are both in the wrong. The true course is not to wager at all.'" (p. 136)

Fowler tells Vigot that he ought to have been a priest and thinks that Vigot looked at him with compassion "as he might have looked at some prisoner for whose capture he was responsible undergoing his sentence of life."(p. 138)

3.8.7 The tragedy of Pyle is a 'lamentable comedy' as his success is fraught with tragic suggestions. The comedy in Greene's writing keeps on rising bearing testimony to the fact that his genius is taking more and more disquieting forms of comedy, subduing the tragic to a less effective place., Fowler sees him as a Quixote figure with his ideas of the Third Force imbibed from the theories of York Harding and the high-sounding words like democracy learnt in the lecture hall and the library. The comic is evident in the innate contrast between the chief actors. Fowler is aware of the comedy that underlies existence and his cynicism could at times be very comic. Fowler asks the Economic Attaché if he has heard of Harold C. Pyle, Alden's father.

> 'No.'

> 'He's the world authority on under-water erosion. Didn't you see his picture on the cover of the *TIME* the other month?'
>
> 'Oh, I think I remember. A crumbling cliff in the background and gold-rimmed glasses in the foreground.'
>
> 'That's him. I had to draft the cable home. It was terrible. I loved that boy like he was my son.'
>
> 'That makes you closely related to his father.'
>
> He returned his wet brown eyes on me. He said, 'What's getting you? That's not the way to talk when a young fellow...'
>
> 'I'm sorry,' I said, "Death takes different people in different ways.' (p. 30)

The comic touches a high point in blending with the serious when Fowler sees Pyle who comes seeking him into the battlefield:

> 'I thought I ought to take a look at it. To tell you the truth. I was a little ashamed of Granger.'
>
> 'I see. As simple as that.'
>
> 'Well, there wasn't any real difficulty, was there? He began to play with his bootlaces, and there was a long silence. 'I'm not being quite honest,' he said at last.
>
> 'No?'
>
> 'I really came to see you.'
>
> 'You came here to see me?'
>
> 'Yes.'
>
> 'Why?'
>
> He looked up from his bootlaces in an agony of embarrassment. 'I had to tell you — I've fallen in love with Phuong.'
>
> I laughed, I couldn't help it. He was so unexpected and so serious. I said, 'Couldn't you have waited till I got back? I shall be in Saigon next week.'(p. 56)

The scene where the French Colonel speaks to the press is full of comedy with Granger trying to break his suavity and the Frenchman breaking all of a sudden into English. After returning to Saigon Fowler finds the congratulatory telegram of his promotion waiting for him and tells himself: "Dante never thought up that turn of screw for his condemned lovers. Paolo was never promoted to purgatory."(p. 66) Fowler once again finds in Pyle a comic figure with his crew-cut trimmed and a loud Hawaii shirt serving the function of male plumage. Pyle's dog always annoys Fowler and increases his contempt for the American. The dog 'Duke' in the background makes Pyle a ludicrous figure:

> His black dog sat on the floor taking up too much room, panting: its tongue looked like a burnt pancake. Pyle said vaguely, Oh, you know, we want to get some of these local industries on their feet, and we have to be careful of the French. They want everything bought in France.'
>
> 'I don't blame them. A war needs money.'
>
> 'Do you like dogs?'
>
> 'No.'
>
> 'I thought the British were great dog-lovers.'
>
> 'We think the Americans love dollars, but there must be exceptions.'
>
> ... ...
>
> 'Could you ask your dog to be still?' I said.
>
> 'Oh, I'm sorry, Duke. Sit down Duke.' Duke sat down and began noisily to lick his private parts. I filled our glasses and managed in passing to disturb Duke's toilet. The quiet lasted a very short time; he began to scratch himself.' (pp. 72-73)

What follows in the scene with Phuong entering it rises to a farce when Fowler has to act as an interpreter for Pyle who does not know French. Fowler asks Pyle if he wanted him to add a little fire to what he said but Pyle, ignorant of the irony, replies:

> 'Oh no,' (he said) 'just translate. I don't want to sway her emotionally.'
>
> 'I see.'
>
> 'Tell her I want to marry her.'
>
> I told her.
>
> 'What was that she said?'
>
> 'She asked me if you were serious. I told her you were the serious type.'
>
> 'I suppose this is an odd situation,' he said. 'Me asking you to translate.'
>
> 'Rather odd.' (p. 75)

and the dialogue shifts and the comedy begins to crackle:

> 'She can always get passion,' I said 'with your chaffeur when you are away at the office,'

> Pyle blushed. He got awkwardly to his feet and said, 'That's a dirty crack. I won't have her insulted. You've no right to...'
>
> 'She's not your wife yet.'
>
> 'What can you offer her?' he asked with anger.
>
> 'A couple of hundred dollars when you leave for England, or will you pass her on with the furniture?'
>
> 'The furniture isn't mine.'
>
> 'She's not either. Phuong, will you marry me?'
>
> 'What about the blood group?' I said. 'And a health certificate. You'll need hers, surely? May be you ought to have mine too. And her horoscope — no, that is an Indian custom.'
>
> 'Will you marry me?'
>
> 'Say it in French,' I said. 'I'm damned If I'll interpret for you any more.' (pp. 76-77)

Even the first incident of the bicycle-bomb is comic in a way. "The whole affair, as it turned out, was not worth more than a paragraph, and a humorous paragraph at that ... Before I had time to adjust my camera the comic and inexplicable action had been accomplished."(p. 139) Comedy could be painful and Fowler in spite of his avowed position of *dégagé* is not immune to suffering. After trying to see Pyle in the legation and not finding him Fowler tells Phuong's sister there in his sardonic humour "I hope you've had the settlement witnessed by the notary public and the American Consul and the Church of Christ Scientist." Then follows the painful confession:

> 'I went into the passage. There was a door opposite me marked Men. I went in and locked the door and sitting with my head against the cold wall I cried. I hadn't cried until now. Even their lavatories were air-conditioned, and presently the temperate tempered air dried my tears as it dries the spit in your mouth and the seed in your body.' (pp. 145-46)

It is perhaps hard to put across the tragic horror of reality without in some way attracting the shades of comedy. When Dominiguez asks him to file something as a follow-up on the bomb, Fowler tells him: 'Oh, work one out for me, Dominiguez. I don't know how it is - being there on the spot, perhaps I got a bit shocked. I can't think of the thing on terms of a cable." (p. 173)

3.8.8 Plenty of devices are commissioned to use to play up the comic strand which has by now emerged as a more powerful force than the tragic. The primary device is one of contrast exemplified in the ruthless portrayal of Pyle and Fowler. While Pyle's dreams cost him his life, Fowler's egotism costs him his position of degage. The same device of contrast is implied between Phuong and the unseen wife of Fowler, Helen. Phuong is a delicate flower that hangs from the stalk without which it would wither the next moment. Helen, a Catholic, is strong. She warns Fowler that the girl is going to be his prey and her long argument conveying a 'No' in peroration is a piece of effectively economical characterization. Comedy is also evident in the anti-American flare up in Fowler who is himself conscious of it as a complex. "I began almost unconsciously - to run down everything that was American. My conversation was full of the poverty of American literature, the scandals of American politics, the beastliness of American children. It was as though she was being taken away from me by a nation rather than by a man." (p. 138) The happy ending to the book once again signifies the triumph of the comic though subdued to some extent by the lurking dissatisfaction in Fowler: "Everything had gone right with me since he had died, but how I wished there existed someone to whom I could say I was sorry.' (p. 187)

3.8.9 Greene includes in his introduction to the novel issued in the Collected Edition in 1973 his journal entries during his stay in Saigon. While working on *The Quiet American*. Greene made four trips to Indo-China,[44] staying there twelve months in all. Once in Saigon, after four pipes he has a dream followed by a nightmare:

> I was coming down the steps of a club in St. James's Street and on the steps I met the Devil who was wearing a tweed motoring coat and a deerstalker cap. . . The Devil stopped me and asked whether I would like to have a year to live again or to slip a year and see what would be happening to me two years ahead. Immediately the Devil vanished and I was holding in my hands a letter - it was from some girl whom I slightly knew. It was a very tender letter, a letter of farewell. Obviously during that missing year we had reached a relationship which she was now ending. Looking down on the woman in the car I thought, 'I must not show her the letter, for how absurd it would be if she were to be

44. See Greene's introduction to *In Search of a Character* (London: Bodley Head 1961), p. 9

> jealous of a girl whom I hardly yet know because of the future.' I went into my room (I was no longer in the club) and tore the letter into small pieces, but at the bottom of the envelope were some beads which must have had a sentimental significance. I was unwilling to destroy these and opening a drawer put them in and locked the drawer. As I did so it suddenly occurred to me, "In two years' time I shall be doing just this, opening a drawer, putting away the beads, and finding the beads are already in the drawer." Then I woke.

Whatever might be its psychological implications, the dream shows that Greene is becoming more and more poignantly aware of the comic element and the absurd underlying not only in what he actively sees around but also in what he dreams of. *The Quiet American* is in a way the exemplification of the central point that dreams could be disastrous. Pyle's innocence makes him dream that a Third Force could be a panacea to the evils of threatening communism. When individual happiness itself is a delusion, collective happiness could not be anything except a chimera. Mere good intentions, without the knowledge of human nature and an understanding of the human situation, could result only in meaningless suffering. Moral intelligence in itself cannot work wonders without its being tutored by some superior power. A happy life in this world would require a correct amount of dreaming and though Pyle dreams he has no way of restricting or controlling his dream with the aid of the awareness of human nature and existence. In his failure to adjust the dream to reality he causes the deaths of several and loses his own life.

3.9 A happy life is a matter of successfully playing the clown. It could also be a matter of dreaming but the correct measure for it is difficult to determine. Dr. Hasselbacher in *Our Man in Havana* (1958) tells the Englishman, Wormold, "You should dream more, Mr. Wormold. Reality in our century is not something to be faced." *Our Man in Havana* is a fantastic comedy, the lightest of light-hearted books, making very plainly a mockery of secret service. The entertainment sways between dream and reality. Lechers and murderers are part of reality, while idealists and humanitarians are part of the dream in Greene's conception. Sin and squalor are aspects of reality which we apprehend more readily and easily than sweetness and light which belong more to the dream. Innocence is a part of the dream since we are corrupted by experience. Dreams disappoint by never coming true, and reality is not something to be encountered in our circumstances; either way it is a harrowing experience. The best thing is to remain in an indeterminate state between dream and reality. Dr. Hasselbacher dreams too much and gets killed. Wormold's success must be attributed to the manipulation of reality to suit his dream and to his ability to play the clown. In this novel, the comic gets the better of the tragic and reinforces the impression that life tends to move more and more towards the comic.

3.9.1 In his introduction to *Our Man in Havana* in the Collected Edition Greene writes: "I had the idea of writing a secret service comedy based on what I had learned from my work in 1943-4 of German Abwehr activity in Lisbon" and gives the factual details which made him think of the fiction in the book. Havana this time provides the backdrop for what Greene wanted to put across and he justifies the choice at length: "Suddenly it struck me that here in this extraordinary city, where every vice was permissible and every trade possible, lay the true background of comedy." The tragedy of war had been ignored totally and Greene is ready with his apology: "I realized that I had been planning the wrong situation and planning it at the wrong period. The shadows of the war to come in 1938 were too dark for comedy; the reader could feel no sympathy for a man who was cheating his country in Hitler's day for the sake of an extravagant wife. But in the fantastic Havana, among the absurdities of the cold war (for who would accept the survival of Western capitalism as a great cause?) there was a situation allowably comic, all the more if I changed the wife into a daughter ... I had not wanted too black a background for a light-hearted comedy, but those who had suffered during the years of dictatorship could hardly be expected to appreciate that my real subject was the absurdity of the British agent and not the justice of his revolution, not did my aesthetic reasons for changing a Captain Ventura into a Captain Segura appeal to them." Greene makes it clear that the book is almost meant to be a fairy tale. The tragic is deliberately set aside with the intention of making a rich harvest of comedy.

3.9.2 The plot is about a vacuum-cleaner agent in Havana, an Englishman. He is recruited much against his will as an 'agent' in the Carribean network. He sends made-up reports to the Head Quarters if only to earn a bit of money to support his dear daughter. The secretary, sent from London to assist him, falls in love with him. His daughter rejects the love of the police-officer, Captain Segura, who has finally to deport the girl and her father. The chief of the British Secret Service has nothing more than an OBE to recommend Wormold for.

3.9.3 The comic pervades the elements of the popular thriller in the book: secret agents, naked girls in night clubs; charming secretaries and sprightly love affairs. Dr Hasselbacher who fought for the Kaiser in Germany before he became a doctor tells Wormold: "... if you are interested in life it never lets you down. I am interested in the blueness of the cheese" and advises him "You should dream more, Mr. Wormold. Reality in our century is not something to be faced."(p. 10)[45] It is against intellectual discussions of this type that Wormold continues life after being left by a wife whose child he had promised to bring up as a Catholic. Milly, his seventeen-year-old-daughter, is sweetly comic: "He could distinguish the approach of Milly like that of a police car from a long way off. Whistles instead of sirens warned him of her coming. She paid no attention to the whistles, they only made her step the higher, seeing her walk you could almost believe in levitation."(p. 15) Years ago when she was thirteen at the convent-school she set fire to a boy and here is the explanation:

> 'I was tempted by the devil,' she said.
> 'Milly, please be sensible.'
> 'Saints have been tempted by the devil.'
> 'You are not a saint.'
> 'Exactly. That's why I fell.'

Here is another example of her liveliness:

> 'Are you smoking in secret?' he asked her.
> 'No.'
> Something in her manner made him re-phrase the question.
> 'Have you ever smoked at all, Milly?'
> 'Only cheroots,' she said.

While Hasselbacher believes in dreaming, Wormold believes in playing the clown. He tells Milly: "... If only we had been born clowns, nothing bad would happen to us except a few bruises and a smear of white wash. Don't learn from experience Milly. It ruins our peace and our lives."(p. 32) It is in this sense that Wormold is the "sadman" of the epigraph who is "the cock of all his jests".[46] He

45. Page numbers refer to *Our Man in Havana*, Penguin edn. 1967.

46. The following lines from the opening stanza of George Herbert's "The Church Porch" (from his *Temple* (1635)) provide the epigraph:

> *A sad wise valour is the brave complexion*
> *That leads the van, and swallows up the cities.*
> *The giggler is a milkmaid, whom infection*
> *Or a fir'd beacon frighteth from his ditties.*
> *Then he's the sport: the mirth in him rests,*
> *And the sad man is cock of all his jests.*

plays a joke without getting himself entangled in it as a victim. He has the 'wise valour' to come up victorious. The 'wise valour' consists in his comical perspective on life which at this point marks a gathering maturity in Greene's understanding of life. The book is full of humourous scenes where there is a lot of clowning. The scene laid in the Gents where Hawthorne plugs Wormold into the Carribean network of spies is one such. The tap is turned on to confuse the mike that might be there:

> 'Please will you explain...?'
>
> 'Can't be careful even in a Gents, when I come to think of it. A chap of ours in Denmark in 1940 saw from his own window the German fleet coming down the Kattegat.'
>
> 'What gut?'
>
> 'Kattegat. Of course he knew then the balloon had gone up. Started burning his papers. Put the ashes down the lav and pulled the chain. Trouble was - late frost. Pipes frozen. All the ashes floated up into the bath down below. Flat belonged to an old maiden lady - Baronin somebody or other. She was just going to have a bath. Most embarrassing for our chap.'
>
> 'It sounds like the Secret Service.' (pp. 26-27)

A fantasy, it has been pointed out, must be judged by its power of invention. Thanks to his power, Wormold learns to be successful very fast. Explaining his presence in the street at ten o'clock in the night in Santiago, he makes good use of his creative imagination. The name of Captain Segura works a miracle. The scene in the Shanghai theatre where Wormold takes Beatrice to warn his non-existent agent Teresa is a hilarious farce:

> 'Yes. What do you want with me?' the thin girl demanded, coming forward holding one stocking. Her little breasts were the size of pears.
>
> 'Who are you?'
>
> 'Soy Teresa.'
>
> Beatrice said, 'Is that Teresa? You said she was fat like that one with the mask.'
>
> 'No, no' Wormold said 'That's not Teresa. She's Teresa's sister. *Soy* means sister.' He said, 'I'll send a message by her.' (p. 123)

The next scene in the professor's house is an imbroglio. The girl dancing with the professor is mistaken to be the wife. When

Wormold refers to Beatrice the professor finds himself in real trouble.

> 'I absolutely assure you, dear, that I know nobody called Beatrice. Nobody.'
> The young woman gave a tigerish laugh.
> 'You seem to have come here,' the Professor said, 'with the sole purpose of making trouble.' It was his first complaint and it seemed a mild one under the circumstances. 'I cannot think what you have to gain by it,' he said and walked into the house and closed the door.
> 'He's a monster!' the girl said. 'A sexual monster. A satyr.'(p. 132)

Another greatly farcial situation is the scene in the Chief's office in London. Wormold thinks that there is going to be a courtmartial for all that he has done. But he is given the job of a Lecturer and recommended for a decoration: "I think in your case - you were not there very long we can hardly suggest anything higher than an O.B.E." (p. 215) "There was always another side to a joke, the side of the victim" (p. 72), we are reminded. Raul and Dr. Hasselbacher die for no fault of theirs as a result of the dangerous joke of Wormold but the focus is not on that. It is on the clowning, the madness and the dreaming. Only a clown can stand the vagaries of chance and circumstance in a world swayed by unseen powers. Wormold bravely plays the clown while Dr. Hasselbacher dreams too much. The dreams of the doctor help the vacuum-cleaner agent. The game of checkers with miniature whiskey bottles is the Doctor's idea. Beatrice appears to be the most fit for the life of which the book is intended to be a replica. She it is who has the right measure of madness. She sings, though a little out of tune:

> *Sane men surround*
> *You, old family friends -*
> *My madness offends*
> *An orange has pips, they say,*
> *And an apple has rind.*

To the Chief of the service she harangues on the point that for a citizen the country is more a family than a parliamentary system and asked if she believed in it she makes the crucial statement: "Not all of it. They haven't left us much to believe, have they - even disbelief. I can't believe in anything bigger than a home, or anything vaguer than a human being." (p. 217)

3.9.4 The comic in the book is a complex combination of dream, the absurd and the farcial with the tragic seeping in at times. The comic begins taking over right from the beginning with Hawthrone coming to recruit Wormold, gaining in intensity in the portrait of Milly sans her duenna, culminating in Wormold's realization that what matters is not experience but being a clown. The interludes in London with Miss Jenkinson and the monocled Chief lend enough to the absurdity of the fantasy. It is Beatrice, once again, who has the real insight into the things. "The world is modelled after the popular magazines now-a-days. My husband came out of ENCOUNTER. The question we have to consider is to which paper *they* belong." She gives us the impression that the more realistic world is that of the BOY'S OWN PAPER. Faith is not enough for it eludes mere formulas. She admonishes Milly mildly: "Milly, dear Milly. Beware of formulas. If there's God, he's not a God of formulas." (p. 186) What matters is being a successful clown: to laugh while being laughed at. Beatrice says: "London seems pretty silly. And Hawthorne. Do you think I would ever have left Peter if once - just once - he'd made a fool of UNESCO? But UNESCO was sacred. Cultural conferences were sacred. He never laughed. ... Lend me your handkerchief" and wipes away a tear adding "I'm laughing."(p. 189)

3.9.5 *The Times Literary Supplement* reviewer writes:[47] "The weakness of the book is that the writer has attempted the impossible conjunction of comedy and farce;; but concludes: "The essential complaint against the book is that Mr. Greene is wanting in sense of form, but such criticism becomes feeble when confronted with the cardinal fact that the author has set out to do something extremely difficult and has abundantly succeeded in doing it." The success lies in the recognition of the fact: "Somebody always leaves a banana-skin on the scene of a tragedy." Ignoring tragedy all the attention is given to the consequences of the banana-skin.

3.9.6 *The Power and the Glory, The End of the Affair* and *The Quiet American* are important steps in the mounting comic sense. In the tale of the whisky-priest a kind of balance is achieved between the tragic and the comic forces, in *The End of the Affair* comedy pervades more effectively than at any time before and in *The Quiet American*, Greene begins to realize forcefully that existence is comic. The realization gets crystallized in *A Burnt-out Case*.

47. 10 October, 1958.

Chapter 4

The Crystallization

> *"In all writers there occurs a moment of crystallization when the dominant theme is plainly expressed, when the private universe becomes visible even to the least sensitive reader. Such a crystallization is Hardy's often-quoted phrase: "The President of the Immortals ...had ended his sport with Tess."*
>
> *Graham Greene*

4.1 With the publication of *A Burnt-out Case* (1960) Greene's fictional universe conceived in a maturing comic vision becomes more fixed than ever before. The tragic is an outcome of the God-oriented vision while the comic without necessarily denying the existence of God is chance-oriented. Feibleman says that comedy too is God-oriented. God looks at the ways of pitiful mortals and is compassionately amused at the 'erring' and 'extravagant' spirits. The transition between the two is effected via humanism. The humanistic stance of evolutionism is a kind of dignified and serious comedy. The philosophy of hope is common both to evolution and comedy. *A Burnt-out Case* marks the transition. Dr. Colin in the novel serves the end of comedy first by discarding the theological dimension of the universe and secondly by reposing his faith in a continuously evoluting world. In this sense it is a culminating point in Green's career as a novelist. He emerges successfully from the clouds of the tragic into a more sunny region though the sunniest is still to present itself. Philip Stratford[1] writes: "A new comic vision has been developing throughout the plays and entertainments of the '50s to replace the earlier melodramatic outlook, and this is the vision which now underlies this serious novel." In the introduction to *A Burnt-out Case* reissued in the Collected Edition (1974) Greene writes:

> Thirty years before I had read Unamuno's *Life and Death of Don Quixote* with no particular interest. It left no memories. But perhaps the book which I so quickly forgot had continued to work its way through the cellars of the unconscious, in the life of which I was fully aware I was

1. "Greene's Hall of Mirrors", *The Kenyon Review*, Summer 1961 Vol. XXXIII, No. 3.

> making my way with passionate curiosity through the works of theology. Yet *The Heart of the Matter* offended moral theologians. *The End of The Affair, The Living Room, The Potting Shed* caused uneasiness among those of my faith, and at the end of a long journey, without knowing myself the course I had been taking, I found myself, in "A Visit to Morin" and *A Burnt-out Case* in that tragicomic region of La Mancha where I expect to stay. Even my Marxist critics shared a characteristic with Waugh — they were too concerned with faith or no faith to notice that in the course of the blackest book I have written I had discovered comedy.

Greene appears to have clearly judged the position that he is likely to remain in. His novels show his progress to a region where the tragic is absorbed by and integrated into the comic.

4.2 Richard Noxon[2] sees Kierkegaard's stages of existence in *A Burnt-out Case* - the aesthetic, the ethical and the religious:

> Connecting these existence spheres are two transitional stages, the first of irony, the second of humour. It is by virtue of the ironical attitude that the aesthete may come to recognize the futility of his way of life, and thereby realize ethical maturity. If the aesthete should be a hedonist he comes to realise that he plays a game that time fates him to lose. It is the ironical fate of the man who lives for variety and excitement to become the victim of the most profound boredom. It is humour, a bitter sardonic humour, that precipitates the ethical man towards the religious level. Humour reveals the transitoriness of all human designs, the comic futility of all human striving. From the perspective of eternity, a man's existence appears as a brief moment whose significance is absurdly exaggerated. The ethical man plans and works as if he would live for ever while knowing that he must die — a contradiction apparent to the mind of the humourist.

Querry, the chief character in *A Burnt-out Case*, has been an aesthete, a Catholic architect of genius, and he has at the same time had a fling at sex and in that sense has been a hedonist. He realizes ethical maturity by an ironical attitude which exposes the futility of

2. "Kierkegaard's Stages in *A Burnt-out Case*", Review of English Literature, Vol. 3, No. 1, January 1962.

his art. His humour makes him perceive that his way of life is fated to fail. He realizes further that basically both his art and sex have always been only a means of self-gratification. This realization leaves him a victim of profound boredom. Querry in the opening pages of the novel is on the threshold of irony. As an aesthete and a hedonist, from the aesthetic level, he reaches by way of irony a kind of ethical level. He progresses to the second transitional stage of humour when he is cut off from attaining the religious level. The humour in his case is a bitter sardonic humour which becomes mirthful towards the end. Dr Colin is ethical which makes him an essential pragmatist. He plans and works as if he would live for ever and the humorist in Querry begins to laugh when the contradiction becomes strikingly apparent to him.

4.3 Querry is disillusioned by his achievement in art and in sex. He resorts to Africa which has been recommended as a cure for the sick heart.[3] At the beginning of the book he writes in his diary (a way of trying to clarify his motives and understanding himself) a parody of Descartes: 'I feel discomfort, therefore I am alive.' The heat, the mosquitoes an the boredom are only viewed as matters of discomfort. Even the crew of the Bishop's boat try to evade the boredom with a game of *Quatre cent Vingt et un* 'wordlessly like a ritual mime'. The captain, a little intrigued by Querry's travel tries to draw him out translating the song of the boatmen and gets the inadequate explanation: 'The road was closed by floods. This was the only route.' Querry's discomfort grows into an irritation on board the boat when the priests indulge themselves in laughter. He tells himself that he has come to the end of everything. The superior at the leproserie is not curious. When Querry tells him that he has come .o the end of suffering he says with a Churchman's habitual coolness: "Oh well, you know suffering is something which will always be provided when it is required."(p. 17)* To Dr Colin who asks him if he is stopping there, Querry replies "The boat goes no further." If free will drives Fowler into a corner, belief in Catholicism (the course of the 'disease' after which he becomes a burnt-out case figuratively) drives Querry to a stance that existence is absurd and farcically comic. Hearing the sound of prayers from the chapel next door he feels the panic of abandonment. The chant reminds him of an illness from which he had long recovered. A

3. "How strange it is that for more than a hundred years Africa has been recommended as a cure for the sick heart." Graham Greene, *In Search of a Character*, Bodley Head, 1961, p. 30

* Page numbers refer to *A Burnt-out Case*, Penguin edn., 1966.

disease leaves one in the company of doctors and nurses; the faith of which Querry is cured leaves him in the incongruous company of priests and nuns. But the humorist in him begins slowly to come alive. He tells Dr Colin that he should be glad to be of use. In the continent of heat and misery, a symbolic externalization of his spiritual condition, Querry struggles hard to find his moorings afresh. By gradual stages he realises that existence is comic and the stages are illustrated by his various efforts to laugh successfully. In a dream he tells a girl who strikes him in the face for having broken a vase she loved, "I'm sorry, I am too far gone, I can't feel at all, I am a leper."(p. 32) Dr Colin, the practical atheist, understands Querry when he opens what is left of his heart to him: "I don't deny my profession meant a lot to me. So have women. But the use of what I made was never important to me. I wasn't a builder of council houses or factories. When I made something I made it for my own pleasure."(p. 45) He tells him further that self expression eats everything, even the self. He writes in his journal: "I haven t enough feeling left for human beings to do anything for them out of pity."(p. 51) His rough and disjointed notes to Dr Colin make clear his mental condition:

> What I have built, I have always built for myself, not for the glory of God or the pleasure of the purchaser. Don't talk to me of human beings. Human beings are not my country. And haven't I offered to wash their filthy bandages?"(p. 52)

Dr Colin, however, does not bother to pay much attention to these notes and he simply says "Who cares?" That very night Querry has a dream. He is a priest in his ridiculously urgent search of sacramental wine troubled by the obsessional phrase "Who cares?" The comic underlies the fact that Querry does try to make himself generally useful in the hospital not withstanding his telling himself that he has lost interest in everything. Religion, art and sex effectively gone dry in him, he drifts into a new life at the leproserie and by slow stages returns to a kind of normalcy. The first stage is marked by his going out in the darkness of the forest in search of his boy, Deo Gratias. In the discussion that follows Querry's act of humanity Dr Colin tells him that hope is always connected with youth but sometimes it can be one of the diseases of age. He says: "These people are all dying — oh, I don't mean of leprosy, I mean of us. And their last disease is hope." "You know where to look for me," Querry says, "if I should be missing." (p. 61) An unexpected sound makes the doctor look up and Querry's face is twisted with 'the rictus of a laugh'. This can be viewed as the first stage where

Querry realises the absurdity of hope of happiness. It has taken a long while of boredom and inefficacious suffering to arrive at this and from now on a new awareness runs through him making him progressively human. In other words he is returning to normalcy however slow the progress might be. From the 'rictus of a laugh' to a 'rudimentary smile' is significant progress. While 'pendele' occupies a lot of his conscious thinking, Mme Rycker comes to the leproserie with the intention of inviting him to their house on her husband's behalf. The Superior tries to warn him of her arrival and comes to Querry who has been reading a letter from a former mistress. Querry expresses his disgust for Rycker and Mme Rycker who overhears the conversation leaves abruptly. Later the Superior and Querry engage themselves in a long discussion:

> 'She's been taken a long way from Pendele,' he (Querry) said.
>
> 'What's Pendele?
>
> 'I don't know - a dance at a friend's house, a young man with a shiny simple face, going to Mass on Sunday with the family, falling asleep on a single bed perhaps.'
>
> 'People have to grow up. We are called to more complicated things than that.'
>
> 'Are we?'
>
> '"When we are a child we think as a child."'
>
> 'I can't match quotations from the Bible with you, father, but surely there is also something about having to be as little children if we are to inherit ... We've grown up rather badly. The complications have become too complex - we should have stopped with the amoeba - no, long before that, with the silicates. If your god wanted an adult world he should have given us an adult brain.'
>
> 'We most of us make our own complications, M. Querry.'
>
> 'Why did he give us genitals then if he wanted us to think clearly? A doctor doesn't prescribe marijuana for clear thought.' (pp. 79-80)

Querry's realization that it is impossible for sex-ridden human beings to think clearly is at once serious and ludicrous. After the discussion Querry asks the Superior to keep that girl and her bloody tears away. He wants to stay unresponsive, not to be drawn out, not to be involved. Comically enough the Superior discusses the

Christian virtues in his next sermon. Querry and Dr Colin listen to it from the steps of the hospital in the cool of the early day. Querry remarks to Dr Colin: "I really believe he's answering something I said to him" with a twitch of the mouth that Dr Colin recognizes as a rudimentary smile. It is a sign for the Doctor who thinks in the leprologist's metaphor that mutilation can be avoided.

4.4 When Querry confesses to the doctor that it was curiosity and pride and not Christian love that set him following his boy into the forest Dr Colin replies that liking is a good deal better and safer than love for it does not demand victims. Incidentally he asks Querry who his latest victim is and is told that he has none since he is cured and safe. Father Thomas with his religious scruples tries to make a spiritual Schweitzer of Querry. He thinks that Querry has been given the grace of aridity and that perhaps he is walking the dark night of the soul in the footsteps of St. John of the Cross. Father Thomas's request to Querry to pray for him sounds odd and brings into a sharp focus the fact that no human being can ever understand another. The whole novel is an extended gloss on the subject of human inability to understand. If Querry comes there in quest of self-understanding - the most ambitious of all quests - and fails to understand the priests, who for him are more interested in electricity and building works than the human condition, the priests too fail to understand him. The comic incongruity lies in the disparate attempts of the various people to understand Querry. Notwithstanding his failures in the larger context of understanding himself and others Querry approximates to a condition of contentment slowly. He tells Dr Colin: 'You know I am happy here'. But we are reminded: "He closed his mouth on the phrase too late: it had escaped him on the sweet evening air like an admission."(p. 99) To make the tangle of human misunderstanding more complicated, Parkinson, the absurd figure of farce, comes in with his thirst for headlines and a portable Remington. The very first sentences he utters mark him as a clown though his stupid obstinacy is to become apparent later. "'I'm Parkinson," the man said firmly as though he were the sole survivor of a whole tribe of Parkinsons. "Am I dying?"' Querry, who does the grotesque job of the interpreter (like Fowler interpreting for Pyle, the man who costs him a lot of happiness), has an instant dislike that he normally has for one clowning without even the simple excuse of amusing others. He comes in with his own theory and would not care what his subject thinks of him and still less of what publicity could cost him. The very initial scene shows Parkinson as the obtuse journalist who sees only what he wants to see without knowing what others might think of him:

> 'It's bloody hot,' Parkinson said. He looked at Querry.
>
> 'Thank God there's someone here at least who speaks English.' He turned his head towards the Remington and said, 'The white man's grave.'
>
> 'Your geography is wrong. This is not West Africa.'
>
> Querry corrected him with dry dislike. 'And Stanley never came this way;' Querry went on, without attempting to disguise his antagonism.
>
> 'Oh yes, he did. This river is the Congo, isn't it?'
>
> 'No, you left the Congo a week ago after Luc.'

Dr Colin anticipates what is to come with Parkinson's widely syndicated articles and warns Father Thomas who does not give up his own theory:

> 'Publicity can be an acid test for virtue. Personally I am convinced that Querry...'
>
> 'I have never enjoyed blood sports, father. And a man hunt least of all.'(p. 113)

Dr Colin is the raisonneur of the piece, the sober man, who preserves his sanity by hardwork and by abstaining from cerebration. He it is who realises that Querry too is a patient and speaking in his habitual metaphor calls him a burnt-out case and gives Father Thomas the ineffectual warning "Where now will he be able to find his therapy? Limelight is not very good for the mutilated."(p. 114) But in a world swayed by absurdity, one should despair of reason. His momentary fear of Parkinson overcome (he has come to the end of fear too), Querry tells Parkinson "Men with vocations are different from others. They have more to lose. Behind all of us in various ways lies the spoilt priest. You once had a vocation, admit it, for it was only a vocation write."(p. 115) He tries to shock Parkinson into an awareness of the absurdity of his presumption by telling him that he had several women after Marie Morel. He confesses: "I've never really loved. I'd only accepted being loved. And then when the worst boredom settled in. Because if I had deceived myself with women I had deceived myself with work too."(p. 118-119) Even after Parkinson's arrival Querry is unaware of the comic fate that would overtake him. Ironically he feels a sense of security. From the conditions of happiness (which he inadvertently admits to Dr Colin he has achieved) he comes to the state of contentment. The doctor believes in the cure he is effecting — the first stage being the curiosity Querry, the patient, has shown in another human being if only in the physically burnt-out Deo Gratias. The second stage is in the curiosity he shows in Dr Colin and his vocation. The central dialectic of the novel occurs at this point. Problems of existence and problems of leprosy get commingled. While the fathers of the Church believe in Christian truth, Dr Colin believes in a Christian myth. Evolution, he believes, had lodged itself in the brains of man. Hundreds of millions of years passed between the dinosaurs and the primates but in our own age we have seen the change from diesel to jet, the splitting of the atom, the cure for leprosy. The Christian myth is a part of the ninth evolutionary wave which can produce Hitlers as well as St John of the Cross. He concludes: "I have a small hope, that's all, a very small hope, that someone they call Christ was the fertile element, looking for a crack in the wall to plant its seed. I think of Christ as an amoeba who took the right turning. I want to be on the side of progress which survives. I'm no friend of pterodactyls."(p. 131) This surprises Querry who in turn asks the doctor if he is a happy man. Dr Colin replies that he supposes he is, thought it is not a question he has ever asked himself. The spiritual ennui coupled with sensual exhaustion makes Querry lose his moorings. The epigraph makes his condition very clearly analogous to that of the speaker in Dante's *Inferno: 'Io non mori, a non remasi vivo.'* (I did not die, yet nothing of life remained). The comic pervades the book in the surprising lucidity of the raisonneur without recourse to theological dogma. There is a comic reversal of roles: the superficially atheistic doctor consoling and reassuring the man who has lost his faith and the spiritual specialists bewildering him. When Father Thomas speaks to him of Europe with the theatres, friends, restaurants, bars, books, shops, the company of equals — the fruits of whatever that means - Querry replies: "I am content here."(p. 133)

4.5 From a sense of aridity and sensual exhaustion arriving at any kind of contentment is rehabilitation itself. Only after the darkness of total negation, affirmation begins to dawn. This is illustrated in a dream which could be interpreted as a deep metaphor:

> He thought he was with the Superior on the boat going away, but in his dream the boat took the contrary direction to that of Luc. It went on down the narrowing river into the denser forest, and it was not the Bishop's boat. A corpse lay in the Bishop's cabin and the two of them were taking it to

> Pendele for burial. It surprised him to think that he had been so misled as to believe that the boat has reached the farthest point of its journey into the interior when it reached the leproserie. Now he was in motion again, going deeper. (p. 137)

The end is not the end really as it turned out to be a beginning. But the quiet he gleans from the sense of contentment is rudely disturbed by the interfering fool Parkinson as much as it has been by the irritating palm-oil manager, Rycker. Parkinson's conclusion that he is the hermit of Congo stings Querry into action: another bit of evidence of the growing human feeling in him. He knows that Rycker must be silenced for he has come a long way and he has nowhere to go if he leaves the leproserie. Comically enough Father Thomas does not try to understand him in his presumptuous effort at creating Querry as he thought he is. Querry tells him that he had no good motive in coming to the leproserie except the one of looking after himself as he had always done. Surely even a selfish man should not be denied the right to happiness. Father Thomas who always tries to see through his theological spectacles says: "You have a wonderful quality of humility."(p. 142)

4.6 The comedy that has been permeating the book underlying the tragedy of Querry's loss right from the beginning comes to a climax under dramatic circumstances. Querry goes to the palm-oil plantation to warn Rycker against doing him any further damage. Mme Rycker tells him that he cannot see him since her husband is in bed down with fever and draws his sting. 'I can hardly strike a woman' he says and a sudden rictus round his mouth startles her. He tells her how he has been persecuted first by her husband, then by herself and last of all by Parkinson. Listening to his tale of unhappiness she breaks down into telling him of her own trouble. The private hell of the child-woman treated like a school girl by her husband makes Querry more human than ever. He has always been loved without loving anyone or anything. The only sign of his love is his going after Deo Gratias and then follows his taking Mme Rycker to Luc to a doctor without her husband being aware of it. Querry's intention is to get a doctor confirm the suspected pregnancy. The husband does not know about it and in his characteristic stupidity draws his own conclusion. The very sardonic confession to Rycker incongruously undoes Querry at the end. He tells him that he has given up his talent just as he has given up women adding a caustic remark : "After all there are only thirty-two ways of driving a nail into a hole."(p. 151) The man who considered himself to have come to the end of everything begins to act. In the hotel where they occupy adjoining rooms he thinks she is crying and goes in. She tells him that she has been laughing. She hopes that her stomach-ache could be the curse and Querry pities her. He finds it impossible not to treat her as a child. He thinks that Rycker instead of rupturing her virginity has sealed it down safely once and for all. She appeals to him as a child and he tells her a story apparently to pass time. The story can be viewed as an inverted account of himself. The zenith of his artistic achievement leads him all the while to a kind of vacancy, disquietude and a feeling of abandonment. When Marie Rycker says that she does not like parables and that she does not like his hero, Querry tells her that he does not like him himself. When he attempts at an inverted self-revelation with "His King existed objectively and there was no other King but his" (p. 161), Marie is reminded of her husband. She asks him about the climax of the story and if it is going to be a happy ending. Fond of sensation she asks him about his women. In Marie, Querry sees a dilemma which he has encountered before. "I tell you it is not easy leaving a profession any more than you would find it easy leaving a husband." With his tale told Querry becomes a somewhat enlightened man: 'In the early hour of coolness he thinks "The King is dead, long live the King."' His unbelief, he wonders, could after all, be a conclusive proof of the King's existence. The tangle of the impossible assumes the proportions of an imbroglio when Rycker comes in search of his wife and finds the smears of her lipstick on Querry's towel. The moment Querry hears of his arrival (Parkinson tells him of that) he leaves. Little does he know of the absurd situation he would be in. When Marie runs away to the nuns and tells them that the child she is with is Querry's and accosts him with the statement, Querry's anger drains out of him: "It would have been easier if he had felt anger, but he felt none: to lie is as natural at a certain age as to play with fire." The explanation which Marie gives him marks the point where the comic becomes subversively prominent.(p. 191)

> 'You know very well that was nothing at all. We drank some whisky. I told you a story to send you to sleep.'
> 'Yes. Once upon a time, That was when I fell in love. No, it wasn't. I'm afraid I'm lying again,' she said with unconvincing humility. 'It was when you came to the house the first time. *In coup de foudre*.'
> 'The night you told them we slept together?'
> 'That really was a lie too. The night I slept with you properly was after the Governor's party.'

'What on earth are you talking about now?'

'I did not want him. The only way I could manage was to shut my eyes and think it was you.' (pp. 191-2)

With the mystery solved thus incongruously he looks at her with a kind of respect. "It would have needed a theologian to appreciate properly the tortuous logic of her argument, to separate good from bad faith, and only recently he had thought of her as someone too simple and young to be a danger."(p. 192) It is at this point that Querry realises that his suffering is a sign of his life. Confronted for the first time with an egotism as absolute as his own, he remembers the priest on the river talking of suffering which will always be provided when it is required. When Dr Colin is told about the incident in Querry's characteristic way, the doctor only assures him that in his case no further skin tests are required. There is the comic again in full operation in the discussions among the priest and the nuns. With the horns of a cuckold romantically thrust on his head Rycker comes down like an absurd fury. Smelling strongly of whisky he demands to see Querry. When Father Thomas tells him he is at home he makes for the door: "He stood there for a moment as though he were on a stage and had forgotten his exit line."(p. 199) Querry hears his own name called in the darkness outside and is poignantly aware of the comic absurdity of what might ensure: "'What a grotesque it is," Querry said, "That this should happen to me. The innocent adulterer. That's not a bad title for a comedy.'" His mouth moves in the effort of a smile. With Rycker on the scene, with Father Thomas, Dr Colin and Brother Philipe (who comes in running to warn Querry of Rycker's gun), the tragedy of Querry loses its sting and peters out into broad comedy. The scene is the brilliant climax of Querry making fun of Rycker with a view to waking him up: "Are you here for a religious argument? I'll admit you know much more than I do about the love of God.' When in the middle of the altercation Brother Philipe entreats Rycker to come to the mission where they would put up a bed for him so that he could talk in the morning after a cool shower Querry laughs again. Rycker fires and the lamps falls with Querry. Fetching a cushion for Querry's head in the darkness when Rycker says that he should not have laughed, the doctor says that Querry does not laugh easily. The last words of the enigmatic Querry are an enigma never to be conclusively solved: "Absurd," Querry said, "this is absurd or else ...' but what alternatives theological or psychological he had they never knew.' (p. 205) The alternatives are left unclarified suggesting that Querry has ripened to a stage where dawns the realization that the human situation is absurd. It is debated whether Querry's ending is happy. The Superior opines "Everybody will have got what they wanted — it's really quite a happy ending, isn't it? Rycker feels he has been important both to God and man ..." Dr Colin, interjects: "You can hardly say it was a happy ending for Querry." "Wasn't it?" the Superior asks. All human beings are happier dead and happiness is a term which has relevance only to the living. Absurd forces entangle the human situation and all efforts at disentangling it are fraught with absurd consequences. Querry is aware of the fact that the whole situation is grotesque, a comedy. Illogical, irrational events crop up subverting the comedy. If this is the situation, either God is not there at all or it must be an absurdity. It is in this context that God is viewed as a practical joker who must have made the world in play.

4.7 Institutional Catholicism appears to be abandoned in this book with a faint mockery. Faith here at the leproserie is converted into a routine business. The priests are more secularly professional than religiously intellectual. They married God but their marriage too became domesticated. Analysis of motives is never taken into their domain and they absurdly glory in the fact. The Bishop asks at the cocktail party if Querry can play bridge and the authorial comment runs: "The Bishop's question was taken to mean that the Church in her wise and traditional fashion reserved her opinion."(p. 66) If the priests ar e victims of religious numbness, Rycker is a victim of religious hysteria. It turns out to be more hideous than the former. His spiritual vanity is appalling as his question to Querry would reveal: "Have I given up priesthood for nothing at all?" Greene makes a burlesque of Rycker's religious sentiment. The frogs around in the darkness seem to croak with Rycker's hollow phrases "Free will, Grace, Love." When stung by ridiculous jealousy he is reduced to a figure of farce, the comic Vice of a Morality play. Light-hearted comedy reigns in Rycker's treatment of his wife. We are reminded of a rigid school mistress and a rather perceptive child intent on making fun of her inescapable teacher:

> Rycker said 'When Mme Guelle asks you what you will drink, say a glass of perrier.'
>
> 'Not an *Orange pressee*?'
>
> 'Not unless you see a jug of it on the side board. We mustn't inconvenience her.'
>
> **Marie Rycker took the advice seriously in and when turned her eyes from her husband and stared at the dull forest wall.**

The only path led inside was closed with fibre mats for a ceremony no white man must see.

'You heard what I said, darling?'

'Yes, I will remember.'

'And the *canapes*. Don't eat too many of them like you did last time. We haven't come to the Residence to take a meal. It creates a bad impression.'

'I won't touch a thing.'

'That would be just as bad. It would look as thought you noticed they were stale. The usually are.'(p. 63)

The interior comment of the author runs that the chastity Mme Rycker has been taught at the convent was something which she connected with clean white garments and light and gentleness, while his was like old sack cloth in a desert:

"You are not even interested when I tell you my deepest feelings."

She said miserably, 'Perhaps it was a mistake.'

'Mistake?'

'Marrying me. I was too young.'

'You mean I am too old to give you satisfaction?'

'No - no. I didn't mean ...'

'You know my kind of love, don't you? Do you suppose that's the kind of love saints feel?'

'I don't know any saints,' she said desperately.

You don't believe I am capable in my small way of going through the Dark Night of the Soul? I am only your husband who shares you bed. ...'

She whispered, 'I don't understand. Please, I don't understand.' (pp. 69-70)

There is a great deal overtly comic in their relationship and Marie Rycker complicates the comedy in the extreme. She has a furtive look at Querry's photograph on the cover page of TIME before she joins her husband in bed. Rycker lies stretched naked inside the mosquito tent of the double bed under the wooden body of the cross. He looks like a drowned man fished up in a net. "A Christian marriage, how often she had been told it by her religious instructors, symbolized the marriage of Christ and His Church." (p. 72) In this 'sub-plot' of Rycker one can see the tangled web of a complex comedy made of sensuality and misconceived religious notions. Greene has illustrated earlier that innocence could be dangerous; here he illustrates that misconceived piety could be deadly. If Rycker does not think of Querry in terms of a saint and if he does not pride himself in his intellectualist theology there would have been no novel - or at least the novel could not have been as it is now. Its artistic excellence is accounted for by the 'open' ending which sets the reader thinking about the insoluble question mark Querry leaves.

4.8 The insoluble enigma of the persistent question mark that Querry is a grotesque exaggeration which belongs to the domain of the comic. His notes to Dr Colin, his admissions to Rycker, Parkinson and Father Thomas, and his fable narrated to Mme. Rycker are all attempts at self-revelation made again and again. They reveal his persistence to convince them of his condition which grotesquely enough no one appears to be convinced of. The battlefield motif, of people fighting in the fog in their circlets, is very much in evidence here. Father Thomas believes in the good that the publicity of Querry's stay there would bring them: Rycker with his abortive seminarian background believes in the opportunity to discuss his theological problems with him: Parkinson believes in his great mission, and all are ludicrously wrong. In this sense they all became comic figures. As irony would have it the innocent looking Mme Rycker shatters the little home that Querry thinks he has successfully made in the far off leproserie. Querry's cries that he has nowhere to go if he leaves there — like those of a dumb leper who has lost his bell — are of no avail. The priests are rendered comic figures in their worldly preoccupations. Only the Superior soberly warns Father Thomas against considering Querry a live saint. "Don't let us recognize them before the Church does."(p. 92) In spite of his commonsensical approach he is made a figure not serious enough as would befit his station. He becomes an absurd figure showing Mme Rycker the picture of a bidet thinking it to be a novel footbath. More incongruously she remembers the ambiguous jokes of her more daring companions at school. Both Querry and Dr Colin have their fling at him. When the Superior says that remorse is a kind of belief, Querry retorts: "Oh no, it isn't. You try to draw everything into the net of your faith, father." (p. 80) When the Superior tells him that Querry was beginning to find his faith again when he had been sadly cut off, Dr Colin answers: "You try too hard to make a pattern, father." (p. 207) Comic forces thus go on obliterating the impressions of Querry's private tragedy in the course of the narrative. Fundamentally the comic lies in the reversal of the assumption that religion can be a healing force and by the fact that ethical rationalism has been given the last word. For the child of three to whom the Superior offers only sweets, Dr Colin is sure of a cure in a year or two.

4.9 With the comic intensified in the novel, the tragicomic mode gains further in its interest making the response it evokes more complex than ever before. In *The End of the Affair*, Bendrix, despite his cynicism, is sentimental and *A Burnt-out Case* shows a tremendous progress since the tragic in it is rightly swallowed up into a comic perspective. Though the recipe for a tragedy is all too evident in the Rycker affair, Greene holds it under the comic light by pulling it out into melodrama, with a mixture of farce thrown in. Querry's tragic end is subtly blunted by the grotesque smile that looms on his face in the end. His death in a melodramatic situation helps to bring out the unmistakably absurd and comic in the nature of things.

Chapter 5

The Novels of the Third Phase

Contrary to common belief, truth is nearly always funny. It's only tragedy which people bother to imagine or invent.

Doctor Humphries in 'The Honorary Consul'

5.1 Laughter has the power to heal and Comedy is the fountain spring of laughter. The capacity to laugh is a matter of the comic sense which sharpens one's awareness of the grotesque, the absurd, the farcical and fantastic. These disparate manifestations of the comic are as much a part of reality as the tragic is. Tragedy deals with confrontation while comedy implies and necessitates adjustment and acclimatization. The perspective of comedy is inclusive while that of tragedy is necessarily restricted. Comedy is wide and it can take into its fold tragedy and assimilate it without disintegrating itself. Aldous Huxley[1] writes that while tragedy tells only partial truth, the epic can embody the whole truth. What Huxley says about the epic may be applied to comedy in that it is inclusive. While comedy can contain tragedy also, tragedy cannot easily absorb comedy- the comic relief that playwrights provide intensifies only the tragedy. Tragedy, it is seen, may be experienced as part of a larger comedy. It is the comic spirit alone that can contain and embrace in its fold the antinomies and polarities of the whole expanse of reality. The tragic sense reveals a preoccupation with evil while the attitude of comedy reveals a simultaneous perception of both good and evil, the beautiful and the grotesque. The comic provides the vantage point which enables one to conceive the tragic without entangling and sacrificing oneself. It has the supreme advantage of furnishing one with a deep insight into reality as well as a strong defence against its dangerous and disagreeable aspects

5.1.1 *The Comedians* (1966) embodies Greene's sunny comic vision in its full bloom. The metaphysical anguish and the dilemma of tormented soul proceeding from the sense of Evil are left behind. Evil is looked in the face with the awareness offered by the perspective of comedy. While tragedy demands heroes, in comedy there are only comedians. Heroism of the sort needed by tragedy is

1. Aldous Huxley, "Tragedy and the whole Truth", *Music at Night and other Essays*, Penguin, 1953, p. 12.

impossible in the contemporary context. Since tragedy is excluded thus, we are only left with comedy. The heroism of the sort exhibited by the Smiths in the novel is sadly comic and that is why when Smith remarks that he may think of them as comic figures, Brown replies that they are not comic but heroic. In terms of Brown's thinking, there is no antithesis between the tragic and the comic; the comic can enlarge itself into the heroic to include the greater dimensions of the tragic within itself.

5.1.2 Duvalier's Haiti is the perfect objective correlative to the terror of life. Greene with his eye for the special trouble spots in the world to match them with the degrees of complexity in the human condition chooses Haiti as yet another example of the terrible "aboriginal calamity" in which Newman saw the human race implicated. Greene writes in his foreword to a book of Haitian History:[2]

> There is something peculiarly Roman in the air of Haiti: Roman in its cruelty, in its corruption and heroism. ... We are nearer to Europe of Nero and Tiberius than to the Africa of Nkrumah. ... that is why Haiti is the scene of classical tragedy in the contemporary manner. We feel sometimes that we are witnessing a tragedy by Racine played by coloured actors - or at the worst moments *Titus Andronicus.*

Haiti is a land stormy with colour, though there may be little food in that country. Young Philipot, the failed poet in the novel, recites Baudelaire to Brown near the swimming pool of the latter's hotel, the Trianon:

> "Quelle est cette ile triste at noire? - C'est Cythere Nous dit-on, un pays fameux dans les chansons Eldorado banal tous les vieux garcons. Regardez, apres tout, c'est une pauvre terre."

Brown, the narrator-actor in the novel, says that only nightmares are real in the place. Doctor Magiot says of his country that they are an evil slum floating a few miles from Florida. He tells Brown: "In this Island the Catholic prayer is very apt. 'The Devil is a roaring lion seeking whom he may devour." (p. 87)[3] Referring to Doctor Philipot's death, he says: "Violent deaths are natural deaths here. He died of his environment." (p. 90) The whole land is poverty-stricken and corruption raises its hydra-heads everywhere. The nightmare republic is ruled by Doctor Duvalier, the horror-inspiring

2. Al Burt and B. Diedrich, *Papa Doc* (London: Bodley Head, 1969)
3. Page numbers refer to *The Comedians*, Bantam Books, 1967.

president, assisted by his bogey-men whose cruelty is described by Brown to the passengers on board the *Medea*. The driver who tried to kidnap the President's children was burnt alive. The chief characters are eyewitnesses to an interrupted funeral. The hearse is stolen after an act of savage vandalism. In a dictatorship, we are shown, one does not have a right even to a dead husband. Asked by Mr. Smith if there is no law in the country, Doctor Magiot replies that the Tontons Macoute are the only law. The new Minister for Social Welfare does not know words like "bail" and "Habeas Corpus". Horror and cruelty have corroded and eaten into the body politic of Haiti. The new Secretary for Social Welfare symbolises the corruption of the State for which Greene uses the symbol of dental decay: "... his teeth were very big and white and separate, like tomb-stones designed for a much larger cemetary. A curious smell crossed the desk as though one grave has stayed open." (p. 48) Brown has a victim of the conditions of Haiti in his presence - his servant Joseph treated by the Tontons Macoute. "In a nightmare anything, however cruel or grotesque, is possible," we are told by the narrator. Nothing said about and shown in Haiti is an exaggeration. Greene tells his friend in the dedicatory letter: "Poor Haiti and the character of Doctor Duvalier's rule are not invented, the latter not even blackened for dramatic effect. Impossible to deepen that night." But when Brown says, "I could understand why it was these men wore dark glasses - they were human, but they mustn't show fear: it might be the end of terror in others." (p. 117) One suspects that the whole edifice of horror is raised on the sandy foundations of fear, and for all its grimness, the whole situation sounds not only melodramatic but even comic.

5.1.3 "... aspects are within us and who seems most kingly is the King."

These lines from Thomas Hardy figure as the epigraph for the novel. The title does not refer merely to the strolling players in the French sense of the word: it is used more in the traditional and theatrical sense denoting roles and masks. The narrator tells us that with the names Smith, Jones and Brown, the situation was improbable. He finds people around him comic. He thinks of Jones: "I thought of him as someone who, having packed in a hurry brought the wrong uniform, for he certainly did not mean to be conspicuous. With the little black moustache and the dark Pekinese eyes I would have taken him for a Frenchman - perhaps someone on the Bourse - and it was quite a surprise to me when I learnt that his name was Jones." (p. 5) Brown himself is something of an anamoly. The purser tells him: "You don't look like an hotelier. You look like ..." "But his imagination failed him" comments the narrator. (p. 26) Brown is constantly aware of his role as a comedian. When he introduces himself to Jones and Smith as Brown he tells us: "I felt as though I were making a bad joke." Making love to his German mistress Martha he feels that he is playing the role of a comedian affording comic relief: "She laughed and held me still and kept me. I responded as well as I could, but the corpse in the pool seemed to turn our preoccupations into comedy. The corpse of Doctor Philipot belonged to a more tragic theme; we were only a sub-plot affording a little light relief." (p. 50) He recounts in a flash-back the way he lost his virginity in a hotel room in Monte Carlo to a woman fifteen years his senior whom he met in the casino. She helps him remove his make up and Brown is aware of the theatricality: "I saw Frere Laurent disappear wrinkle by wrinkle in the mirror above the shelf where lay her lotions, her eyebrow pencils, her pots of pomade. We might have been two actors sharing a dressing room." (p. 54) Not only does Brown think in terms of actors but also in terms of spectators: "He [the British Charge] was the perfect spectator - the spectator of whom every actor must sometimes dream, intelligent, watchful, amused and critical in just the right way, a lesson he had learnt from having seen so many performances good and bad in indifferent plays." (p. 95) He is uncomfortable when he imagines what the Charge must think of him if he knew of his affair with the Ambassador's wife for "the act belonged too closely to the theatre of farce." (p. 96) When the Charge tells him that his interference about Jones may not be politic saying: "I have a feeling that this is not the first police-cell Major Jones has known. We mustn't exaggerate the situation", Brown feels like the player King rebuked by Hamlet for exaggerating his part." (p. 96) Towards the end of the book Brown remembers.

> I sat in the hotel through the whole afternoon in case she came, but I was glad she stayed away. I remembered how twice before our love-making had been disturbed by the dead-first Marcel and then the *ancien ministre*. Now it was Doctor Magiot who had joined the dignified and disciplined ranks; they rebuked our levity. (p. 272)

5.1.4 The leitmotif is overtly brought into focus in a discussion at the Ambassador's residence. The participants besides Luis, the Ambassador, are Brown, young Philipot and Martha. Brown tells them how once he persuaded a London restaurant to believe that he had been a waiter at Fouquet's wondering whether Jones isn't playing the same game and whether both of them are comedians. Young Philipot says that he is a comedian with his verses. The ambassador asks them to cheer up and proposes that they should all be comedians together. He says that even Papa Doc is a comedian.

> "Oh no," Philipot said. "He is real. Horror is always real."
>
> The ambassador said, "We mustn't complain too much of being comedians - it's an honourable profession. If only we could be good ones the world might gain at least a sense of style. We have failed - that's all. We are bad comedians, we aren't bad men."
>
> "For Christ's sake," Martha said in English, as though she were addressing me directly. "I'm no comedian." We had forgotten her. She beat with her hands on the back of the sofa and cried to them in French now, "You talk so much. Such rubbish. My child vomited just now. You can smell it still on my hands. He was crying with pain. You talk about acting parts. I'm not acting any part. I do something. I fetch a basin. I fetch aspirin. I wipe his mouth. I take him into my bed." (p. 125)

A few minutes later Martha tells Brown in their privacy:

> "Perhaps we won't have to be comedians any more." "You said you were no comedian." (Brown replies) "I exaggerated, didn't I? But all that talk irritated me. It made every one of us seem cheap and useless and self-pitying. Perhaps we are, but we needn't revel in it." (p. 126)

For Brown the role of a comedian implies pretension and for young Philipot a mistaken course of behaviour. For the ambassador the profession of a comedian is honourable since what matters most is being a good comedian. Failures make us bad comedians but not bad men. To Martha's mind suffering and life are real and she refuses to accept being a comedian. Her remark: "Perhaps we won't have to be comedians any more" implies that they need not play-act innocence. The role of a comedian provides immunity from damage. Comedy can include horror since it is really a matter of perspective at a point of the tragedy-comedy scale. At the correct point between the two even horror is absorbed. The Tontons Macoute are a case in point. The dark glasses help them hide their own fear. Remove their glasses, their masks are shed, the horror disappears. It is the ambassador who has a correct grasp of comedy. "If only we could be good ones [comedians] the world might gain at least a sense of style." If everyone were to play the individual parts assigned well, life would not be insufferable. Evil is oppressive because the sense of proportion and equilibrium are upset. If mankind learnt the art of playing comedians well, evil will be reduced to be a less threatening phenomenon. Greene is testing as it were the resources of comedy and the depths he has discovered in it are evident in the use of this metaphor of theatre and role-playing.

5.1.5 Martha is the central philosopher of comedy and the exemplum of its metaphysic. She agrees with her husband that a comedian's is an honourable profession. Though there are comedians who are cheap, useless and self-pitying, she certainly is not one of them. Her sense of comedy would include charity and love. Comedy, for her, is not mere appearance - it is reality itself put within reach of everyone's comprehension - provided the individual has understanding and a correct perspective on things. She wants to oblige Brown once out of generosity. When the foot-steps of the ambassador are heard on the stairs, she is neither fussed nor upset. Without hustling herself and with perfect grace she walks out of the room before her lover and calls out to her husband "I'm just showing Mr. Brown the rooms up here ..." It is in this context that Brown realizes that she proved to be the best comedian of them all. Martha's philosophy of life is based on the principle of charity - the greatest of all virtues. In a letter to Brown in New York she writes:

> "perhaps the sexual life is the great test, if we can survive it with charity to those we love and with affection to those we have betrayed, we needn't worry so much about the good and the bad in us. But jealousy, distrust, cruelty, revenge, recrimination ... then we fail. The wrong is in that failure even if we are the victims and not the executioners. Virtue is no excuse." (p. 131)

The sexual life has a vital role in human life. If one can show charity on sexual life with reference to one's own behaviour and that of others, in other areas of life showing charity would be much more easy. After realizing that Martha is an excellent comedian Brown feels that he played his part less well. He is painfully aware of the fact that he has not learnt the trick of laughter. Martha gives him a new awareness of life:

> We lay down in a shallow declivity under the palms like bodies given a common burial, and I remembered another death, Marcel hanging from the Chandeliers. Neither of us would ever die for love. We would grieve and separate and

> find another. We belonged to the world of comedy and not of tragedy. The fire-flies moved among the trees and lit intermittently a world in which we had no part. (pp. 153-154)

A few moments later lying side by side they discuss life and Martha enlightens him saying: "The situation [in Germany] is not abnormal. It belongs to human life. Cruelty is like a search light. It sweeps from one spot to another. We can only escape it for a time. We are trying to hide now under the palm trees." (p. 154) Brown tells us that he sometimes wondered whether that was not the happiest moment they knew together. In the role of a jealous lover he loses the balance of being a good comedian. He is a Bendrix without knowing that jealousy is absurd in the world they inhabit, though he thinks he is able to see the comic pervading everything. Martha, once again, comes out victorious with her attitude of perfect comic detachment. A perfect player can discern not only the comedy of the lightest variety but also the profound comedy underlying things. She sees Jones in the Volendam skirt come as their first refugee, and laughs till her eyes are filled with tears. With Jones in the embassy, the comedy around Martha's life gains another dimension when Brown becomes an absurdly jealous lover. When at first she realizes that he is tormented by irrational jealousy she tells him with her habitual sweetness: "Darling, he makes us laugh, that's all." When he goes on baiting her, she explains with gentleness that he should have been a novelist and that he is inventing all of them. When Brown does not see her point and relent, she flares up:

> "My darling, be careful. Don't you understand? To you nothing exists except in your thoughts. Not me, not Jones. We're what you choose to make us. You're a Berkeleyan. My God, what a Berkeleyan. You've turned poor Jones into a seducer and me into a wanton mistress. You can't even believe in your mother's medal, can you? You've written her a different part. My dear, try to believe we exist when you aren't there. We're independent of you. None of us is like you fancy we are. Perhaps it wouldn't matter much if your thoughts were not so dark, always so dark." (p. 219)

5.1.6 Though Brown fails to play the role of an accomplished comedian and causes the pathetic death of Jones with his jealousy and distrust, at the end of the book he realizes Jones's excellence as a comedian:

> Perhaps, under the circumstances, it was only natural that I dreamt of Jones. He lay among the dry rocks on the flat

> plain beside me and he said: "Don't ask me to find water. I can't I'm tired, Brown, tired. After the seven hundredth performance I sometimes dry up on my lines - I've only two lines." I said to him, "Why are you dying? Jones?"
>
> "It is in my part, old man, it's in my part. But I've for this comic line - you should hear the whole theatre laugh when I say it. The ladies in particular."
>
> "What is it?"
>
> "That's the trouble. I've forgotten it."
>
> "Jones, you must remember."
>
> "I've got it now. I have to say - just look at those bloody rocks - 'This is a good place,' and everyone laughs till the tears come. Then you say, 'To hold the bastards up?' and I reply, 'I didn't mean that.' (p. 274)

From the Latin scholarship of the Jesuit school, through a failure of vocation into a graduation via the world of adultery and deceit into the profession of a mortician, Brown's is a difficult progress. He had drifted away from faith and arrived at a position where human life is viewed as a matter of playing roles wearing masks. His rootlessness helps him play his role with the degree of success he has. He is aware of being a phoney and a fake: "I suppose those of us who spend a large part of our lives in dissembling, whether to a woman, to a partner, even to ourselves: begin to smell each other out." (p. 34) Just as he sees in Jones a man acting a part, he sees in Petit Pierre an actor who has to enact the 'gaiety of despair':

> He giggled up at me, standing on his pointed toe-caps, for he was a tiny man. He was just as I had remembered him, hilarious. Even the time of the day was humorous to him. He had the quick movements of a monkey, and he seemed to swing from wall to wall on ropes of laughter. I had always thought that, when the time came, and surely it must one day in his precarious livelihood, he would laugh at his executioner, as a Chinaman is supposed to do." (p. 37)

Brown's stay with the Jesuits gives him an awareness of religion and though he tells himself and believes in conscious life that he has done away with faith and religion once and for all by dropping the roulette-token in the collection box, religion haunts him in dreams when the subconscious has the sway. He dreams that he is a boy kneeling at the communion rail in the college chapel in Monte Carlo. "The priest came down the row and placed in each mouth a borbon biscuit, but when he came to me he passed me by." (p. 137)

The comfort which religion brings to many is denied to Brown. When he tells Martha "I am nothing" and she tells him that she is not a Catholic nothing but a Protestant nothing, Brown falls into a kind of reverie:

> I had a sense of coloured balls flying in the air, a different colour for every faith - or even every lack of faith. There was an existentialist ball, a logical-positivist ball. "I even thought you might be a Communist nothing." It was gay, it was fun so long as with great agility one patted the balls ground; it was only when a ball fell to the ground one had a sense of impersonal wound, like a dog dead on an arterial road. (p. 214)

He believes in living from day to day and takes things as they come. He wants to give the impression of a man who wants to live in the present alone. "Transcience is my pigmentation," he says. (p. 214) When Martha tells him "Perhaps you are a *pretre manque*" he retorts that she is laughing at him and says "The genitals have no theology." Later he broods: "I mocked myself while I made love. I flung myself into pleasure like a suicide on to a pavement." (p. 214) He is aware that he is not so successful a comedian, but he does not know wherein his fault lies. At a moment, thinking of Marcel's dying for his mother, he feels that death is a proof of sincerity thinking perhaps that he is not sincere enough. But his failure is occasioned not by his lack of sincerity but by a lack of sufficient detachment which his role calls upon him to show. He knows that he is playing the role of a lover but cannot keep away the prowling jealousy. He devises a perfect plan for sending away Jones permanently. Martha with her native intelligence rebukes him: "But I don't like your motive." (p. 244) There is comic irony in his being forced to become a mortician in the end. He is plainly puzzled at the end for he could not grasp the essence of comedy: "While I was a boy the Fathers of the Visitation had told me that one test of belief was this: that a man was ready to die for it. So Doctor Magiot thought too, but for what belief did Jones die?" (p. 274) Perhaps he died for the belief that he is playing the role of a comedian. Brown's failure is a matter of maladjustment and death may not be very important for one who learns to play his role well.

5.1.7 Born in Assam of an English planter and an Indian woman, Jones is a comedian par excellence. He is a fake but he makes no bones about practising deceit. He goes about with his moustache and the fake title boasting that he has a flair for smelling water, that he has lost a platoon once and that he can work miracles with a dozen men in guerilla warfare. For all we know he may be running away from debtors or some woman trouble. He does not look beyond his nose and symbolically enough he has been reading in paper-back *No Time like the Present*. Whatever others may think of him he has an essential knowledge of himself. "One never knows" is the phrase which conveyed his research into life. He frankly lives on his wits. The cocktail shaker from Asprey's, which he values next to his life, is one bought on a bad cheque. He is content with the little rakings off in salon bars. Both in appearance and choice of words he strikes one as anomalous. In a long dialogue with Brown he explains how he divides the world into two sorts - the toffs and the tarts. While the toffs can do without the tarts, the tarts cannot do without the toffs. He says proudly that he is a tart himself and explains to Brown that the toffs have a settled job or a good income. They have a stake somewhere. The tarts make a living here and there with their eyes skinned and ears open. The toffs have reason, intelligence, character. In a country of tarts down from the President it is one danger the more for men like Jones. A tart can spot another. The end of Jones is occasioned by his pathetic switching of the role, from a tart to a toff. He knows that playing a toff is the hardest part of all for him. 'I find myself laughing at the wrong moment ... I get scared sometimes too. I lose the way. It's frightening to be lost, isn't it, in a strange city, but when you get lost inside yourself ... Have another lager." (p. 19) The ellipsis is a clear confession of his confusion. Jones is a more successful comedian in spite of it. Everyone around him likes him and remembers him. At the *bordel* Brown asks the girl they call Tin Tin why she liked Jones and is told: "He made me laugh." (p. 132) Martha says the same about him: "Darling, he makes us laugh, that's all." (p. 21) Reporting the last of him young Philipot tells Brown: "He (Jones) was a wonderful man. With him we began to learn, but he didn't have enough time. The men loved him. He made them laugh." (p. 268) Mr. Smith is glad to hear of Jones's prospering and says: "I have always felt that Mr. Jones has great character." (p. 152) Jones has a knack of winning friendship and there is something sweet in him. With his brown eyes like copper coins and moist with some kind of emotion he tells Brown of the dream of his life: 'to get into money and set up a golf course with a bar attached to it'. He endears himself even to the Tontons. Brown is even puzzled by his flair for winning popularity. He says to Martha: "It's strange to me, how easily he makes friends. Luis and you. Even Mr. Smith was fond of him. Perhaps the crooked appeals to the straight or the guilty to the innocent, like blonde appeals to black." (p. 233) With his moustache shaved off to come back into safety, Jones looks more reliable to Brown. "When once the great sacrifice had been made, he entered with a kind of expert enthusiasm into the spirit of the charade." (p. 207) When things go beyond cheering up, 'shut-eye' is the solution according to Jones. He does not fight shy of playing a role thrust on him by Brown owing to his obsessive jealousy. At the proper time Jones makes a confession to Brown. "If I had a dog here tonight instead of you, I'd confess to the dog." (p. 251) He confesses first that Martha has been one of the fifty women whom he had not the courage to touch. He never saw a forest; he was only in charge of entertaining the troops in the war. As if to validate his confession he is sick, when he sees a dead man. If Brown fumbles owing to his lack of detachment, Jones succeeds with it. We are told that he has paid for the modest stone that commemorates him on the far side of the international road "with his life." He is in perfect contrast with Smith. When he says that he and Mr. Smith are "Horses out of the same stable" Brown wonders what a saint possibly could have in common with a rogue. Jones escapes the evil around him with laughter as long as he can. The supreme virtues in him appear to be his capacity for friendship and laughter. His greatness lies in evading terror. Comedy and good humour help him to get along. We must remember what he asks for of his friends when they visit him in the prison cell.

5.1.8 If Jones appears a fake at first sight, Mr. Smith is genuine throughout. "His eyes were of clear washed blue and he had homely sprouts of grey hair from his nose and ears. He was a genuine article, if ever there was one, a complete contrast to Jones." (p. 6) He has a firm conviction that vegetarianism would solve the problems of acidity and violence. He tells a friend: "Vegetarianism is not only a question of diet, Mr. Brown. It touches life at many points. If we really eliminated acidity from the human body we would eliminate passion." (p. 15) Brown retorts with his cheap cynicism "Then the world would stop" and is gently reproved: "I didn't say love." Brown's attitude towards Mr. Smith changes once and for all with that reproof. He is never comfortable in his presence, for Mr. Smith stood always as a standing reproof of his levity and flippancy. Mr. Smith is the most serious among the comedians and it takes quite long to Brown to realize his greatness. Mr. Smith is fortunate in his wife who lives with her husband a life of open charity. She is upright and gentle and she shares her husband's convictions as faithfully as an ideal wife. The Smiths are exposed to cruelty, violence and terror but they play their roles with a real tenacity of purpose. The treatment meted out to Doctor Philipot's hearse, the visit to Duvalierville, or even the executions of the prisoners cannot shake their faith. Brown is full of admiration for the heroism they show. "Reality could not touch him [Mr. Smith]. Even the scene in the Post Office had not sullied his vision. The Haitians, freed from acidity, poverty and passion, would soon be bent happily over their nut cutlets." (p. 148) Mr. Smith is committed not only to his own convictions but also to his friends. He would, if it came to that, ring up the President himself to intervene on behalf of Mr. Jones. Brown wonders: "Wasn't it possibly a flaw in character to believe so passionately in the integrity of all the world?" (p. 152) With his genuine charity and goodness he strikes both Jones and Brown as a father figure:

> "I wish I'd seen more of them," Jones said. "There's something about him..." He added surprisingly, "He reminded me of my father. Not physically, I mean, but ... Well, a sort of goodness."
>
> "Yes. I know what you mean. I don't remember my father."
>
> "To tell you the truth, my memory's a bit dim too."
>
> "Let's say the father we would have liked to have." (p. 185)

With his fundamental goodness and charity Smith encounters reality. Rising from the swimming pool, he appears like a myth. He and his wife are a perfectly matched pair of idealists. Their idealism and innocence are perfect antidotes to the evil which encompasses them. Mrs. Smith knows that he stood no chance of winning the election which he bravely contested against Turman in 1948. Mr. Smith is modest and he does not like his 'mission' to be called a mission. He calls it 'hope' with delectable modesty. If Don Quixote is a myth in the Spanish reality, Smith is his counterpart in Haiti. He is never dejected. With gentility and patience he tries to win people to his side. He has a firm conviction that with acidity removed conscience gets an elbow room. When conscience is awakened vegetarianism grows to be capable of being a religious aid. He is realistic despite his idealism. His defeat in the election, which for him is only a 'gesture', does not depress him. When Brown subtly warns him that he may be disappointed in Haiti, Mr. Smith replies with profound wisdom: "Most things disappoint you till you look deeper." He is not baffled by the horror in Haiti: "When you look properly at things they are pretty bad everywhere." That evil is baffling should not deter one from right action, though action is fraught with comic failure. Mrs. Smith too is majestically tender in accepting their defeat. "Mr. Smith came here with such high hopes," she says and consoles both herself and her husband saying "One lives and learns. It is not the end." (p. 182) Mr. Smith is humbly apologetic to have sounded disappointed: "Learning comes easier to the young. Forgive me, Mr. Brown, if I sound dejected." With a blow mercilessly dealt to their idealism, the Smiths do not consider their goodness and faith misplaced. They leave Haiti sadder and wiser not despairing of idealism but with a determination to persist in an unconditional gesture of humanity. The Haitian episode only makes them the more sympathetic and charitable than before. In terms of Greene's thinking Mr. Smith's is the happiest life. "Dona nobis pacem" is the prayer but Mr. Smith never needed it. Smith is the only character in the entire range of Greene's fiction who has peace. He appears to be born with peace and he lives in it and breathes it in spite of the endless turmoil around him. His charity is endless: "When a man knocks on the door we don't ask him about his politics." (p. 264)

5.1.9 While the Smiths and Jones deal with evil, wearing the masks of comedians and armed with the weapons of their ideals or idiosyncracies, Doctor Magiot, the raisonneur in the novel, remains absolutely unperturbed in his majestic thoughtfulness. While Smith is humanitarian, Doctor Magiot is a humanist. He is a slowly matured version of Doctor Colin. Suggestively enough both of them are medical men by profession. Maladies, their diagnosis, prognosis and treatment belong to their domain — not only the physical but also the political and intellectual ones. Doctor Magiot is the one character in the novel who can see through the 'isms' into the truth and into the heart of the matter. Though he knows what is wrong with the state of Haiti, like a true doctor he is affected neither by a sense of disapproval not by a sense of horror. He does not either despair of or glory in the future of Haiti. Though a born Catholic, he can admire suicide as 'the clear headed act of a mathematician' since it is not theological despair that drove Doctor Philipot to it. He understands the death and delivers his report: "He died of his environment." He believes only in certain economic laws but has insight into and sympathy for religion: "Religion can be excellent therapy for many states of mind." He is a Communist believing in it as a system of philosophy. His attitude is positive. He explains to Brown in a letter written during the last moments of his life:

> "Communism ... is more than Marxism, just as Catholicism— remember I was a born Catholic too — is more than

> the Roman curia. There is a *mystique* as well as a *politique* ... if you have abandoned one faith, do not abandon all faith. There is always an alternative to the faith we lose. Or is it the same faith under another mask?"(pp. 273-74)

Doctor Magiot is a humanist and he is far above the routine 'isms'. For him faith which does not necessarily imply any standard 'ism' is essential for human life and progress.

5.1.10 La Comtesse, Brown's mother, is the forerunner of the delectable Aunt Augusta of *Travels with my Aunt*. Leaving her son with the Fathers of the Visitation at Monte Carlo she roams about and lands finally at Haiti. Seeing her son before her death has been perhaps as accidental as his birth. She is thoroughly and unabashedly sensual. Doctor Magiot tells her son that, if asked what she wanted out of life, she would have replied 'fun'. Though she is well past seventy she might have passed for a woman in her late forties. She summons her son to her side with a post card which could have easily gone astray but for the comedy that life is. She tells her son: "They say that to be dead is about as quiet as you can get. I don't see any point in my anticipating death. It lasts a long time." (p. 65) She is aware of playing a role all her life switching over from one role to another. When her son kisses her, she closes her eyes in an artificial gesture of love and when he is opening the door to go out, she giggles and says: "You really are a son of mine. What part are you playing now?" These happen to be her last words and Brown is always puzzled when he thinks of them. The son and the mother know one another instinctively though they have been little together. Brown with a gift for perceiving comedy everywhere sees in her "an accomplished comedian". Doctor Magiot who knows her fully says that 'Fun' included almost everything, even death, for her. She dies in 'fun'. In a letter, which her son finds in Marcel's pocket, she writes: "Marcel, I know I'm an old woman and as you say a bit of an actress. But please go on pretending. As long as we pretend we escape. Pretend that I love you like a mistress. Pretend that I would die for you and that you would die for me." Against the background for Monte Carlo, perhaps, it is only her pretension that has seen her through life with the success she had. Where reality is terrifying, pretension could make living fun.

5.1.11 Critics are not slow to recognise the shift in Greene's outlook. *The Times Literary Supplement*[4] reviewer writes: "A strong current of

4. January 17, 1966.

optimism runs through the book." David Lodge in his article[5] identifies Greene's progress:

> The idea, deriving from existentialist thought, of human life as "absurd" has had the effect on contemporary literature of breaking down traditional genre categories and displacing potentially tragic materials into disquieting forms of comedy. The title of Mr Greene's new novel is suggestive in this context, and so is the following observation by the narrator: "When I was a boy I had faith in the Christian God; life under His shadow was a very serious affair; I saw him incarnated in every tragedy ... Now that I approached the end of life it was only my sense of humour that enabled me sometimes to believe in Him."
>
> While respecting the Dedication's injunction not to confuse Brown with the narrator of another color, one cannot but see this passage as some kind of comment on the latter's progress from the fiction based on a 'tragic' conflict of human and divine values to fiction conceived in terms of comedy and irony in which the eternal verities are obscured by confusions and contradictions of modern life.

While tragedy requires identification for appreciation, comedy can be appreciated with detachment. Comedy and tragedy are appreciated from two different perspectives. *The Comedians* is a crystallised form of Greene's outlook which has undergone a process of evolution. Mark Schorer writes in a foreword that a novel is an "image of life and an author's selective interpretation concretely embodied." The 'selective interpretation concretely embodied' in Greene's *The Comedians* is comic. It is an affirmation of the possibilities of life regardless of one's religious faith and existential situation. The novel embodies a sense of life as viewed through the tears in the nature of things without the tears leaving a sense of depression behind. The tears themselves signify the sense of the comic — we sometimes laugh till the tears come. Laughter and comedy could be antidotes to evil and the resultant anguish. Heroic grappling with evil is fraught with tragic potentialities but an awareness of evil and an acclimatization to it could make life worthliving. It is the comic sense that sharpens the awareness and makes acclimatization feasible. This novel distinctly effects the shift in Greene's artistic centre of gravity. The tragic is no more an undermining power; it is

5. "Behind the Mask: Graham Greene's Comedians', *Commonwealth* 25 February 1966, p. 605.

reduced to its rightful place in a larger perspective of comedy. Nor does comedy undermine Greene's basic integrity as an artist with a profound moral sense and preoccupation with the "aboriginal calamity". There is a marked re-integration of the artistic imagination. Comedy in fact helps him in the affirmation of faith.

5.1.12 *The Comedians* exemplifies Greene's metaphysic of comedy. The various planes of comedy are manifest in the characters. Brown is conscious of playing a role but he has a limited insight into comedy. He succeeds as long as he is aided by chance but flags and fails when confronted with reality in his personal relationship with Martha. His comic detachment gives way when he becomes possessive in love like Bendrix. Merely an awareness of comedy is not enough without a conscious practice of detachment implied in it. Brown holds a theory without realizing that he must try it out in his personal life. He has not interiorized it and for that reason becomes an author of tragedy in contriving Jones's death for purely selfish reasons. He reduces his personal situation to an awkward melodrama by failing to see comedy as a key to smooth life. It is not a failure of characterization but Brown's own failure to realize the full implications of the philosophy of comedy. His character is enough to show that Greene is not merely toying with comedy but trying to make it a model for the mitigation of the "aboriginal calamity" evident even in Brown's jealousy. The death of Jones which follows as an outcome of Brown's failure serves to illustrate how the irresponsible comedian tries to escape reality altogether for a long time: Jones can be viewed as the victim of a nemesis for playing irresponsible comedy. Reality seems to assert its claim when his death is almost devised by Brown. We are shown that comedy does not compromise with irresponsibility and self-aggrandizement. Tragedy, seen in the deaths of young Philipot and Jones, and the horror of the situation of which the minister's suicide is a part, serve as a tragic counterweight to comedy. There is no substitute to maturity. Chance may aid comedy but comedy cannot escape reality. Escapism or mere deceit will not do. The Smiths, a contrast to Jones, are not escapists and there is a sweet comedy in their idealism in the fact of horror. The Smiths have insight into the apparent incongruity in things as they are and as they should be. They make a sincere attempt to bend the actual towards the idea. Though they do not fully succeed, their idealism is not ridiculous. Comedy does not mar the beauty of their 'heroism'. Greene's progress in the metaphysic of comedy can be measured in the progress Brown achieves as compared to his predecessors. Scobie, Bendrix and Fowler are victims, in a way, of the tragic but Greene has succeeded to a large extent in visualizing a metaphysic of comedy, though the tragic substance still remains at least half-untractable. But it is a further progress from *A Burnt-out Case* where comedy is merely suggested. Brown, the central character and the central consciousness of the novel, is a battered individual at the end though Martha, eventually a minor character, is shown to be one who has a larger share of the joy of life. Martha's success can be attributed to her capacity to hold in balance the disparate forces of tragedy and comedy. She combines in her role the polarities of reality and a modicum of happiness. *The Comedians* is a very significant experiment which advances Greene's comic vision; though it is replete with tragic material it is surrounded by an exuberant comic sense.

5.2 *Travels with my Aunt* (1969) is a full-blown comedy untrammelled by any dark shades of tragedy. A complete freedom from any theological preoccupation with things seems to contribute to this flowering. With no religious convictions as such, Henry Pulling says on one Christmas eve: "I could be there [in the Church] without hypocrisy since I always enjoyed the more poetic aspects of Christianity. Christmas, it seems to me, is a necessary festival; we require a season when we can regret all the flaws in our relationships; it is the feast of failure, sad but consoling." The essence of religion is a charitable disposition towards imperfection and frailty. A sympathetic regret for all the failures, including the failure to understand our fellow men, perhaps, is all that we need to have. Greene's comic vision is manifest in charity and maturity. In *A Sort of Life* he writes: "The experiences of a long life may possibly increase one's intuition of human character ... I cannot be bothered to remember (the intellectual exercises) - I accept. With the approach of death I care less about religious truth. One hasn't long to wait for revelation or darkness."[6]

5.2.1 *Travels with my Aunt* is a rich harvest of comedy. The tragic strain is completely absorbed by the sense of the comic in this novel as nowhere else in Greene's fiction. Old age and death are pathetic but then action and liveliness are age-old antidotes. The novelist here echoes the idea that life is worth living at whatever cost, with whatever morality or religion. As the poet Browning puts it in his poem, "Saul": "How good is man's life, the mere living." The alternatives appear for the septuagenarian aunt to be 'edging day by day across to any last wall' or be found by the wall effortlessly. It is the

6. Graham Greene, *A Sort of Life* (London: Bodley Head, 1971), p.165

effort and the sad edging that mar life that ought to be a comedy. From beginning to end the book is replete with comic sense. The funeral with which the novel opens loses its touch of the tragic the moment the undaunted aunt makes everything serve her purpose. A powerful sense of *joie de vivre* is infused into the book and whatever sad overtones there are are submerged completely. Greene has successfully recreated the myth of Don Quixote though with a difference in the aunt with her own brand of knight-errantry. There is a direct reference to Don Quixote: the prematurely retired bank manager tells us: I felt as though I were being dragged at her heels on an absurd knight-errantry, like Sancho Panza at the heels of Don Quixote but in the cause of what she called fun instead of chivalry."(p. 103)[7] The quality of quest the novel inheres is different from that of the classic it resembles in a way. If the world of the Don is one of tragic dedication to values lost irretrievably, the world of the aunt is unashamedly realistic with its built-in deceit and hypocrisy and a craving for success at any cost. The Spanish classic is a vaster comedy rounded off with the conversion of the Knight of the Sorrowful Countenance abdicating suddenly his dearly held convictions. *Travels with my Aunt* is one in the same genre which has the circumvention of the unpleasant facts of death and old age as its basic theme.

5.2.2 There is no preoccupation with death. Prolonging life is the thing. Aunt Augusta, Jo Pulling, Charles Pottifer, each in his or her own way seeks to prolong life. It is finally asserted that a healthy attitude to life is a matter of adjusting one's lenses. Henry finally adjusts his lenses the way the 'aunt' would like. The chief character of the novel is the majestic aunt of the title, Aunt Augusta, a 'young' lady of seventy-five. She has a philosophy of her own, sparklingly vivacious and charmingly fresh. When her sister dies around eight-two and Henry calls that old age she replies 'accusingly', "She was only twelve years older than I am." Old age is a reality which has to be faced but a sense of victory can be enjoyed even in a surrender provided it is graceful and provided the thing is viewed in the correct perspective. The Aunt is a pleasantly amusing type who wishes to defy death. She is thoroughly practical and absolutely unsentimental. She remains a picture of supreme self-confidence and bubbling enthusiasm for life. Quite early in the novel she tells Henry: "Age, Henry, may a little modify our emotions — it does not destroy them". (p. 18) Her practical sense is seen in her remark: "... at my

7. Page numbers refer to *Travels with my Aunt*, Bodley Head, 1969.

age one has ceased to expect a relationship to last. Think how complicated life would be if I had kept in touch with the men I have known intimately." (p. 42) Henry slowly gravitates to her and she reveals him slowly but unmistakably that she had a series of lovers: the senior Pulling, Jo Pulling, Curran, Dambreuse, and Mr Visconti.. There is Wordsworth too, if only a stop-gap. She is really attached to none till seventy-five when she comes to the journey's end and gets united with her staunch lover Mr Visconti. Augusta in her freedom from sentimentality offers a poignant contrast to Miss Paterson, the school teacher, who cannot forget Henry's father. The pale sentimental woman fades into insignificance before the brilliant aunt with her saga of adventures. At seventy-five the great Augusta still breathes the fragrance of life: "I haven't reached nightfall yet." Life is a matter of memories of happy and joyful living — not sentiment and cerebration. 'A long life," she enlightens the 'nephew', "is not a question of years". She knows the joy of life and so the value of living. She appreciates fully the efforts of Jo Pulling and Charles Pottifer to prolong life and attain what share of immortality they can. She accepts the fact of old age with grace and ease and defies it with cheerful heroism at the same time. Henry says: "One of the few marks of age I noticed in my aunt was her readiness to abandon one anecdote while it was yet unfinished for another... like an American magazine." Mr Visconti shares the aunt's wanderlust and that is perhaps the reason why he can stay young at eighty. Travel could be an antidote not only to boredom but also to old age. Henry's father, in aunt Augusta's words, had his own way of travel: "He travelled from one woman to another ... all through his life."(p. 65) Augusta wheedles Henry to stay with her explaining to him the importance of living: "My dear Henry, if you live with us, you won't be edging day by day across to any last wall. The wall will find you of its own accord without your help, and every day you live will seem to you a kind of victory." (p. 271) She professes philosophy of longevity: "A long life is not a question of years. A man without memories might reach the age of a hundred and feel that his life has been a brief one." (p. 65) She has lots of memories accumulated during her seven decades of intense living and she loves people with a zest for life for she shares it with them. She is eager to narrate to Henry the anecdote relating to Charles Pottifer who devised yet another means of prolonging life. Not believing that death is the end of life he made an arrangement with the answering service of the telephones. If life is a matter of accumulating experience, travel is a fabulous means to accumulate experience. The secret of the aunt's never-fading youth lies in her travels. Journeys end in lovers' meetings and

Aunt Augusta meets Mr Visconti at the end and they finally decide to marry and settle down. After a life of what the French call *mouvemente* yet many more days of happiness remain for the spirited couple. The pace of death is something which cannot be arrested absolutely but it is not impossible to neutralize it. The aunt, Jo Pulling and Charles Pottifer in their hankering after prolonging life to the best of their ability spurn tragedy as it were and make intelligent bids to enact a delightful comedy.

5.2.3 Greene is a myth-maker and Aunt Augusta is something more than a mere character. She is in her own may a myth like the Presidential candidate, Mr Smith, in *The Comedians*. Henry, meeting her at his mother's funeral for the first time after fifty years, is surprised by her appearance: "I was surprised by her brilliant red hair, monumentally piled, and *her two big teeth* which *gave her a vital Neanderthal air*."(Emphasis mine) Age has mellowed her and whetted her appetite for zestful living. There is always a twinkle in her sea-deep blue eyes and she is not ashamed to live according to the dictates of her taste. She could be coarse without so much as a blush and she has a flair for speaking with incredible frankness. When Henry looks at the very large double bed as curlicued as the Venetian glass she tells him: "I am especially attached to Venice because I began my real career there, and my travels. I have always been very fond of travel." She does not hide the fact that she has had a series of lovers and she is not shy to let the 'nephew' have an inkling of what pleasures she had. "Your father had spells of activity."(p. 25), she tells Henry. What surprises most in her is her supreme self-confidence: "Oh, it will need an atom bomb to destroy us."(p. 47) She can be surprisingly ribald:

> *Hatty*: "I see a knife — or it might be a syringe."
>
> *Augusta*: "Or it could be something else, Hatty, you know what I mean."(p. 49)

Asked if she is a Roman Catholic she replies promptly and seriously: "Yes, my dear, only I just don't believe in all the things they believe in." (p. 181) Conscience for her is something which weakens a man and Henry is astounded to hear when she tells him happily that Mr Visconti has not got a conscience. Religion never took a serious hold on her imagination, it served only the purpose of convenience: "I call myself that [a Catholic] for convenience. It belongs to my French and Italian period." (p. 51) She can poke fun at Catholicism at times as when she says: "I sometimes believe in a Higher Power, even though I am a Catholic."(p. 101) Perhaps it is the freedom from serious belief in religion which has helped her acquire an insight into human nature. At a point in her self-revelation she tells her ward: "I've always been interested in human nature. Especially the more imaginative sides of it." (p. 80) This is not merely an histrionic boast but a fact. If religion is a matter of understanding, the aunt has great religion in her. She knows what she really is. Nightfall is real but luckily it is still a long way off. She is in perfect contrast to her sister Angelica the putative mother of Henry whom she calls the virgin, *La Pucelle*: "Poor Angelica, she never understood men." Angelica was straight-laced and she drove her husband to other women. Aunt Augusta is full of unsentimental pity for Henry's father who died in the arms of the school teacher Miss Paterson in Boulogne. Henry is amazed at being told: "The two A's were called. People used to say my name [Augusta] fitted me because I seemed proud as a young girl, but no one said my sister's name fitted her. A saint she may well have been, but a very severe saint. She was certainly not angelic."(p. 67)

5.2.4 Apart from memories accumulated over several decades of rich life, Augusta has a flair for recounting with apparent zest anecdotes which reveal her consistent perspective on life bound up with a philosophy of living. She harangues Henry on the subject of economy:

> "You retain the spirit of a bank-manager, even in retirement. Understand once and for all that I am not interested in economy. I am over seventy-five so that it is unlikely I will live longer than another twenty-five years. My money is my own and I do not intend to save for the sake of an heir. I made many economies in my youth and they were fairly painless because the young do not particularly care for luxury. They have other interests than spending and can make love satisfactorily on a Coca-Cola, a drink which is nauseating in age. They have little idea of real pleasure: even their love making is apt to be hurried and incomplete. Luckily in middle age pleasure beings, pleasure in love, in wine, in food. Only the taste for poetry flags a little but I would have gladly lost my taste for the sonnets of Wordsworth (the other Wordsworth I mean of course) if I could have bettered my palate for wine. Love making too provides as a rule a more prolonged and varied pleasure after forty-five. Aretino is no writer for the young."(pp. 85-86)

With all this insight into life she is absolutely unsentimental. When Henry appears to have been moved by Miss Paterson's devotion to his father she flares up with her characteristic vehemence: "That little sentimental creature? She doesn't know what love is."(p. 190) There is nothing cynical in her unsentimentality. She offers Henry guidelines to happy living: "You must surrender yourself first to extravagance. Poverty is apt to strike suddenly like influenza, it is well to have a few memories of extravagance in store for bad times."(p. 186) The sedate Henry is blown off his feet by the 'experience' of his aunt. He tells himself: "My aunt had obviously spent many years abroad and this had affected her character as well as her morality." (p. 87) With a continental training she finds something in common between a school and a brothel: "A brothel after all is a kind of school and not least a school of manners. I have known several madames of real distinction who would have been just as at home in Roedean and have lent distinction to any school.'(p. 83) She is for newness in metaphor: "All the world is a stage of course, but a metaphor as general as that loses all its meaning... People who like quotations love meaningless generalizations." (p. 127) Nothing can put out the ever-kindling enthusiasm in her and she is the genuinely pleasure-loving woman in Greene's fiction with a philosophy: "A little honest thieving hurts no one, especially when it is a question of gold. Gold needs free circulation." She adds: "You mustn't think me straight-laced. I am all for a little professional sex." (p. 82) She does not disguise her dislike for Henry's prudence and wonders: "I don't know from which side of the family you inherited prudence. Your father was lazy, but never, never prudent."(p. 77) There is enough justification in her outburst since she herself is never prudent. Another admirable quality in her is her frankness even with regard to her sexual preferences and habits: "I have always preferred an occasional orgy to a nightly routine."(p. 99) She believes that what distinguishes a man is his being a man. When Henry with his conventional morality is angry with Monsieur Dambreuse and blurts out: "But surely, Aunt Augusta, you couldn't bear the man after you had discovered how he had deceived you all those months?" She is furious: "You young fool, Monsieur Dambreuse was a *man*, and I only wish you had been given a chance of growing up like him."(p. 102) She enlightens Henry that women would fall for a man who can make them laugh. "It's the best way to win a woman. They think of the period that must elapse between one love-making and another."(p. 125) The amazed Henry misinterprets her profession during her Italian period and Augusta is too lady-like to call a brothel a brothel, though conventional morality disgusts her. She breaks out into a lecture when Henry suggests that she must have detested Mr Visconti who cheated her:

> "I despise no one, no one. Regret your actions, if you like that kind of wallowing in self-pity, but never, never despise. Never presume yours is a better morality. What do you suppose I was doing in the house behind the *Messagero*? I was cheating, wasn't I? So why shouldn't Mr Visconti cheat me? But you, I suppose, never cheated in all your little provincial banker's life because there's not anything you wanted enough, not even money, not even a woman. You looked after other people's money like a nanny who looks after other people's children. Can't I see you in your cage, stacking up the little fivers endlessly before you hand them over to their proper owner? Angelica certainly brought you up as she wanted you. Your poor father didn't have a chance. He was a cheat too, and I only wish you were. Then perhaps we'd have something in common."(p. 131)

It is only occasionally that she remembers her old age: "I loved chocolate once. I'm growing old." (p. 136) But she is confident that she has not reached the lavatory floor yet. She has great versatility besides her vivacity. She can acclimatize herself to new situations with a surprising flexibility. It is beyond Pulling's capacity to understand her constancy to Mr Visconti. She dreads a life of conventional respectability: "Two touchables together, what a terrible life they always make of it, two people suffering, afraid to speak, afraid to act, afraid of hurting."(p. 131) She confesses: 'I like men who are untouchable. I've never wanted a man who needed me, Henry ... Your father was pretty untouchable too."(p. 268) Age matures her and restores a semblance of sentiment. In her letter to Henry from Paraguay she writes: "Come as soon as you can, for I get no younger. I do not suffer from gout like an old friend who I met the other day on a packet boat, but I feel nonetheless a certain stiffness in the joints. I want very much to have with me a member of my family whom I can trust in this bizarre country."(p. 225) Once settled down with her husband and son she is aware of having made a happy innings: "I am so happy Henry, that you are here and Mr Visconti is safely returned. Perhaps I'm getting old, for I shall be content with a spell of family life."(p. 289)

5.2.5 Augusta has in her the harmonious combination of the reality of old age and the sense of conquest. The victory lies in her graceful surrender. So great is her sense of contentment and feeling of joy that the fear of death does not bother her at all. The tragedy of death is spurned or integrated into the realm of the comedy of a prolonged life. The romantically sad self-sacrifice of Wordsworth is ignored along with his death: "Yes, dear, all in good time, but can't you see that now I am dancing with Mr Visconti."(p. 317)

5.2.6 Henry Pulling, the prematurely retired bank manager of Southwood, is in his late forties. He has never married, he has always lived quietly and apart from an interest in dahlias he has no hobby. Living a sedentary life and brought up in the straight-laced morality of Angelica, his 'aunt's' behaviour appears strange to him; he slowly gravitates to her and gets absorbed in her world. The bank conditioned him and apologetically he says: "If I seem to the reader a somewhat static character he should appreciate the long conditioning of my career before retirement." (p. 18) The bank has taught him that any whim can end only in bankruptcy. He having come to the aunt, slowly his attitude changes. After a couple of 'travels' he discovers for the first time 'a streak of anarchy' in him. Slightly afterwards, electrified by the saga of the aunt's adventures and with the unaccustomed wine singing in his head he reflects: "What did the truth matter? All characters once dead, if they continue to exist in memory at all, tend to become fictions. Hamlet is no less real now than Winston Churchill, and Jo Pulling no less historical than Don Quixote." (p. 74) There is comic irony in the inversion manifest in Henry speaking to the aunt in terms of generations: "Dear Aunt Augusta, it helps sometimes to speak of another person. I know I belong to a different generation, perhaps a more conventional generation." There is comic reversal of the generation gap. Judged by her temperament it is the aunt with her Bohemianism, promiscuity, sensuality and nymphomania who should have belonged to the contemporary generation of youngsters. But it is Henry who belongs, temperamentally, to the Victorian age with his sentimentality and respectability. Nonetheless, Henry is aware of the comedy of his following the aunt in her travels: "I felt as thought I were being dragged at her heels on an absurd knight-errantry, like Sancho Panza at the heels of Don Quixote, but in the cause of what she called fun instead of chivalry."(p. 103) Representing originally the mental make-up of the Victorian Age, Henry feels hopelessly out of depth when Miss Tooley talks in terms of culture and human experience. Modern literature has never appealed to him. To his mind it was in the Victorian age that English poetry and fiction reached the highest level. He is content with Tennyson and Browning. After a slow transformation in Augusta's company and after being rebuked once by her not to presume his to be better morality, he realizes that she is one of the life-givers. Uncle Jo and Senior Pulling could have been invented by her but still they are no less real. Once drawn into the aunt's world he regrets being left and there is a wistful note in this:

> Beyond Latimer Road there stretched another world - the world of Wordsworth and Curran and Monsieur Dambreuse and Colonel Hakim and the mysterious Mr Visconti who had dressed up as a monsignor to escape the allied troops, yes, and of my father too saying, 'Dolly Darling' to Miss Paterson with his last breath on the *auberge* floor and gaining a life long devotion by dying in her arms. To whom now could I apply for a visa to that land with my Aunt gone?"(p. 201)

Fearing the worst-that the old lady might be dead — he feels the most interesting part of his life might be over. He notes sadly: "I had waited for a long while for it to arrive, and it had not lasted long." (p. 219) His new found attachment to his aunt makes him look at things afresh. He begins to ponder on the secret of everlasting youth and the utility of Christmas. Though religiously lukewarm in spite of his regular attendance at the Church for the sake of respectability which his profession demanded of him, he finds Christmas a necessary festival. "We require a season when we can regret all the flaws in our human relationships: it is the feast of failure, sad but consoling." (p. 204) He imbibes a tolerance verging on charity and hoodwinks all the faults in the aunt. "All my working life I had been strictly loyal to one establishment, the bank, but my loyalty now was drawn in quite another direction. Loyalty to a person inevitably entails loyalty to all the imperfections of a human being, even to the chicanery and immorality from which my aunt was not entirely free. I wondered whether she had ever forged a cheque or robbed a bank, and I smiled at the thought with the tenderness I might have shown in the past to a small eccentricity."(p. 212) From this to the total approval of the aunt's performances is a significant progress, a progress towards understanding and charity. Reading Wordsworth's great Ode in Palgrave's Golden Treasury he reflects: "I had been born as a result of what my stepmother (Angelica) would have called an immoral act, an act of darkness. I had begun in immoral freedom. Why then should I have found myself in a prison-house? My real mother had certainly not been imprisoned anywhere." (p. 245) Henry is not far from understanding and charity when he says: 'I would have certainly called her career shady nine months ago, and yet now there seems to be nothing so very wrong in her curriculum vitae, nothing so wrong as thirty years in a bank."(p. 280) It is not merely in his thinking that there has been a transformation. The transformation embraces his actions too. Locked in the prison cell in Paraguay, like Mr Jones the arch comedian in The Comedians, remembering the aunt's words about the 'wall' he feels that he has trained himself to be thankful that the wall has kept its distance. The aunt's way of life is totally approved of and accepted and with that he accepts her as his mother. When, at the end of the book, he calls her 'Aunt Augusta' she does not respond. He takes a few more steps towards her and calls 'Mother' and she immediately responds. Characteristic of a comedy there is a family reunion: "A flash bulb broke the shadows up. I have the photograph still - all the three of us petrified by the lightning flash into a family group. You can see the great gap in Visconti's teeth as he smiles towards me like an accomplice. I have my hand thrown out in frozen appeal, and my mother is regarding me with the expression of tenderness and reproof."(p. 318) Having wedded a life of happiness Henry falls in love with Maria, the daughter of the Chief of Customs. Though there is a considerable difference in their ages (Maria will be sixteen the next year) he finds her gentle and obedient and they plan to read Browning together in the warm scented evenings:

God's in his heaven
All's right with the world.

5.2.7 With *Travels with my Aunt* Greene's customary hero has undergone a total transformation. Henry Pulling is vastly different from the principals preceding him. Bendrix is unsentimental to some extent and he desired to live the life of a natural human being as opposed to figures like the whisky priest and Scobie who are steeped in sentiment. Fowler scores an advance over Bendrix and cultivates a studied indifference to everything except his comfort. Querry is deliberately negative in his outlook though the direction he suggests to be taking is towards comedy. Brown in *The Comedians* has a greater awareness of comedy in life and Henry Pulling marks the highest point of the growth of the comic sense. The magic touch of the aunt transforms him and a new awareness is infused into him. His transformation is a growth in that it is characterized by gentleness, tenderness and a greater degree of hope. He acquires a keener appreciation of human weaknesses and a fine sense of humour. Journey after journey leads him into new areas of experience against which formerly he has insulated himself. Though there are moments when he wants to leave Augusta and return to the life of Southwood with his dahlias, the gravitational pull of the spirited woman finally succeeds. Greene makes it evident here that experience holds out an irresistible fascination to innocence. The acclimatization is not without nagging doubts. In Istanbul amid the dancers in the West Berlin Hotel Henry wavers: "I was like an outsider at some religious ceremony of which he couldn't interpret the symbols ... My aunt ... had a world of her own to which I would never be admitted, and I would have done better, I told myself, if I had stayed with my dahlias."(p. 154) Temporarily separated from the aunt he suddenly finds to his dismay that he has lost his taste for dahlias. He is eager to join his aunt whatever may be her faults. He attains great tolerance and becomes capable of looking at things from a point of view beyond the customary ethics. Human love can get over the problems of evil by embracing evil into the fold of life as a necessary part. In the sense that he exercises gentleness and tolerance preached by religion, Henry is a Greene hero with a difference. The transformation in him is complete and irreversible. He finds it impossible to write the letter he mentally composes to Miss Keene in the prison cell in Paraguay for she would be quite unable to reconcile the writer with the man she had known. (p. 282) But the decision is not regrettable. He returns to his mother's affection and is assimilated into the family. The lesson that Henry learns is one of acceptance. He watches with wisdom and amused irony a world of events mysteriously groping towards harmony. Problems of death and problems of morality are just by-passed.

5.2.8 The brightness of the comic vision is richly in evidence even in the minor characters. Miss Tooley, James O' Toole, and Mr Visconti are illustrative of the comic vision. Miss Tooley with her enormous wrist watch trying a long journey and smoking pot to get 'it' off is comic. Frank and outspoken to an alarming degree, she takes Henry unawares. The conversations between her lover and herself which she faithfully repeats to Henry are delightful in their own way. Nothing shocks her and nothing corrupts her. With his newly acquired sense of comedy Henry tells Tooley's father that his wife did not succeed in corrupting her though she brought home her boy friends. Tooley has a philosophy of her own. Having majored in English Literature, she loves irony as a literary device. She wants to do things 'in depth.' She tells her father that he sees the world horizontally which is superficial. She wants to see the world vertically. She is thoroughly uninhibited and she comes into the sunny world of comedy breaking her good news: "The curse. I've got the curse. I was right you see. The jolting of the train, I mean, it did do it. I've got a terrible belly-ache, ..."(p. 150) She shows her genuine affection for Henry by asking him permission to call him Smudge, the name of the dog she once had. She is close to the world of the aunt. Henry is not slow in assessing her: "She was closer to my aunt. She would never, I felt sure, have criticised Mr Visconti: she would have accepted him, as she accepted Julian's project, a voyage to Istanbul, my company, her baby."(p. 135)

5.2.9 James O'Toole, the CIA agent is yet another comic character. With his urinary research as a cover for his job he is weighed down by his responsibility of fathering a child like Tooley. He confides to Henry: "People talk about the age of reason. There is no such thing. When you have a child you are condemned to be a father for life. They go away from you. You can't go away from them."(p. 235) Separated from his wife who divorced him and separated from his daughter who roams about with her boyfriend, he is a sadly comic figure. When Henry tells him that she still calls herself Tooley, he says with a kind of 'questioning hope': "I guess she must think of me sometimes?"(p. 241) Sadness and comedy can go together. To borrow the words of the aunt his *is* a very sad story in its special way but it's rather funny too.

5.2.10 Mr Visconti is a robust figure of comedy in his early eighties. He is a war criminal and the great thing about him is his complete lack of conscience. Escaping the allied troops in the guise of a monsignor he enacts a hilarious comedy in which the General is left behind and the dog which loved him fatally run over. Nothing can daunt him for he has such a capacity for deep understanding. Aunt Augusta calls him an 'untouchable' and for that reason is ready to slave for him. He has a flair for escapades both serious and hilarious. The police could get nothing from him in spite of their lie-detectors. Truth drugs are ineffective to get truth from him. He perfects a theory all his own of getting at truth. "Champagne, if you are seeking the truth, is better than a lie detector. It encourages a man to be expansive, even reckless, while lie-detectors are only a challenge to tell lies successfully." He is a real Machiavellian. He has a true insight into the comic aspects of existence. Asked to explain the absence of his teeth he once explained that he had exchanged them for cigarettes. "I cannot think what I would have done without these teeth when I had to run away. Before I reached Milan and Mario's Jesuits I was down to the last tooth." He makes a dig at religion saying that scepticism is inbred in a Catholic. He thinks of an ingenious plan to sell the two million unsold plastic straws with his insight into psychology: "Any Catholic knows that a legend which is believed has the same value and effect as the truth. Look at the cult of the saints." (p. 314)

5.2.11 The harvest of comedy that *Travels with my Aunt* offers is not merely from characters. The whole novel is steeped in the comic spirit. Parody, inversion, exaggeration, the important comic modes are all deployed here. Doggie's Church founded by Curran with the help of Hatty and Augusta is a parody of religion. The sacramental church is parodied. "The Church knows all the rules but it does not know what goes on in a single human heart" says the priest at the end of *The Heart of the Matter* but now the element of seriousness is completely washed out by the comic tilt. Another interesting parody is Mr Visconti's theory of rats. Doctor Colin and Querry have a long discussion on evolution in *A Burnt-out Case*. Here is a parody of the discussion and the theory of the survival of the fittest. Mr Visconti is a lover of rats. Defending his craftiness and yearning for survival, he says: "The future of the world lies with the rat. God, at least as I imagine him, created a number of possibilities in case some of his prototypes failed — that is the meaning of evolution."(p. 296) The discussion takes place between Henry and Mr Visconti. A kind of light-hearted satire can be read into Mr Visconti's theory directed against human beings devising ways of destroying their own species. A rat does not kill another. The rat exists longer (even after the atom bomb) which fact bears testimony to its intelligence. Rats survive because of their superior intelligence. They survive because they are the fittest. Flashes of humour illuminate the book. A short sampler should be enough. "Bolt the door on the inside when you go out" is humorous. Hiccups are said to be cured by a sudden shock but Henry feels that they can equally be caused by one. Asked who Wordsworth is the Aunt replies: "Let us say he attends to my wants. A very gentle sweet strong person." There is an anecdote in which the police arrest Hamlet's uncle for the real murder that is committed on the stage following the story. Wordsworth knew a loader who had keys to every kind of suitcase but he was baffled once by a Russian one. A brothel is like a school. Henry has a habit of moving lips which once led him into an odd situation. The flight of Mr Visconti dressed up as a monsignor during which he has to listen to sweet confessions, and the dog, run over looking like a biscuit, typing mistakes like Gone with the Qind and Dutch Deformed are instances of delightful wit. The aunt says once: "Politics in Turkey are taken more seriously than they are at home. It was only quite recently that they executed a Prime Minister. We dream of it, but they act." Miss Paterson speaking of her children scandalizes Aunt Augusta. At times the humour is Rabelaisian.

5.2.12 A work of imaginative literature has always to be put to the ultimate test of the complexity of the response it evokes. Greene's *Travels with my Aunt*, judged by that criterion, is a rich book. Pathos which is evident as in Jo Pulling's death and that of Wordsworth is absorbed into the world of comedy. Jo Pulling's unavailing attempts at prolonging life and Wordsworth's yearning to continue as his bebi-gel's lover responding to her enthusiasm for delectable 'jig-jig' lose the poignancy of the tragic and the shadows cast by them are dispelled by the festive illumination at the end of the novel. The inclusive comic vision absorbs the graver, the sadder and the tragic undertones. Evidence for this can also be seen in the inversion of some stock symbols in Greene. Two big front teeth give Augusta vital Neanderthal air as opposed to the carious teeth of the mestizo in *The Power and the Glory*. When they christened Pinkie (*Brighton Rock*) the holy water did not *take* and like him Henry did not howl the devil out. Still he remains a sober, sweet person. With *Travels with my Aunt* Greene seems to effect a conquest of tragedy by comedy. Death nearly disappears as a significance. Treachery blooms into a comic intrigue. Falsehood looks like a form of truth. The Night of Tragedy breaks into the Day of Comedy. However, Greene does not seem so much to be evading reality as playing it with a wise kind of amusement. The creatures of tragedy can be the masters of comedy if only one looks through another end of the magical telescope. Life yields to you if you do not yield to death, Greene seems to be saying.

5.3 After *Travels with my Aunt* Greene in all probability should have discarded tragedy altogether and indulged in pure comedy. But instead, in *The Honorary Consul* (1973) he plunges back into the world of tragedy playing out those very old these only to realize the difficult truth that not withstanding the pressure of tragedy, what really matters is the salvaging of life, a delicate sense of comedy. The provincial Argentinian town of *The Honorary Consul* is all of a piece with the bleak, abandoned country of loveless passion, heartless betrayal and absurd hope seen hitherto in the world of Greene's fiction set in Mexico, Sierra Leone, Belgian Congo and Haiti. The tragedy of passion and betrayal remains the same. But the sting and the bitterness are mitigated by a very delicate blend of the comic.

5.3.1 With *The Comedians* Greene's grasp of comedy is thorough and *The Honorary Consul* marks an advance in the combination of the comic and the tragic with a further complexity. In this novel,

Greene seems to deepen both his comic and serious constituents. In a way, *The Honorary Consul* takes one back to *The Comedians* and then to *A Burnt-out Case* and then to some extent to the earlier landmarks like *The Power and the Glory*. The new novel appears to a tightly organized symposium of both his serious and comic components together, almost with a deliberate system of echoes from his earlier work. The problem of evil is totally absent from *Travels with my Aunt*, while God is here *as* evil. Here is a further attempt to explore the nature of evil. Father Rivas's refusal to cut himself away from the Church on the grounds of his marriage may be viewed as a kind of progress in maturation. That is the serious and so the darker side of the novel, the serious substratum. The comic triumph lies in raising Fortnum to the stature of a hero, a gimmick already used successfully in *The Comedians* with Jones. The sentimental honorary consul, surrounded by a host of sentimental characters like the novelist and the poet, who are steeped in *machismo*,[8] a Spanish-European quality, returns to faith in simple love and things that go with it and weds a young girl from a brothel. This confirms the impression that Greene would not take the way of unadumbrated fantasy without enriching it with far-reaching insights. He struggles to unravel, in retrospect as it were, his whole cumulative vision of life and things.

5.3.2 An inherently comic situation is the backbone of the plot. Paraguayian rebels in a bid to kidnap the visiting American Ambassador, with a view to using him as a hostage to force their government to release political prisoners, abduct the wrong man, the honorary consul. The doctor who helps them only with information gets caught in the web. He finds himself in a mess being the lover of the consul's wife when he comes to realise that no one would lift a finger to save the hostage. The novel deviates from the merely melodramatic and strays into the regions of the purely comic. The novelist-character Saavedra ridicules the doctor in the novel: "You might as well expect me to write a story about kidnapping of Senor Fortnum." Greene seems to have taken up the challenge to write a contemporary political novel. With the predominantly human factor of important personal attachment, Greene disproves Saavedra's theory that dealing with contemporary politics would limit the novelist's achievement.

5.3.3 Personal attachments figure as most important issues in the novel. Filial attachment, never seen with any intensity hitherto in

8. Masculine pride

Greene's fiction, is given a delicate importance here. The figure of father looms large here. Henry Plarr, the doctor's father, leaves his family inconsiderately and takes to his commitment to the poor as an *abogado*. He sets his sights high and ideals come first to him. Doctor Plarr for all his professed cynical detachment is influenced by his absent father. When Saavedra asks him if he chose the place of his practice on the ground of being nearer to his father he replies:

> "You are a perceptive man, Saavedra. Yes, it may have been my father's nearness which brought me here. In the *barrio* of the poor I am aware of doing something he would have liked to see me do, but when I am with my rich patients - I feel as though I had left his friends to help his enemies."(p. 166)[9]

With great affection for his father the doctor prays: "God help you, father, wherever you are" but the face he conjures up when he prays is not his father's but Fortnum's. When Colonel Perez reveals to him that his father had been killed, Doctor Plarr remembers the man in Buenos Aires who was illegitimate. After years of ardent search the man learnt his father's name as that of an international banker who had been dead a long time. His quest having come to an end thus, he said to Plarr once, "You cannot imagine how empty I feel now. What is there to interest me?"(p. 180 The same kind of emptiness leads Doctor Plarr to get trapped with the ill-fated revolutionaries. Oddly enough, he begins to worry that his child has to grow up under Fortnum. Fortnum's remark that he is a 'cold fish' stings him into thought for his child embedded in Clara's womb. He wonders: "What effect did it have to have a cold fish for a father. It might have been better if they could have exchanged fathers. A cold fish would have been his proper parentage rather than a father who cared enough to die."(p. 212) The father image goes right up to the end of the book. Father Leon Rivas tells Doctor Plarr:

> "We all seem to live with dead fathers, don't we? Fortnum hated his, I think I may have loved mine, perhaps. How can I possibly tell? The word love has a slick sound. We take credit for loving as though we had passed an examination with more than average marks."(p. 217)

5.3.4 Beyond sixty though he is, Fortnum does not forget his father. As a boy he had a traumatic experience of being thrown off a horse. Apparently on the verge of death he tells Doctor Plarr: "It is better

9. Page numbers refer to *The Honorary Consul* (Penguin, 1974)

for him [Clara's child] to be along with a mother than a father. I know that well. I was left alone with my father and it was never any fun. Always horses, horses ..."(p. 202) In spite of his father's drunken carelessness, Fortnum does not hate him. "I used to be angry with my father. He didn't understand me, I thought, or care a nickel about me. I hated him. All the same I was bloody lonely when he died. And now," (he lifted the glass) - "I even imitate him. Though he drank more than I do. All the same a father's a father."(p. 115)

5.3.5 The father figure is prominent in Aquino's verse. He has written a poem with the refrain: "I see my father only through the bars." He talks symbolically of the father. "In my poem the father went on following the child all through his life — he was the school master, and then the priest, the police officer, the prison warder, and last he was General Stroessner himself."(p. 122) Liberty is his dream and to achieve it he has to escape from behind the bars and rise in revolt against the father. His authority has to be destroyed. While this is the type of father Aquino envisages, Fortnum stands as a symbol of another type of father, charitable, understanding and forgiving. A father is not only a progenitor but also an insignia of love. For him to forgive is all. Once a father, always a father. As James O'Toole says sadly: "When you have a child you are condemned to be a father for life - They go from you. You can't go away from them." (*Travels with my Aunt*, p. 235) The complexity of the comic strand lies in the fact that Fortnum is raised to the stature of a father though the child that Clara bears is not his own.

5.3.6 Doctor Plarr becomes a grotesque figure professing the non-existence of the word love in his vocabulary. Born of an English liberal and a Spanish mother and brought up by his mother in Buenos Aires, he is still in his thirties. He plays deliberately the comedy of a lover out of curiosity and physical desire. But the word love itself is repellent to him. He surprises Fortnum by telling him that he is not quite sure what the word love means:

> "Has no woman ever loved you, Ted?" Fortnum inquired. A kind of *paternal anxiety* in his voice irritated Doctor Plarr (Emphasis mine)
>
> "Two or three have told me so, but they had no difficulty in finding someone else after I said good-bye. Only my mother's love of sweet cakes isn't likely to change. She will love them in sickness and in health till death do them part. Perhaps that's the real true love."

> "You're too young to be a cynic."
>
> "I'm not a cynic. I'm curious, that's all. I like to know the meaning which people put on the words they use. So much is a question of semantics..." (p. 71)

His unsentimentality is thorough-going. His apartment is bare and truthful like a police cell (In this quality he reminds us of Scobie). He never used 'I love you' to any women he slept with. He prefers to think of himself as a painstaking diagnostician. Love is a malady he attributed to loneliness, pride, physical desire or even a simple sense of curiosity. However, his rationality does not protect him from getting himself sexually entangled. Too logical and rational to 'fall' in love, he realizes that he has fallen into an obsession. The author comments underlining the comedy of the tangle: "An obsession may sleep a while, but it doesn't necessarily die, and in less than a week he wanted to see her again." (p. 74) His love for Clara is never spontaneous. They never kiss on the mouth (it was part of the brothel training for her). Once following her into the bed room he becomes thoughtful:

> In a real love affair, he thought, you are interested in a woman because she is someone distinct from yourself; then bit by bit she adapts herself to you, she picks up your habits, your ideas, even your turns of phrase, she becomes a part of you, and then what interest remains? One cannot love oneself, one cannot live for long close to oneself - everyone has need of a stranger in bed, and a whore remains a stranger. Her body has been scrawled over by so many men you can never decipher your own signature there.(p. 90)

Doctor Plarr dreads being asked "Do you love me? When he is afraid of the question Clara's mind is elsewhere. Herein lies the comedy of the situation. While he wonders if she would ask him the question, she keeps thinking of her husband. His love, even at the purely physical level, is wrought with the comic as her:

> *Clara*: "I don't think I want to make love."
>
> *Doctor Plarr*: "No, of course, I understand." (p. 95)

The unspontaneousness of their sexual relation is carried to the point of absurdity. At a point in the narrative he becomes aware of the fact that there seemed to be no point in playing the game since he knew what moves he had to make to win — the moves were sympathy, tenderness, quiet, the counterfeiting of love. His clinicality is carried to the extreme when he wants to probe even his mother's love: "Had she ever felt any love for his father or himself, or had she just played the comedy of love like Clara? He had grown up, during the years he spent alone with his mother in Buenos Aires, to despise comedy." (p. 141) Comedy, in Doctor Plarr's terminology, means pretension and play-acting. The very scenes in which he merely performs love are scenes of an absurd comedy — not scenes of life-giving sentiment. Here is an example:

> "Anything. Why not tell me how much you love me." They had been sitting on a sofa and her husband was sleeping in an armchair... Senor Escobar sat astride him as though she were a child playing ponies. (p. 147)

Even till the last moment of his life which comes more as an absurd surprise than a logical sequel Clara's question haunts him:

> "You love me a little?" She corrected herself quickly, Do you want to make love to me?" (p. 170)

She knows that the word Love is taboo to him and the insight perhaps is owing to her brothel background. After a bout of love-making she forgets herself and asks the question which haunts Doctor Plarr:

> "Do you remember that time at the camp when I told you I was pretending? But, *caro*, I was not pretending. Now when you make love to me I pretend. I pretend I feel nothing. I bite my lip so as to pretend. Is it because I love, Eduardo? Do you think I love you?" (p. 171)

But love is a claim he would never meet, a responsibility he would refuse to accept. "Love" is a word, according to him, used always for asking something in return, either obedience, an apology or an unwilling kiss.

5.3.7 Doctor Plarr is the artistically logical development of a series of men like Bendrix, Fowler, Querry and Brown. He has something in common with everyone of these principal characters in Greene's novels. He combines in him, in varying degrees, Bendrix's unbelief, Fowler's refusal to be involved, Querry's boredom and Brown's view that existence is comic. Taking sex casually he defines love as a whore's comedy for the client. Curiosity is the driving force behind his escapades and a cold fish as he is, he could never learn to love. His prayer like Bendrix's at the end of *The End of the Affair* is significant: "For heaven's sake, let this comedy end in comedy. None of us are suited to tragedy." (p. 234) Tragedy assumes human dignity and in the doctor's view human dignity is non-existent. He feels that honour means nothing to the hungry for they have to wage a more serious fight for mere survival. His attitude to life is doomed to sadness. He sadly leaves the insight into love for the betrayed husband to glean. He tells Fortnum proudly: "My job is to turn up stones. Guess work is not much good when you make a diagnosis." (p. 51) He knows that only a chain of errors could follow a wrong equation. The 'comedy' he sees around can be rationalised only in one way. There is a great practical joker somewhere who plans the jokes. In spite of this realization, he, like Scobie under different circumstances, finds himself in a dilemma. Having walked away from Clara's appeal and being told by Perez that his father was killed, when the bell rings he knows that he has to make a choice and go either to Clara or to the kidnappers:

> The small patch of marble floor on which he stood seemed like the edge of an abyss; he could not move one step in either direction without falling into the darkness of involvement or guilt ... He felt giddy on the ledge of the marble parquet. He couldn't stand motionless forever. (p. 178)

Closely guarded in the hut by the very men whom he wanted to help, when one of the guards approaches the door he wonders with a sense of resignation, even or relief, whether there would be a burst of firing as the climax of the whole absurd affair. Having realized that standing motionless is impossible, he flares up at Aquino when he refuses to release Fortnum:

> "It's your damned *machismo* again, isn't it? Who invented *machismo*? A gang of ruffians like Pizarro and Cortes. Can't any one of you for a moment escape your bloody history? You haven't learnt a thing, have you, from Cervantes? He had his fill of *machismo* at Lepanto." (p. 223)

In a sort of ennui like D. in *The Confidential Agent* and Brown in *The Comedians*, he tells Fortnum:

> "Nothing is ever what we intend. They didn't mean to kidnap you. I didn't mean to start the child. You would almost think there was a great joker somewhere who likes to give a twist to things. Perhaps the dark side of God has a sense of humour.

Though he is aware of the comic holding sway over things it is with a sense of sadness that he comes to his end. He tells Aquino: "I'm jealous because he [Fortnum] loves her. That stupid banal word, it's never meant anything to me. Like the word God. I know how to fuck - I don't know how to love. Poor drunken Fortnum wins the game." (p. 251) When he is shot in the head, Leon says he is sorry and begs forgiveness. Doctor Plarr musters his humour and whispers "*Ego te absolvo*". Then we are told:

> "He intended to laugh, to show Leon he was only joking - that he had often joked when they were boys at the unmeaning formulas the priests taught them to use - but he was too tired and the laugh shrivelled in his throat." (p. 253)

This reminds us of Querry's enigmatic laugh before his death. Querry skids into tragedy by his attachment to cynicism. But Doctor Plarr's case is different. He finds himself involved in a tragedy and deprived of his cynical stance, when he is betrayed into a real feeling of jealousy. He belongs to the tragic band in the tragic-comic spectrum. Though his cynical stance gets him into the orbit of comedy, his consequent death pulls him out into the world of tragedy.

5.3.8 Fortnum, the son of a drunkard and a drunkard himself, believes that successful living is a matter of the 'right measure', of whisky. Once he tells Doctor Plarr "You mustn't think I am always as happy as this, but it's the measure that counts." (p. 45) His father advised him to conquer fear lest it should conquer him. But fear, he says, is part of human nature and it is a bit like the balance of nature. If all the spiders in the world were killed, we would be suffocated under the weight of flies. Knowing human limitations and being a victim of them himself he does not want to analyse too much. He learns tolerance and sympathy. With tolerance he ignores the doctor's jibe at his sennility and tells him: "When you get to my age you accumulate a lot of regrets. It's not a bad thing to feel you've made at least one person a little happier." The author adds a comment: "It was a kind of simple, sentimental and self-confident statement which Doctor Plarr found embarrassing. No reply was possible." (p. 72) The novelist Saavedra understands Fortnum. He tells the doctor: "He was drinking, I think, for the same reason that I write - to escape the darkness of his spirit. He confided to me that he was in love." (p. 156) On the edge of death he wants to stay awake for he has a lot of things to think about and not much time. Let out from the hiding place, with Doctor Plarr killed along with the kidnappers, the freedom he finds does not cause him any jubilation. The very whisky he loved, Long John, loses its taste. But he becomes wiser and comes out victorious as a lover. Doctor Plarr's incongruous cynicism bewilders him and draws his sympathy for him at the end as much as his own father's drunken unperceptiveness. It is a shock for him that Clara does not shed a single tear for her lover. When he finds that Clara has no feeling for Doctor Plarr he becomes acutely aware of the meaninglessness of life. Still he could not bring himself to love Clara any the less.

> A kiss was worth nothing from someone who was incapable of loving even her lover. And yet, he asked himself, what fault was it of hers? You don't learn about love from a customer in a brothel. And because it was not her fault he must be careful never to show her what he felt. It would have been a lot simpler, he thought, if she had loved Plarr. (p. 259)

No wonder his warmth and charity draws from Clara tears for her dead lover though she told herself emphatically not to say 'I love you'. Fortnum's supreme understanding is evident in the following dialogue:

> "There's nothing wrong in love, Clara. It happens. It does not matter who with. We get caught up," he told her, and remembering what he said to young Crichton, he added, "We get kidnapped," attempting a feeble joke to reassure her, by mistake."
>
> "He never loved me," she said. "To him I was only a girl from Senora Sanchez."
>
> "You are wrong." It was like pleading a cause; he might have been attempting to bring two young people to a closer understanding.
>
> "He wanted me to kill the baby."
>
> "You mean in your dream?"
>
> "No. No. He wanted it killed. He really wanted it. I knew then he could never love me."
>
> "Perhaps he'd begun, Clara. Some of us .. we are a bit slow. ... it's not so easy to love. ... we make a lot of mistakes." (p. 267)

Fortnum admits to her that he too had been deficient in love and makes a human noise to win her agreement. Finally the moment of mutual comprehension dawns and Clara opens her heart to him and speaks to him of her brother. The last word belongs to Fortnum and not to the rationalistic doctor.

5.3.9 The intellectual Father Leon Rivas tries to perfect a personal theory of God. Active religion involves active belief and not dead rules. Religion ultimately is a personal affair and the discussion between the failed priest and the clinical doctor marks a high point in the novel. Paradox and irony, two predominantly comic modes, help us get at Greene's insight into existence. Leon tells Doctor Plarr: "We have Jehovah in our blood. We can't help it. After all these centuries Jehovah lives in our darkness like a worm in the intestines." (p. 218) A revolutionary not only in politics but also in his religion he says that his marriage is not a desertion but a temporary separation. "I have told you - I never left the Church. Mine is only a separation, Eduardo, a separation by mutual consent, not a divorce. I shall never belong wholly to anyone else. Not even to Marta." (p. 219) It is not ideological riddles and cavilling on the point of a hair in offering a solution and arguing it out that constitute insight into truth but a painful delving into the nature and origin of things. Here is the realization: Christ was a man. The Romans killed the man, the carpenter from Nazareth:

> "Some of the rules he laid down were only the rules of a good man. A man who lived in his own province, in his own particular day. He had no idea of the kind of the world we would be living in now. Render unto Caesar, but when *our* Ceasar uses Napalm and fragmentation bombs ... The Church lives in time too... I think sometimes the memory of that man, that carpenter, can lift a few people out of the temporary church of these terrible years, when the Arch bishop sits down to dinner with the General, into the great Church beyond our time and place, and then ... those lucky ones ... they have no words to describe the beauty of that Church." (p. 220)

Even the unbelieving doctor is shocked when Leon says:

> "Was it love which sent six million Jews to the gas ovens? You are a doctor, you must often have seen intolerable pain — a child dying of meningitis. Is that love? It was not love which cut off Aquino's fingers. The police stations where such things happen ... He created them." (p. 221)

The shocked doctor mumbles: "I have never heard a priest blame God for things like that before." and is told with equanimity: "I don't blame Him. I pity Him." (p. 221) Here is pity *par excellence*. Scobie in *The Heart of the Matter* is said to have wondered: "If one knew the facts would one have to feel pity even for the planets, if one reached what they called the heart of the matter?" (p. 117) But Father Leon Rivas goes one step higher and pities God. This is a high comedy with a capacity for illumination, not merely laughter. Along with insight goes a deeper understanding and along with it a greater tolerance and a large-hearted forgiveness. The existence of evil is no argument to disprove His existence. When Marta, his wife, asks Leon about the Father who slept with women, with great tolerance he replies: "He could go to confession and sin again and go to confession. I am not responsible for his conscience." (p. 225) Mere clap-trap is no religion. The lapsed priest does admit that the money for candles would have fed half the poor people there. Doctor Plarr asks him about man's duty to love God: 'It's like the duty of a German to love Hitler. Isn't it better not to believe in that horror up there sitting in the clouds of heaven than pretend to love Him?" With composure Leon replies: "It may be better not to breathe, but all the same I cannot help breathing. Some men, I think, are condemned to belief by a judge just as they are condemned to prison. They have no choice. No escape. They have been put behind the bars for life." (p. 226) Then comes the question finally: if he believes in God so much why kill Fortnum? Here is the answer: "Saint Paul answers the question. 'What I do is not that which I do, but something which I hate.' He knew all about the nightside of God. He has been one of those who stoned Stephen." (p. 229) Perhaps it is through the odd combination of being both a husband and a father that he could achieve the wisdom to profess a private theory of God and evil. He is baffled by the mystery of evil and the professional spiritualists offered him no help. "They just sat comfortably down in the presence of the horror like the old Archbishop at the General's table and they talked about man's responsibility and free will. Free will was the excuse for everything. It was God's alibi. They had never read Freud. Evil was made by man or Satan. But I could never believe in Satan. It was much easier to believe that God was evil." He explains his theory at length. God made man in his image and so man's evil is His evil too. God too is divided like man and tempted like man. The God he believes in must be responsible for all the evil as well as all the saints. Horror and evil represent the nightside of God and a time will come when the nightside will wither away. Then the simple daylight of God will prevail. The Christian Church with its rules formulated centuries ago will undergo a transformation and "the great church beyond our time and place" will shape itself with an indescribable beauty. Leon's personal religion is an attempt to negotiate evil in life in a personal if not in a perennial way. A priest turned revolutionary, a cynical doctor caught in a web, a novelist with machismo offering himself as a hostage, are the cast in the plot.

The characters are full of paradoxical stances and they become comic the moment they reveal themselves in their roles and their theories. Doctor Plarr who sees comedy everywhere tells Leon after discovering their mistake: "It's really rather comic". "He looked from one fact to another," we are told, "but no one smiled in return." (p. 31) Deficient in political tact and clinging to his vocation in an odd inverted way Leon is as incongruous as his bat-ears. As elsewhere it is the physical deformity in him that defines his character. Incongruity is deliberately introduced to stave off the feeling of tragedy. When Doctor Plarr teases him saying that he is no criminal except for an abortion or two, with the intention of disturbing him, without wincing Leon replies: "In a wrong society the criminals are honest men." (p. 103) He is more used to enduring pain than inflicting it. The hot coffee that Fortnum throws in his face, though scalding his cheek, does not anger him. Leon is talked about in terms of a bull in the arena, a familiar Greene trope. The characters around the priest are like picadors pricking the bull's hide to make the beast more active before he dies. The word 'Father' is flung at him 'like darts inserted to pierce the skin'. Doctor Plarr wonders: "Why do we want to destroy him - or are we hoping to destroy ourselves? - it is a cruel sport." There is evidently something shockingly absurd in Leon's face which Doctor Plarr sees: "In the innumerable lines of premature age which criss-crossed the face he thought he could detect a tangle of agonies, like a tangle of fighting snakes." (p. 201) There is comedy in Leon's reading a paperback detective novel and contrasting the world in it with the one which he lives in: "What a wonderfully peaceful novel this one is. Everything is so well ordered. There are no problems. There is an answer to every question." This reminds us of Arthur Rowe's feeling as a child (in *The Ministry of Fear*). The apparent lightness with which he formulates his religious theories is the other extreme to which a Pinkie can go. It is the duty of a man committed to religion to contemplate and acquire an insight into religion. Leon's convictions, however odd they may seem, are painstakingly arrived at.

5.3.10 The minor characters bear testimony to the comic spirit. Doctor Humphries is one. Living in his seedy apartment with a leaking *douche*, he reminds us of the remittance man, Minty, in *England Made Me*. He propounds the theory: "Contrary to common belief the truth is nearly always funny. It's only tragedy which people bother to imagine or invent." (p. 21) The doctor's mention of x-ray to know the truth about him makes him hastily add: "I only want the truth about other people. It's always other people who are funny."

Another minor but equally comic character is the failed poet and failed rebel, Aquino. He reminds us of the young Philipot in The Comedians. A victim of police persecution in a prison cell where he lost his fingers, he has a firm conviction in the dignity of being a rebel and he believes that he has a protocol to observe. He is all emotion and energy: "I hate things which are slow. I would rather be a mouse than a tortoise, even though the tortoise lives a longer time." (p. 121) Though he is for putting an end immediately to their hostage, the idea of death daunts him. When Fortnum taunts him what he would do with his body he replies: "Senor Fortnum, why talk about disagreeable subjects? I write about death - yes but only death the great abstraction. I do not write about the death of friends." (p. 124) Even Marta, the priest's wife, contributes to the sad comedy by pressing her husband to say a Mass. The English Ambassador recovering from a bad breakfast, worried by a slash in the entertainment allowance and deprived of a siesta, is another comic figure underlining the comedy of Fortnum's inconsequence. "Thank God it's no longer", the Ambassador said. "Next week it will all be over. He'll be either dead or freed." (p. 132) Pitiably small beer as Fortnum is, in his place he would prefer a quick death. It is the idea of the Ambassador that Doctor Plarr should send a letter to the British press from an Anglo-Argentine Club.

5.3.11 Greene seems to be in agreement with Doctor Humphries' view that truth is always funny. Human dignity and human grandeur are no longer possible in the contemporary society and comedy is the only thing that describes the truth of men and matters. Greene seems to say with his insight that life is pathetic, ironical, grotesque - in a word more comic, than tragic. He wrote in a film review in 1936[10]: "The truth is seldom tragic, for human beings are not made in that grand way. The truth may be sad but truth is nearly always grotesque as well." He is interested in being human. Human beings are creatures of vanity and weakness. There is no tragic flaw but an incongruous weakness in the comic man. C.C.O'Brien in his "A Funny Sort of God" draws a parallel between the careers of Greene and P.G. Wodehouse. Evelyn Waugh, he recalls, once maintained that God was essential to Greene's work as Jeeves was to Wodehouse's. Over the years, the valet has grown "rather less funny and Mr. Greene's God rather more so."[11] Greene is impatient with novels like Saavedra's which inflate life to make it a tragedy which it

10. *The Pleasure Dome*. (London: Secker and Warburg), 1972. p. 45.

11. *New York Review of Books*, XX, No. 16 (Oct. 18, 1973), p. 59.

is really not. Doctor Plarr is right in being impatient of Saavedra's heroic ideals. Greene implies that Saavedra does not write about real people or real events. Doctor Plarr, we are told, has sometimes a longing to 'exclaim' to his 'melancholy patient', Saavedra:

> "Life isn't like that. It isn't noble or dignified. Even Latin American life. Nothing is ineluctable. Life has surprises. Life is absurd. Because it is absurd there is always hope. Why, one day we may even discover a cure for cancer and the common cold." (p. 16)

5.3.12 What predominates in the novel is the tragic substratum: the weird political situation; the extraordinary realistic approach of Father Leon Rivas's theology; the poetry of death composed by Aquino; the novels written by Saavedra steeped in *machismo*. All these from a massive and dark background to the delicate attachment that is formed between Fortnum and Clara. The very attachment would have been untenable without the tragic death of Doctor Plarr. One even suspects that the doctor is almost punished for his cynicism. A plausible reason for Greene's naming the novel after the frail, fictional, unrespected, wasting and dubious honorary consul appears to be that Fortnum has the fortune to exist. To exist is perhaps the supremely important thing. He has the advantage of survival and the philosophy of comedy depends heavily on the philosophy of survival. The fittest may not really survive but when they do, they seem to be the fittest. The secret of Greene's choice of Fortnum as his protagonist seems to be that Greene cannot be shaken out of his new found faith in comedy. This faith in comedy seems to be constituted of faith in the reality, genuineness and weakness of personal and mutual attachment. Whether God is good or evil, whether it is Communism or Democracy, whether poets and novelists glorify or decry the state of things, or whether politics has brought down chaos into the world, what finally matters is that one indestructible living cell of life, the beautiful flicker of mutual love surrounded by the flood of destruction. This is a step ahead in the understanding of human significance. This is also a non-tragic evaluation of life. One cannot afford to throw away precious life either in faith or in cynicism. Comedy is but another name for reverence for life.

5.3 *The Human Factor* (1978) takes the shape of a novel drawing its inspiration to some extent from Kim Philby, the British spy in Russian pay, who defected to Russia. There was a campaign of denigration when Philby's treason was discovered. Greene offered in an article[12] a personal and sympathetic reflection on the man making out a plea for a just and humane treatment to the 'traitor' for his conscious 'disloyalty'. In *The Human Factor* spying as a profession and Communism as a political philosophy are utterly subsidiary, the focus having been kept on the human factor which is central both to the novel and Greene the novelist. Castle, an Englishman, is a cheat in the sense that, though working in the British Secret Service, he is a Russian agent. His duplicity is of a kind which Greene fervently and convincingly suppresses. Of an age when one should be past both passion and pride, Castle is considered a "dullish man, first class, of course, with files." (p. 38)[13] Before the novel opens he fell in love with one of his agents in Africa, where he also worked, a black girl and married her though she had already been pregnant by a lover belonging to her own race. Out of a sense of gratitude to a Communist called Carson who helped him to get Sarah and Sam out of the country, Castle agrees to be a double agent telling himself that he is a Russian agent only where African affairs are concerned. Greene for the first time in *The Human Factor* attempts the portrayal of marital felicity. Castle is happily married though for the reader the felicity may appear fraught with a touch of the comic. Unlike Querry or Doctor Plarr, he cares and cares deeply. With his pro-African sympathies reflected in the book he is mentioned to have been writing on apartheid and confirmed later by his marriage, Castle becomes a 'naturalised black'. When Sarah is deported he follows her to England and gets established in M I 6. Castle's unambitiousness and dullness make him appear harmless. Davis's love of port and *Penthouse* point him out as being a possible leak and thanks to the enthusiasm of the fly-fishing Doctor Percival, a lethal dose of a toxic substance hitherto untested on human beings is used on him and he is successfully eliminated. Daintry, the chief of the section, himself an unhappy man is wild with fury but is helpless. After the unfortunate end of Davis which Castle knows should have been his own and the arrival of Cornelius Muller whom Castle knew and hated in Africa, the moment of crisis arrives. As a sign of burying the hatchet, Muller gives Castle some notes on Operation Uncle Remus, an American programme for military operations to retain Africa. Castle with his love of Africa, in a bid to save innocent African lives writes his last report and defects leaving behind Sarah

---

12. Graham Greene, "Reflections on the Character of Kim Philby", *Esquire*, LXX, No. 3. September 1968, p. iii.

13. Page numbers refer to *The Human Factor*, Bodley Head, 1978.

and Sam with the hope of their being enabled to join him in Moscow. In the cold flat ('in a snow in which one could expect the world to end') with a disconnected telephone he bides time reading *Robinson Crusoe* and finally loses his temper. He realizes that he is reduced to living on the gratitude of others. Boris, one of his 'controls', tells him that, like love, gratitude needs to be renewed daily lest it should die away. Castle gets connected on the phone to his wife if only for a short while when he tells her of his hopes. But her reply intending to communicate a sweetly human tenderness "Maurice, Maurice, please go on hoping" is never heard by him for the connection has been cut.

5.4.1 Castle is not like Greene's principals who preceded him since he is happily married and does not experience the agonies of having committed sin with the dilemmas of a split-mind super-imposed on them. There is no theological-spiritual tension as such though the pressure owing to the repression of the human mounts insufferably to a climax where a final decision is taken. He is simply human valuing human attachments most. When Daintry, the only man whom he credits with a human interest in the office, asks him to accompany him to his daughter's wedding, Castle does not have the heart to let him down. Like the Assistant Commissioner of Police in *It's a Battlefield* he is baffled by the word justice. He tells Davis: "I haven't the faintest idea what the word justice means." (p. 163) He reminds us of a different kind of Scobie when he falls into a thoughtful mood. For example, remembering how as a child he fell in love with a shy and ugly girl of seven he becomes very thoughtful:

> Why are some of us, he wondered, unable to love success or power, or great beauty? Because we feel unworthy of them, because we feel more at home with failure? He didn't believe that was the reason. Perhaps one wanted the right balance, just as Christ had, that legendary figure whom he would have liked to believe in. "Come unto me all ye that travail and are heavy laden." Young as the girl was at that August picnic she was heavily laden with her timidity and shame. Perhaps he had merely wanted her to feel that she was loved by someone and so he began to love her himself. It wasn't pity, any more than it had been pity when he fell in love with Sarah pregnant by another man. He was there to right the balance. That was all. (pp. 186-7)

Scobie becomes quite a fool in deluding himself into the belief that he is committing suicide to stop giving pain - like Christ dying on the cross. If Scobie met his end by an over-developed sense of pity,

Castle realises that wisdom lies in righting the balance. The intermixture of comedy and tragedy is very complex here. In the context where suicide would be a possible solution Castle knows that for him suicide is out of the question. "He had promised Sarah that one day they would be together." (p. 258) Sarah means more to Castle than God would ever mean to Scobie. Castle's self-searchings and self-communings are always occasioned by the human factor. The tragic absurdity of Scobie is transformed in Castle into a serious human concern. The effect is haunting. This could be perhaps because of the absence of religious convictions in Castle. Unlike Scobie, he is not weighed down by the problem of evil. Castle is not a Catholic, not even a believer. Christ for him is only a legend which he would have liked to believe in. He is more pragmatic and, in a way, down-to-earth. He does not strike heroic postures. He is clear-headed about what he wants and does everything in his power to make his honest dreams come true. He wants a simple life of security, peace, a happy retirement on a good pension. Though he does not hit back at his mother's jibe at his sense of gratitude he tells Sarah why he loved the Communist who helped him:

> "Oh, there were always some things which stuck in my throat. He (Carson, the Communist) used to say I strained at a gnat and swallowed a camel. You know I was never a religious man — I left God behind in the school chapel, but there were priests I sometimes met in Africa who made me believe again — for a moment — over a drink. If all priests had been like they were and I had seen them often enough, perhaps I would have swallowed the Resurrection, the Virgin birth, Lazarus, the whole works ... When people talk about Prague and Budapest and how you can't find a human face in Communism I stay silent. Because I've seen — once — the human face. I say to myself that if it hadn't been for Carson, Sam would have been born in a prison and you would probably have died in one. One kind of Communism — or Communist — saved you and Sam. I don't have any trust in Marx or Lenin any more than I have in Saint Paul, but haven't I the right to be grateful?"(pp. 134-5)

Sleepless later and waiting to make himself sure from Sarah's breathing that she was asleep first, he remembers his childhood hero:

> Then he allowed himself to strike, like his childhood hero Allen Quatermain, off on that long slow underground

> stream which bore him on towards the interior of the dark continent where he hoped that he might find a permanent home, in a city where he could be accepted as a citizen, as a citizen without any pledge of faith, not the City of God or Marx, but the city called Peace of Mind. (p. 135)

It is pledges that make life complicated whether it is to Capitalism or to Communism, Catholicism or Atheism. Without pledges of this sort one could still be human, caring only for a simple life which ensures peace of mind. Here is Castle's dream. He wonders: "... is it possible that one day life will be as simple as childhood, that I shall have finished with buts, that I will be trusted naturally by everyone, as Sarah trusts me — and Sam?" (p. 218)

5.4.2 Duplicity has come to be Castle's profession and the human factor and the professional one rise and submerge alternately like battling forces struggling to surface conclusively. Castle wants the human factor to outweigh everything else but his profession pulls him to the other extreme at the cost of his peace of mind. He is deeply human and loyalty to the beloved comes before all 'isms' for him. Greene's own love of the individual above the established orders is evident once again in Castle. To be human is the thing; the rest is of little consequence. Greene challenges accepted notions about other kinds of loyalty as though offering an extended gloss on Forster's dictum, one should rather betray one's country than one's friends. Castle is surprised that Sarah does not say a word of blame when he tells her: "I'm what's generally called a traitor." She replies: 'Who cares?" and puts her hand in his, a gesture more intimate than a kiss. She reassures him: "We have our own country. You and I and Sam. You've never betrayed that country, Maurice."[14] (p. 238) When, after Castle's defection, Mrs. Castle criticises her son, Sarah rushes to his defence with great warmth:

> "He was trying to help my people. If he hadn't loved me and Sam ... It was the price he paid to save us. You can't imagine here in England the kind of horrors he saved us from."
>
> "A traitor?"
> She lost control at the reiteration: "All right - a traitor to whom? To Muller and his friends. To the Security Police?"

14. We are reminded of Fellows in *The Power and the Glory* saying "Oh treason" and the comment: "There was so much treason everywhere it was like petty larceny in a barracks." (p. 35)

> "I have no idea who Muller is. He's a traitor to his country."
>
> "Oh, his country," she said in despair at all the cliches which go to form a judgement. (p. 336)

Castle finds a kind of extension of his own faith in personal relationship in an oddly contorted way when in Moscow another defector like him called Bellamy replies to his question whether he was happy there: "Yes, I am. Happiness always seems to me a matter of persons not of places, and I have a nice friend." (p. 325)

5.4.3 Castle is a 'traitor' according to customary considerations. Even his mother fails to understand him when the human factor submerges the professional in him ultimately. The novel shows how the individual trapezes between the human and the professional ties. Castle takes care to hide even his capacity for intuitiveness believing that it is safer to be inconspicuous. He plays a part exceedingly well and pulls the wool over the eyes of the investigators. The mask he wears is so rigid and inflexible that until he is thoroughly rattled he does not open up his heart even to Sarah. The professional mask, however, does not impede the illuminating insight. Davis asks him to wish him good luck in his overtures to Cynthia while promising to burn the contents of the rubbish bin as an offering to Cynthia. Castle replies: "Of course, with all my heart." Then follows this :

> The hackneyed phrase came warm and unintended to Castle's tongue. It surprised him, as though, in penetrating a familiar cave, on some holiday at sea, he had observed on a familiar rock the primeval painting of a human face which he had always mistaken for a chance pattern of fungi. (pp. 88.89)

5.4.4 Greene prefaces his novel with this short paragraph:

> A novel based on life in any Secret Service must necessarily contain a large element of fantasy, for realistic description would almost certainly infringe some clause or other in some official Secrets Act. Operation Uncle Remus is purely a product of the author's imagination (and I trust it will remain so), as are all the characters, whether English, African, Russian or Polish. All the same, to quote Hans Anderson, a wise author who also dealt in fantasy, "Out of reality are our tales of imagination fashioned."

This should be applicable to *Our Man in Havana* also but when we read that side by side with this it is two kinds of fiction that we encounter. Wormold is purely fantastic, a comedian with smears of whitewash; but having played the act he miraculously emerges in gleaming silk. *The Human Factor* is a comedy with a difference and it is the difference that marks the distinctive achievement of Greene. The element of seriousness is held in strict control in *Our Man in Havana* giving free rein to the fantastic while the serious is given free play in *The Human Factor.* The comic, as well as the serious, becomes deeper and the combination is more complex and more effective. The epigraph from Conrad would serve to illustrate the point further: "I only know that he who forms a tie is lost. The germ of corruption has entered into his soul." Though Castle's loyalty to Sarah and loving care for her happiness cannot exactly be viewed as a germ of corruption, one cannot say for certain whether Castle is not lost in his tie with her. Alan Ross[15] notes:

> *The Human Factor* reflects on rather than elaborates the Conrad quotation. Castle acts out of gratitude for love in a way that is totally foolish but though in a superficial sense he loses everything he is not 'lost' spiritually because his motives have never been impure. Indirectly he causes the death of a colleague who was wrongly suspected of being the 'leak' and who is callously disposed of by the department but it is he himself who has to live out the consequence of his action. In a communist country, Castle observes, he knows himself to be a capitalist 'with a human face' who achieved for him his years of happiness, and he died in consequence. Once again Greene manages to anticipate a political situation and to illuminate it in terms of personal relationships. Gratitude may seem an inadequate motive to risk a future for, but it has always been the flawed man who has claimed Greene's compassion.

But despite this purity of motive, Castle exiles himself from the very person for whom he lost a world.

5.4.5 T.J. Binyon[16] writes:

> To read *The Human Factor* against the memory of *Our Man in Havana* is a rather disconcerting experience: ... in the earlier book intelligence work is sent up, and here it is played straight. Indeed, the laughs in *The Human Factor*

15. *The London Magazine*, March 1978, Vol. 17, No. 9.
16. *The Times Literary Supplement*, March 17, 1978, p. 301.

> are fewer and thinner than in any of the author's more recent novels: the only comic character is Castle's dog, an unlovable boxer called Buller whose name drives home the South African connection.

The statement is not entirely wrong: it isolates for us the seriousness of the book. *Our Man in Havana* is a fantasy, an 'entertainment'. In the new novel there is a complex interaction of the serious, the pathetic and the potentially tragic. The pathetic inheres in the death of Davis; the serious in the separation of the loving couple Castle and Sarah who have already suffered too much to bear another turn of the screw; the potentially tragic in the bleak hope of Castle to which he is condemned. The human factor accentuated doubly in the lives of Davis-Cynthia and Castle-Sarah has a serious dimension and the condition of man continues to be the driving force in Greene though it is consistently combined with a comic perspective on life.

5.4.6 The usual way things operate in administration is shown in an oddly comic light - odd because of the strange admixture of seriousness. Castle escapes suspicion as much because of his 'dullness' as because of his relationship with another Castle in the Treasury. Comically enough it is the circumstantial evidence that mounts against Davis who is a spendthrift, a race-addict and a lover of vintage port more because he took only a third in mathematics and physics at Reading. The offender escapes and the innocent gets killed. The offender, of course, is not an offender in a way. The professional zeal of Doctor Percival who talks of the whole thing in terms of flyfishing is comic and serious at the same time. There is the comic in the serious and the serious in the comic[17] in the very portraiture of Davis, Cynthia, Castle, Hargreaves, Doctor Percival, Daintry - almost every character in the novel. Davis is a sad clown yearning for Cynthia but debunking marriage:

> "You know very well what they pay us," Castle said, "and I'm married."
>
> "A grave error of judgement." (p. 11)

Davis is spoken of as an actor who has been miscast. "When he tried to live up to the costume, he usually fumbled the part." (p. 10) His death like Jones's in *The Comedians* is sad and sadness in a comedy underlying it haunts the reader's memory. In scene after scene the sad and the pathetic is transfused into the comic. Davis

---

17. This is pointed out to be the unique contribution of Shakespeare to characterization.

calls Sam a bastard playfully and Castle who knows it is true is not offended. Sarah loves Castle more than the man who fathered her child. Here is a bit of dialogue which reminds us of the comic in Mme. Rycker's tale in *A Burnt-out Case*:

> In bed that night she woke from her first sleep and said, as though the thought had occurred to her in a dream, "It's strange, isn't it, your being so fond of Sam."
>
> "Of course, I am. Why not? I thought you were asleep."
>
> "There's no 'of course' about it. A little bastard."
>
> "That's what Davis always calls him."
>
> "Davis? He doesn't know?" she asked with fear. "Surely he doesn't know?"
>
> "No, don't worry. It's the word he uses for any child."
>
> "I'm glad his father's six feet underground," she said.
>
> "Yes, so am I, poor devil. He might have married you in the end."
>
> "No. I was in love with you all the time. Even when I started Sam I was in love with you. He's more you child than his. I tried to think of you when he made love. He was a tepid sort of fish. At the University they called him an Uncle Tom. Sam won't be tepid, will he? Hot or cold, but not tepid." (Emphasis mine) (pp. 28-29)

Mme. Rycker's blatant and outrageous declaration is the height of a complex comedy while sarah's statement is a gentle confession of love. What has been absurd in the former's statement is transformed into the tender with the refined intervention of the human factor.

5.4.7 The discussion that takes place at the country house of the security Chief where Hargreaves, Doctor Percival and Daintry discuss the leak is a brilliant mixture of the serious and the comic:

> Hargreaves lifted his bad leg with both hands and eased it towards the fire. "Suppose we did prove Davis to be the culprit - or Castle or Watson. What should we do then?"
>
> "Surely that would be up to the courts," Daintry said.
>
> "Headlines in the papers. Another trial *in camera*. No one outside would know how small and unimportant the leaks were. Whoever he is he won't rate forty years like Blake. Perhaps he'll serve ten if the prison's secure."
>
> "That's not out concern surely."

> "No, Daintry, but I don't enjoy the thought of that trial one little bit. What co-operation can we expect from the American afterwards? And then there's our source. I told you, he's still in place. We don't want to blow him as long as he proves useful."
>
> "In a way," Percival said, "it would be better to close our eyes like a complaisant husband. Draft whoever it is to some innocuous department. Forget things.
>
> "And what a crime?" Daintry protested.
>
> "Oh, crime," Percival said and smiled at C. like a fellow conspirator. "We are all committing crimes somewhere, aren't we? It's our job."
>
> "The trouble is," C. said, "that the situation *is* a bit like a rocky marriage. In a marriage, if the lover begins to be bored by the complaisant husband, he can always provoke a scandal. He holds the strong suit. He can choose his own time. I don't want any scandal provoked." (pp. 40-41)

The use of metaphor marks out each speaker - Daintry's legal; or C's political or Doctor Percival's scandalous. A serious issue is crowded out by the diverse metaphors and the effect is comic in a situation involving tragic issues.

5.4.8 The scene that follows the registry office wedding at Sylvia's (Mrs. Daintry) flat is the best example of the blend of the comic and the tragic in an almost disconcerting manner. Daintry, dreading to meet his ex-wife, attends the wedding of his daughter knowing full well that he would be an unwanted stranger there. Castle accompanies him hearing a distress note in his invitation. After the wedding they go to Sylvia'a flat. There are more plaster owls than guests in the cluttered rooms. Daintry could not get the name of his son-in-law right. Sylvia greets Daintry and disappears. The miserably uncomfortable Daintry breaks a particularly valuable owl. Castle receives the telephone call announcing Davis's death. Here is the bizarre conclusion of the scene:

> "... Daintry stood alone with a slice in his fingers behind a table littered with owls. He said, "For God's sake, let's be off, Castle. I don't understand this sort of thing."
>
> "Daintry, I've had a call from the office. Davis is dead."
>
> "Davis?"
>
> "He's dead. Doctor Percival ..."
>
> "Percival!" Daintry exclaimed. "My God, that man ..." He pushed his slice of cake among the owls and a big grey owl

> toppled off and smashed on the floor.
>
> "Edward," a woman's voice shrieked, "John's broken the grey owl."
>
> Edward thrust his way towards them. "I can't be every where at once, Sylvia."
>
> Mrs. Daintry appeared behind him. She said, "John, you damned old boring fool. I'll never forgive you for this - never. What the hell are you doing anyway in *my* house?"
>
> Daintry said, "Come away, Castle. I'll buy you another owl, Sylvia."
>
> "It's irreplaceable, that one."
>
> "A man's dead," Daintry said. "He's irreplaceable too." (p. 174)

This scene reminds us of that rich scene in *The End of the Affair* when Waterbury the critic, Sylvia his girl and Bendrix the novelist-narrator are on a bus, Bendrix going to Golders Green. The scene marks a complex emotional centre of the book in that it combines notes of the sad, the comic and the absurd. In *The End of the Affair* Waterbury is purely academic in 'threatening' Bendrix. Sylvia goes on showing consistent human interest in Bendrix while his mind is on the funeral. Bendrix is acutely conscious of the absurdity of the trend of things. Sylvia is ready to fall for him leaving her lover. The critic himself is engrossed in his professional zeal in 'interviewing' the novelist. The scene in *The Human Factor* overlaid with indifferent men and Sylvia's plaster owls[18] is the meeting point of a marriage that is on the rocks, a marriage that is just making a beginning and a marriage that is nipped even before it started budding. The complex combination of the serious, the comic and the absurd all in one reminds us of the scene mentioned how in the earlier novel. Bendrix is on his way to Sarah's funeral in Golders Green. Waterbury is stiffly academic, an obtuse comic figure like Sylvia in the new novel with her passion for plaster owls. Waterbury exclaims that the funeral in Golders Green is in tune with Bendrix's characters, while Sylvia asks with human interest if it is friend. The novelist narrator reflects:

> I could see that she was speculating - man? Woman? What kind of a friend? and it pleased me. For I was a human being to her and not a writer: a man whose friends died and

18. Sylvia's passion for owls reminds us of Mrs. Plarr's passion for porcelain parrots. Both are separated from their husbands.

> who attended their funerals who felt pleasure and pain, who might even need comfort, not just a skilled craftsman whose work has greater sympathy perhaps than Mr. Maugham's though of course we cannot rank it as high as ... (*The End of the Affair*, (p. 146)

The conversation going off in different directions is a strange and complex mixture of different kinds of emotion. Waterbury is insensitive in that the funeral does not evoke in him a touch of sorrow befitting the occasion. The comic suddenly takes over when Sylvia decides to follow Bendrix:

> Sylvia said, "I'm going as far as Hampstead myself. I'll put you on your way."
>
> "You never told me," Waterbury said with suspicion.
>
> "You know I always see my mother on Wednesday."
>
> "Today's Tuesday."
>
> "Then I needn't go tomorrow."
>
> "It's very good of you," I said, "I'd like your company."
>
> "You used the stream of consciousness in one of your books," Waterbury said with desperate haste. "Why did you abandon the method?"
>
> "Oh, I don't know. Why does one change a flat?"
>
> "Did you feel it was a failure"
>
> "I feel that about all my books Well, good bye, Waterbury."
>
> "I'll send you a copy of the article," he said as though he were uttering a threat. (EOA. p. 147)

The critic and the owl-lover, insensitive to the human factor, are in total contrast with Bendrix, Daintry and Castle who realise the sad comedy of the self-absorbed clowns.

5.4.9 Another scene in the novel where there is a rich and an extremely well-balanced combination of the absurd, the comic and the serious is the one where Castle goes to a Catholic church. Oppressed by the insufferable silence imposed upon him by his duplicity, believing that to talk is a therapeutic act, Castle, in sheer desperation, moves towards the box of the confessional with trepidation:

> "Kneel down, man, what sort of a Catholic do you think you are?"

> "I'm not a Catholic."
>
> "Then what business have you here?"
>
> "I want to talk, that's all."
>
> "If you want instruction, you can leave your name and address at the presbytery."
>
> "I don't want instruction."
>
> "You are wasting my time," the priest said.
>
> "Don't the secrets of the confessional apply to non-Catholics?"
>
> "You should go to a priest of your own Church."
>
> "I haven't got a Church."
>
> "Then I think what you need is a doctor." the priest said, he slammed the shutter to, and Castle left the box. It was an absurd end, he thought, to an absurd action. How would he have expected the man to understand him even if he had been allowed to talk? He had far too long a history to tell, begun so many years ago in a strange country. (p. 234)

The priest's literalmindedness and his refusal to talk to the distressed man shows a typical lack of human feeling. Castle's belief that the secrecy of the confessional might guarantee safety to him shows his intense human need exposed to an indifferent world. The combination of the sad and the comic thus evokes a complex response.

5.4.10 The blend is clearly apparent in characterization also. Here is an example:

> Cynthia, the major-general's daughter, came in with two cups of coffee and a telegram. She had something in common with Davis, for she played a comedy too. If faithful Davis looked as untrust-worthy as a bookie, Cynthia, the domesticminded, looked as dashing as a young commando. It was a pity that her spelling was so bad, but perhaps there was something Elizabethan about her spelling as well as about her name. She was probably looking for a Philip Sydney, and so far she had only found a Davis. (p. 53)

This read along with Davis's reaction to Doctor Percival's chit does not bode well to the affair: "This chit *is* signed Percival, Emmanuel Percival, What a name. Wasn't Emmanuel the bringer of good tidings? Do you think they might be sending me abroad too?"(p. 57)

The incongruity in their relationship which never ripens does not leave behind an effect of comedy, though both Davis and Cynthia are deliberately painted in comic terms. The comic is undone by the seriousness it accumulates slowly culminating in the death of Davis.

5.4.11 Emmanuel himself is an ambivalent comic figure whose actions promote sadness and tears. Hargreaves knows that the Doctor's having a conscience is a most unlikely supposition. He asks him: 'Do you never find that you shock yourself, Emmanuel?" (p. 103) The mixture of his ideology and flair for fly-fishing are a dangerous combination. When C. blames him that he should have waited till he returned, the Doctor's flippant answer is an outrage: "When you feel the fish on the line, you don't stand waiting on the bank for someone else to advise you what to do." (p. 207) His attitude to life and things is not less disconcerting:

> "... I don't think Communism will work — in the long run - any better than Christianity has done, and I'm not the Crusader type. Capitalism or Communism? Perhaps God is a Capitalist. I want to be on the side most likely to win during my life-time. Don't look shocked, John. You think I'm a cynic, but I just don't want to waste a lot of time. This side that wins will be able to build better hospitals, and give more to cancer to build better hospitals, and give more to cancer research - when all this atomic nonsense is abandoned. In the meanwhile I enjoy the game we're all playing. Enjoy. Only enjoy. I don't pretend to be an enthusiast for God or Marx. Beware of people who believe. They aren't reliable players. All the same one grows to like a good player on the other side of the board - it increases the fun."
>
> "Even if he's a traitor?"
>
> "Oh, Traitor — that's an old-fashioned word, John. The Player is as important as the game. I wouldn't enjoy the game with a bad player across the table."(p.207)

Doctor Percival's deceptive utilitarian rumblings are a sign of intellectual flatulence. He is no better than the incongruous Ida Arnold and more hateful at a deeper level.

5.4.12 The complex response consequent on the subtle combination of the serious and the comic is evident in short scraps of dialogue like:

> "How I run on, don't I?' Percival said.

> "Never can go straight on the subject. It's like fishing again. You sometimes have to make a hundred false casts before you place the fly."
>
> "I'm not a fish" Daintry said, "and it's after midnight." (p.45)

In this scene Doctor Percival finds that his metaphors from fly-fishing sounded offensive and quickly switches over to painting. But Daintry is no fool. He represents the serious element never to be diluted by any kind of flippancy:

> ...Percival pointed at a yellow square. "There is your Section 6. That's your square from now on. You don't need to worry about the blue and the red. All you have to do is pinpoint our man and then tell me. You've no responsibility for what happens in the blue or red squares. In fact not even in the yellow. You just report. No bad conscience. No guilt."
>
> "An action has nothing to do with its consequences. Is that what you're telling me?"(p.46)

5.4.13 Another piece of dialogue reminds us of the singularly effective combination. The Chief of the Secret Service and Muller from Africa talk about the Communist, Carson, and a cnessplayer who played the game of the profession as long as it was challenging enough. Muller has an intuition that Davis was not the leak but the chief does not own up to his mistakes. He has his own way of making abstractions and believing in them:

> Hargreaves thought again of Melmotte. People talked of courage as a primary virtue. What of the courage of a known swindler and bankrupt taking his place in the dining room of the House of Commons? Is courage a justification? Is courage in whatever cause a virtue? He said, "we are satisfied that Davis was the leak we had to close."
>
> "A fortunate death?"
>
> "Cirrhosis of the liver."
>
> "I told you Carson died of pneumonia."
>
> "There are other motives too. Love of money."
>
> "That certainly does'nt apply to Castle."
>
> "He loves his wife," Muller said, "and his child."

> "What of that?"
>
> "They are both black," Muller replied with simplicity ... (p. 247)

Intuition is a matter of the capacity of the mind and the capacity of being human has nothing to do with it. Though Muller hated Castle and his sympathy for the blacks, he has an insight into Castle's mind, while the chief making abstractions about primary virtue does not have the drive to see the dangerous held under control. Proved wrong in his smug self-satisfaction, Hargreaves could do nothing more than dislike Muller as his wife does:

> "Has that man Muller gone"?
>
> "Yes."
>
> "I don't like him."
>
> "Nor do I." (p. 249)

5.4.14 Helen Gardner writes[19]: "It used to be said as axiomatic that while Greek tragedy is soaked in religious conceptions and concerned with the relation of man to the Gods, Shakespearean tragedy is agnostic and concerned with the relation of man and man." Greene's novels share the qualities of both the Greek and Shakespearean tragedies in their own way. They are concerned in a triangular way with man's relation to God, his environment and his fellowmen. Greene's writing is characterized by the complex and inclusive comedy, the frontiers of which have extended considerably in recent times. The tragic and the comic are no longer disparate elements. They can co-exist and the comic can inhere in the tragic. Wylie Sypher's[20] remark used as an epigraph earlier bears repetition: "Perhaps the most important discovery of modern criticism is the perception that comedy and tragedy are somehow akin, or that comedy can tell us many things about our situation even tragedy cannot." Greene's writing has a delicate but firm texture of the comic, the sad and the serious, beginning specially with *The Comedians* and thereafter. The inclusive frontiers of comedy make this possible. Tragedy is undermined by a broader understanding of reality. The comic itself is transformed by the inclusion of the sad and the thoughtful. The effect is one of richness and ripeness. The responses the varying degree of combinations evoke are complex.

19. Helen Gardner, *Religion and Literature* (London: Faber, 1970), p. 14.
20. Wylie Sypher, *Comedy* (Garden City, New York: Doubleday Anchor Books, 1956), p. 193.

5.4.15 In *The Human Factor* the blend of comedy and tragedy is deeper in the sense that both the constituents are of a higher order than ever seen before. For example, disguise, a usual device used in comedy, is raised to the level of the most thoughtful. Jones in *The Comedians* disguises himself in a Volendam skirt and so does Castle here as a blind man, both to make good their escape. The preoccupations of the two characters are as entirely different as their situations and temperaments. But the comedy of Castle's disguise where he is fighting not merely for survival but for his innermost convictions are struggling to realise the ideal of loyalty to the beloved he cherished most is a subtler one. For that reason the comedy in his case touches an unsurpassed height of thoughtfulness. The subtlety of the comic does retain the tragic, again of a subtle order. Davis's death and the dog Buller's are tragic without any emphasis on guilt which did loom large in Greene's earlier fiction. His new awareness of the comic integrating with and subsuming the tragic under it is responsible for this mature outlook. The final impression is not simply that of a comedy but one verging on tragedy. Castle is saved with a future suspended precariously, with hope flickering at a long distance. The protagonists are saved but the poignancy lies in their being saved apart — with a melancholy stretching of hands across a continent. Here is an anxiety necessitated but the inherent limitations imposed on human existence. The fulcrum of human attachment is used to drive home the basic truth that 'ism's and abstractions do not give the comfort that human beings really need. The need is visualized in Castle who tries to extend this element of the human in as many relationships as possible. The sad strands of love denied in Davis-Cynthia and Daintry-Mrs Daintry episodes accentuate the importance of the human factor. This novel takes a step ahead of *The Honorary Consul* in its poignancy and primacy of a delicate human attachment. In a world where God is an inexplicable factor where human institutions like Capitalism or Communism are but instruments of abuse of humanity, the only core that seems to matter and last is the loyalty of man to man, or more truly, between man and woman. Greene seems to return almost to a fairy-tale simplicity. There is no consummation greater than a happy union in marriage and happiness continued in the simple bond of matrimony. This novel shows inextricable blend of the tragic and the comic almost in perfection. The death of Davis is a touching even: he is a victim of an irrational system whose irrationality is largely a contribution of human beings who do not think enough. Human life is cheap in an absurd system. It is by a miraculous chance that Castle escapes death - his life is strewn with comic incidents and he is a beneficiary of the absurdity of the behaviour of humans and the systems. But there seems to be an enveloping irony that, through all comic guises that lead to his escapes, an unbridgeable gulf is being dug between Castle and his only hope, his wife, who together with him had formed one sweet habitable world. The conclusion is almost unequivocal in suggesting that Castle is left with nothing but hoping. We know that it is hard for him to count with any certainty on a spring to come. The vast and subtle world of human tragedy looms large before us. By its emphasis on hope, it tends to comedy; but by the virtual denial of the reunion of Castle with his wife, it unmistakably tilts into tragedy. Such an inextricable blend of tragedy and comedy, the depiction of a purely human predicament, a situation where man is tantalised by hope in a scheming world where elementary human relations are rendered unsustainable, marks a new advance in the Greeneian art and vision. As a creative artist Greene comes finally to wield a power of laughter and sorrow, like Shakespeare as noted by Dr. Johnson, not only in one composition but in one mind:

> You have seen Sunshine and rain at once; her smiles and tears were like a better way.
>
> (*King Lear*, IV, iii, 17-19)

Chapter 6

Conclusion

> *Finish the tragedy! No. I have finally understood. Certainly everything is ugly, everything is sad, and afterwards we know it. But the soul must be purged by laughter. The only virile attitude to take in the face of the human condition is to laugh at it. And that is comedy.*
>
> *Jean Anouilh, 'La Petit Moliere'*

6.1 Asked in 1963 about the direction in which he liked to work further, Greene told Professor Frank Kermode in an interview:[1] "I would like to be able to write." This does not mean that he has the limited ambition to write disparate individual works without reference to his consistent personal vision. Early in his career, in 1936, Greene wrote about Henry James that "the symmetry of his thought lends the whole body of his work the importance of a system."[2] It is time critics began thinking of Greene's works in terms of his 'system'. It is possible to deduce a 'system' from his novels by considering him a creative artist who has portrayed a well-integrated and self-consistent fictional universe. The abiding interest in Greene lies in the mystique he has created. Greene's basic themes themselves have undergone a transformation owing to the gradual shift in his attitude towards life and things. The earlier preoccupation with betrayal, with squalor and seediness in the outside world as well as in human relations have paved the way to a maturer attitude where love, however imperfect, friendship and companionship are reckoned as essential to make life both happy and pleasurable. The emphasis has been shifted from tragic betrayal to friendship, from sordidness to sweetness and nobility to a degree compatible with the general human condition, and from a failure to a feeling of success and accomplishment, though not in the immediate materialistic sense. The shift is clearly to the inclusive comical perspective. Greene seems to come round to believe that the tragicomic view is more inclusive than the merely tragic and that it is wiser to integrate

---

1. Frank Kermode, "The House of Fiction, Interviews with Seven English Novelists", *Partisan Review*, Spring 1963.
2. Graham Greene, "Henry James: The Private Universe", *The Lost Childhood and Other Essays*. Penguin, 1966, p.20.

the tragical into a comical perspective on life. His mystique of the comic is exemplified in his work without his being doctrinaire in the theoretical construct in itself. The stance is achieved over decades of steady maturation. The projected comical vision bears testimony to Greene's position as a great imaginative artist. A synoptic view of Greene's vision shaped over the years is valuable for a deeper appreciation of Greene as a creative artist. No single play of Shakespeare can be understood, said Eliot, without a study of other plays of Shakespeare.

6.2 There are two aspects of Greene's work - the purely technical one and the one relating to his motive and message in the larger context. As Philip Stratford writes:[3] "Greene's artistic point of view verges on the philosophical and its development can be better studied if it is disengaged from technical considerations." The burden of the critic is to assess the creative artist's intention and measure it against his accomplishment. Greene is a serious artist in the sense that he is committed to portray the reality he has the ability in him to comprehend. The phrase 'religious' artist is apt to be misleading for it smacks of Catholic preoccupations which are relevant only to a few of his novels. Then there are his own assertions stating that he is not a Catholic novelist but a novelist who happens to be Catholic. He may more appropriately be described as a novelist who is a committed humanist, a humanist who has not shut his doors on any flow of light including that from religion. Religion here implies a spiritual inspiration which embraces an eternal and universal value regardless of doctrinal or sectarian limitations. Being a novelist who is also a humanist and a Catholic, Greene has fully realised that religion is an individual affair. Greene felt that it was not enough for an artist "to render the highest kind of justice to the visible universe" unless the word "visible" included the private vision also. Greene's aim remains "to present truth as honestly a possible" and the novel is for him "the most important of contemporary art forms."[4] Greene's personal religion is reflected in the myth he has been creating which is a matter of his innermost convictions. He admired the characters of Francois Mauriac — as against those of even accomplished writers like Forster who 'wandered like cardboard symbols through a world that was paper thin' — for they are not men and women with souls to win or lose. Greene's criticism,

3. Philip Stratford, *Faith and Fiction* (Notredame: University of Notredame Press, 1964), p.137.
4. Graham Greene, "Creative Reading", *Spectator* CLIV Feb. 1935, p.356 Quoted by Philip Stratford.

apart from its justice in relation to Forster's characterization, should serve as a pointer to his serious preoccupations. Asked by Professor Kermode in what sense the 'abiding temptation to tell a good story' is to be regarded inimical to the production of a good novel, he replied: "I'm not sure that one can generalise on that: I feel that it is inimical to my producing a novel. My own wish always is to produce a central figure who represents some idea of reasonable simplicity — a mythical figure if you like." While Miss Murdoch, in the same interview, regarded myth as a great temptation of self-indulgence, Greene thought that myth ought to be concerned with the texture of reality and should form the object of conscious pursuit. Myth consists of the writer's projected world (Abercrombie calls it 'perceived reality') and Greene for all his assertions about the centrality that myth ought to take in any piece of good fiction is a superb plot builder with the result that the myth is hidden under the perfect artefact. He admits to a measure of discomfort in this respect: "And I would like to ascend into myth, but find my boots so often muddy with plot." Plot is said to be in the limbo of discarded conventions and to write plotlessly is the aim of the novelist today. Of course such views are countered by writers like Somerset Maugham in theory as well as in practice. Wilde's witticism about George Meredith that he can do everything with the novel except tell a story keeps alive the importance of plot and story. Myth is the representation of reality, the real truth about the world and there is nothing which matters more beyond that. Greene's mystique is dynamic for it goes on enhancing its facets and enriching itself as he moved from one phase to another in ever deepening maturity. "If I were to choose an epigraph for all the novels I have written," writes Greene in *A Sort of Life*, "it would be from *Bishop Blougram's Apology*:

> *'our interest is on the dangerous edge of things*
> *The honest thief, the tender murderer,*
> *The superstitious atheist, demi-rep*
> *That loves and saves her soul in new French books*
> *We watch while these in equilibrium keep*
> *The giddy line midway.'"*

The lines bring into focus the tragic-comic contradiction which life presents. Greene delicately unravels the difficult strands of life to show how a comprehensive vision of life implies an awareness of the inherent oppositions in life, the antinomies which affirm that though life is fraught with tragic materials, the entire substance is leavened by the comic.

6.3 Doctor Magiot, the humanist and the mouthpiece of Greene's mystique in *The Comedians*, writes in his letter to his friend, Brown: "... if you abandon one faith do not abandon all faith. There is an alternative to the faith we lose." The melodramatic and the tragic of the earlier phases are slowly but surely integrated into a comic vision glorying in the fact that life for all its violence, unhappiness and shabbiness still holds out tremendously varied prospects. A saint will not take our agonies seriously knowing what would come at the end. Here is the seed of the mystic experience in germination which reflects the belief expressed by Saint Juliana of Norwich:

Sin is behovely
All shall be well and
All manner of things shall be well.

Sin or man's incapacity to escape from spiritual errors and suffering can become behovely without disconcerting us if there is proper inward discipline, moral and spiritual, on the part of the human being like the cultivation of charity and compassion. From this point of view, sin may be a stepping stone to spiritual elevation in so far as it arouses this discipline and is a test of man's moral stamina and development. Though one may not attribute a saint's eye-view of things to Greene, the final impression that he seems to leave is one of charity and compassion. He writes from the point of view of the 'black square' as much as from that of the 'white square' and liberates himself from the tyranny he sees in the attitude of the Leningrad group.[5] He believes in the virtue of disloyalty to the extent that loyalty either to the faith or the vocation hinders a comprehensive compassion.

6.4 A study of Greene's novels reveals his dynamism and the inexhaustible powers of growth in him. Comedy which is usually a means of simple enjoyment is reckoned as a serious pursuit by him. "Comedy is essentially a serious activity," wrote L.C. Knights.[6] Greene's comic vision is such that it helps us to interpret ourselves to ourselves and gain an insight into existence. His strategy is one where initially an amount of fantasy is blended with the popular medium of the contemporary thriller. 'Evil' is blown up with a comical zeal and the actuality which somehow always falls short of the ideal is transmuted with a seemingly frivolous distortion inspired by a really deep spirituality. In this sense Greene's novels are comedies with a difference. The inexplicable mystery of the absurd

5. See Greene's *Why do I write?* (London: Percival Marshall, 1948)
6. Cited by Wylie Sypher, op. cit.

and at the same time a God-pervaded world can be understood only with the charity and light-heartedness inspired by comedy. There has been a persistent awareness of this fact in the artist himself or else he would not have talked of 'entertainment', 'fairy-tale', 'frivolity' and 'comedy'. The comic vision that Greene projects is thoughtful: his comedy perplexes and illumines. Adultery and betrayal as much as impotence could belong to the tragic and in fact they have been so in Greene's fiction of the earlier phases. But they are transformed into being agents of charity with the aid of the inclusive comical perception. The under-current of contempt in the treatment of the cuckold, Henry Miles, in *The End of the Affair* is totally overcome in the portrayal of Senor Pineda, Fortnum and Castle. Fortnum's wife sleeps with Doctor Plarr and Castle's wife had a son by an earlier lover but both Fortnum and Castle ignore the infidelities as unimportant. Adultery is tolerated with a measure of charity and even bastards are accepted which are proofs enough to show that merely sexual relationships may be insignificant in the context of true attachment inspired by the inner springs of love. Tolerance is a virtue of the comic sense. Fortnum grows in understanding and he does not love Clara any the less after he discovers her liaison with Doctor Plarr. Castle tolerates the ugly Buller (unlike Fowler who hates Pyle's dog) and loves Sam, Sarah's illegitimate son (unlike Brown who hates Angel, Martha's son). Greene's vision has tolerance, flexibility, wisdom, charity and humility in that it does countenance and absorb the serious twists and painful turns in the irrational way things shape out for man. Though reckoned at times as a practical joker, God is very much here. Ernst Cassirer, the German Philosopher, has written a major comment on the 'sympathetic vision' of the great comic artists who, he says, bring us close to the realities of our human world and dissolve our scorn and doubt in a laughter that liberates us.

6.5 Like tragedy, comedy too is said to be homeopathic in that it cures folly by folly. The Greeneian genre of the inclusive, sympathetic comedy is a prophylactic against anguish and bitterness. It arms us with the capacity to laugh at evil and error thereby enabling us to surmount them. The comic in Greene's vision is a device spiritually inspired to encounter harsh and irrational reality with an even temper. Comedy, as Greene presents it, is as much a philosophical compensation as a psychological one. Like his faith, his comedy can tolerate the miraculous; in his world comic heroes are saints and saints are comic heroes; they face and accept the apparent inconsistencies and irreconcilables in existence. To be human is important and to be human is to be tolerant. It makes us realize that the worm that eats the rose is as much a part of the world as the rose itself. This is the implication of Somerset Maugham's well-known remark about the Lordship at the Old Bailey and the packet of toilet paper beside the bunch of flowers; "It would remind him that he was a man like any other."[7]

6.6 A microcosm of Graham Greene's world of fiction would be made up of a lavatory-eat, a mud hut, a limping dog, heat and flies; darkness and thunder; a battlefield; a hunted man, a waif-like woman, a corrupted child, a policeman and a priest, human beings with varying degrees of not only lechery but also commitment, faith and *joie de vivre*. Passion, ultimately, gives way to love; betrayal to loyalty, and hatred to compassion, however weak, unappreciated and unrecognized the nobler and humane qualities themselves may remain to be. Against a predictably typical setting, the actors enact a drama whose dominant theme is a comedy in the form of the incongruous and the inexplicable. God is very much here - if only in the guise of the practical joker. Man is ordained to face an adult word with the faculties of an infantile brain, enjoined to think clearly in a state of intoxication and forced to act wisely under the pressure and excitement of the genitals. The resultant action could not be anything but funny though at times sad. In the world of Greene's fiction, the human condition is represented with vividness, explained with clarity, and accounted for with understanding. The message is one of charity and large-heartedness. The plea is for a joyfully-knowing and wisely-tolerant perspective; the perspective of comedy deepened by a tragic awareness of the limitations of the human situation.

7. *The Summing Up* (London: Heinemann, 1949), p. 55.

BIBLIOGRAPHY

1. Primary Sources: The Novels of Graham Greene

Greene, Graham. *The Man Within*. London: Heinemann, 1929.

---------------------------- *Stamboul Train*. London: Heinemann, 1932.

---------------------------- *It's a Battlefield*. London: Heinemann, 1934.

---------------------------- *England Made Me*. London: Heinemann, 1935.

---------------------------- *A Gun for Sale*. London: Heinemann, 1936.

---------------------------- *Brighton Rock*. London: Heinemann, 1938.

---------------------------- *The Confidential Agent*. London: Heinemann, 1939.

---------------------------- *The Power and the Glory*. London: Heinemann, 1943.

---------------------------- *The Ministry of Fear*. London: Heinemann, 1943.

---------------------------- *The Heart of the Matter*. London: Heinemann, 1948.

---------------------------- *The Third Man and The Fallen Idol*. London: Heinemann, 1950.

---------------------------- *The End of the Affair*. London: Heinemann, 1951.

---------------------------- *Loser Takes All*. London: Heinemann, 1955.

---------------------------- *The Quiet American*. London: Heinemann, 1955.

---------------------------- *Our Man in Havana*. London: Heinemann, 1958.

---------------------------- *A Burnt-out Case*. London: Heinemann, 1960.

---------------------------- *The Comedians*. London: Bodley Head, 1966.

---------------------------- *Travels with my Aunt*. London: Bodley Head, 1969.

---------------------------- *The Honorary Consul*. London: Bodley Head, 1973.

---------------------------- *The Human Factor*. London: Bodley Head, 1978.

2. Other works of Graham Greene

(a) Short-stories

Greene, Graham. *Twenty-one Stories*. London: Heinemann, 1954.

---------------------------- *A Sense of Reality*. London: Heinemann, 1963.

---------------------------- *May We Borrow Your Husband? And other Comedies of the Sexual Life*. London: Bodley Head, 1969.

---------------------------- *Shades of Greene*. London: Bodley Head, 1975.

(b) Plays

Greene, Graham. *The Living Room*. London: Heinemann, 1955.

---------------------------- *The Potting Shed*. London: Heinemann, 1958.

---------------------------- *The Complaisant Lover*. London: Heinemann, 1959.

---------------------------- *Carving a Statue*. London: Bodley Head, 1964.

---------------------------- *The Return of A.J. Raffles*. London: Bodley Head, 1975.

(c) Travel Books

Greene, Graham. *Journey without Maps*. London: Heinemann, 1936.

---------------------------- *The Lawless Roads*. London: Longmans, 1939.

---------------------------- *In Search of a Character*. London:Bodley Head, 1961.

(d) Essays

Greene, Graham. *The Lost Childhood and other Essays*. London: Eyre and Spottiswoode, 1951.

---------------------------- *Introduction to Three Novels*. Stockholm: Norstedts, 1962.

---------------------------- *Collected Essays*. London: Bodley Head, 1969.

(e) Autobiography
Greene, Graham. *A Sort of Life*. London: Bodley Head, 1971.

(f) Film Criticism
Greene, Graham. *The Pleasure Dome*. London: Secker and Warburg, 1972.

(g) Biography
Greene, Graham. *Lord Rochester's Monkey*. London: Bodley Head, 1975.

3. Books on Graham Greene

Allott, Kenneth and Miriam Farris. *The Art of Graham Greene*. London: Hamish Hamilton, 1951.

Atkins, John, *Graham Greene* (Revised edition). London: Calder, 1966.

Boardman, Gwen. *Graham Greene: The Aesthetics of Exploration*. Gainsville: Univ. of Florida Press, 1972.

Cargas, H.J. *Graham Greene* St. Louis: Herder, 1969.

De Vitis, A.A. *Graham Greene*. New York: Twayne, 1964.

Evans, R.O. (ed.) *Graham Greene: Some Critical Considerations*. Lexington: Univ. of Kentucky Press, 1963.

Hynes, Samuel. *Graham Greene*. Englewood Cliffs, N.J.: Prentice-Hall, 1973.

Kulshrestha, J.P. *Graham Greene the Novelist*. Delhi: Macmillian, 1977.

Kunkel, Francis L. *The Labyrinthine Ways of Graham Greene*. New York: Sheed and Ward, 1959.

Lodge, David. *Graham Greene*. New York: Columbia Univ. Press, 1966.

Mesnet, Marie-Beatrice. *Graham Greene and the Heart of the Matter*. London: Cresset Press, 1954.

Pryce-Jones, David. *Graham Greene*. (Writers and Critics) Edinburgh: Oliver & Boyd, 1963.

Stratford, Philip. *Faith and Fiction: Creative Process in Greene and Mauriac*. Notredame: Univ. of Notredame Press, 1964.

Subrahmaniam, K.S. *Graham Greene: A Study*, Bareilly: Prakash Book Depot, 1978.

Wolf, Peter, *Graham Greene the Entertainer*, Carbondale: South Illinois Univ. Press, 1972.

Wyndham, Francis, *Graham Greene* (Writers and their Work.) London: Longmans, Green & Co., 1966.

4. Essays and Articles

Allen, Walter. "*The Novels of Graham Greene*", Penguin New Writing XVIII, 1943.

Allott, Miriam. "Graham Greene and The Way we live now", *Critical Quarterly* Aug. 1978.

Brace, Keith. "*The Best and Worst of Graham Greene.*" *The Sunday Standard*, April 30, 1978.

Calder-Marshall, A. "The Works of Graham Greene." *Horizon*, Claire V. May, 1940.

Chapman, Raymond. "The Vision of Graham Greene," in *Forms of Extremity in Modern Novel* ed. Scott Nathan A. Richmond Va., John Knox Press, 1965.

Choudhury, M.K. "Graham Greene's *The Power and the Glory*: The Force of the Irrational", *Indian Journal of English Studies* Vol. XVI, 1976.

"The Significance of Caricature in Graham Greene's *The Comedians*", *Punjab University Research Bulletin* (Arts), Oct. 1974.

"Graham Greene's *Travels with my Aunt*: A Picareque Novel," *Punjab University Research Bulletin* (Arts), Oct. 1972.

Cronin, Vincent. "Graham Greene's First Play," *The Catholic World*, Sept. 1952.

Fielding Henry. Author's preface to Joseph Andrws, Buckler W.E. (ed.) *Novels in the Making*. Boston: Houghton Mifflin Co., 1961.

Fytton, Francis. "Graham Greene: Catholocism and Controversy," *The Catholic World*, Dec. 1954.

Hess, Whitcomb M. "Graham Greene's Traversty on "The Ring and the Book", *The Catholic World*, Oct. 1961.

Kenny, Herbert A. "Graham Greene," *The Catholic World*, Aug. 1957.

Kermode, Frank. "The House of Fiction, Interviews with Seven English Novelists," *Partisan Review*, Spring 1963.

"Mr. Greene's Eggs and Crosses," *Encounter*, April 1961.

Krishna Rao, A.V "The Comedians and The Guide: A Study of their Comic Vision," Paper read before the ACLALS Conference, New Delhi, Jan. 2-8, 1977.

Lees, F.N. "Graham Greene: A Comment," Scrutiny, Oct. 1952.

Malagi, R.A. "Graham Greene's *Travels with my Aunt*," *Karnatak University Journal-Humanities*, Vol. XVII, 1972.

"*Graham Greene's Travels with my Aunt*," Karnatak U. Jounal, Vol. XVII, 1973.

Mewshaw, Micheal. "Greene in Antibes," *London Magazine*, June-July '77.

Narayanan, P.S. "Rule of Law and Human Rights," *The Hindu*, April 11, 1978.

Noxon, Richard. "Kierkegaard's Stages in A Burnt-out Case," *Review of English Literature*, Jan. 1962.

O'Brien, C.C. "A Funny Sort of God," *New York Review of Books*, XX, No. 16, Oct. 18, 1973.

Panicker K. Ayyappa. "Symbol and Motif in Modern Fiction," *Onlooker*, Vol. I No. 1, March 1975.

Rama Rao, V.V.B. "An Appreciation of Graham Greene's Style" *Mansas Educational Journal* Vol 1. No. 1, 1975.

"The Creative Artist's Vision in Graham Greene's Novels", *Triveni*, Vol. XLV, No. 2, July-September 1976.

"Graham Greene and the Burden of Childhood" *The Literary Half-yearly* Vol. XIX, No. 2, July 1978.

"The Significance of Epigraphs in Graham Greene's Novels", *Journal of English Studies*, Vol. 10, No. 1, November 1978.

Rewak, William J.	"*The Potting Shed* - Maturation of Graham Greene's Vision," *The Catholic World*, Dec. 1957.
Ross, Alan.	"Notes", *The London Magazine*, March 1978.
Sena Vinod.	"Catharsis or Ecstasy: W.B. Yeats on Tragedy," *The Literary Criterion*, Vol. XI Winter 1974.
Sewell, Elizabeth.	"Graham Greene", *Dublin Review* No. 463, 1954.
Stratford Philip.	"Greene's Hall of Mirrors," *The Kenyon Review*. XXIII, Summer, 1961.
	"Unlocking the Potting Shed," *The Kenyon Review*, XXIV, Winter 1962.
Ziolkowski, Theodore:	"The Telltale Teeth: Psychodontia to Sociodontia," *PMLA* Vol. 91. No. 1, January 1976.

5. Reviews in the TLS

The Man Within:	*The Times Literary Supplement*	20 June 1929.
The Name of Action:	-do-	9 Oct. 1930.
Rumour at Nightfall:	-do-	3 Dec. 1931.
Stamboul Train:	-do-	15 Dec. 1932.
It's Battlefield:	-do-	8 Feb. 1934.
England Made Me:	-do-	4 Jul. 1935.
A Gun for Sale:	-do-	11 Jul. 1936.
Brighton Rock:	-do-	16 Jul. 1938.
The Confidential Agent:	-do-	23 Spet. 1939.
The Power and the Glory:	-do-	9 Mar. 1940.
The Ministry of Fear:	-do-	29 May 1943.
The Heart of the Matter:	-do-	29 May 1948.
The Third Man:	-do-	4 Aug. 1950.
The End of the Affair:	-do-	7 Sep. 1951.
Loser Takes All:	-do-	18 Feb. 1955.
The Quiet American:	-do-	9 Dec. 1955.
Our Man in Havana:	-do-	10 Oct. 1958.
A Burnt-out Case:	-do-	20 Jan. 1961.
The Comedians:	-do-	27 Jan. 1966.
Travels with my Aunt:	-do-	20 Nov. 1969.
The Honorary Consul:	-do-	14 Sep. 1973.
The Human Factor:	-do-	17 Mar. 1978.
A Basement Room and other Stories:	TLS	23 Nov. 1935.
Nineteen Stories:	-do-	26 Jul. 1947.
A Sense of Reality:	TLS	21 Jun. 1963.
The Living Room:	-do-	10 Jul. 1953.
The Potting Shed:	-do-	21 Feb. 1958.
The Complaisant Lover:	-do-	31 Jul. 1959.
Journey without Maps:	-do-	23 May 1936.
The Lawless Roads:	-do-	11 Mar. 1939.
In Search of a Character:	-do-	27 Oct. 1961.
The Lost Childhood and other Essays:	-do-	6 Apr. 1951.
Collected Essays:	-do-	13 Mar. 1969.
A Sort of Life:	-do-	17 Sep. 1971.

Reviews in other periodicals

Our Man in Havana:	*The London Magazine*	Dec. 1958.
The Comedians:	-do-	Mar. 1966.
Travels with my Aunt:	-do-	Apr. 1970.
The Potting Shed:	-do-	Jun. 1958.
The Complaisant Lover:	-do-	Jul. 1960.
Carving a Statue:	-do-	Mar. 1960.
Collected Essays:	-do-	Jun. 1969.
Our Man in Havena:	*Encounter*	Dec. 1958.
The Honorary Consul:	-do-	Dec. 1973.
A Burnt-out Case:	*Partisan Review*	Vol. 28 1961.
A Burnt-out Case:	*The Kenyon Review*	Vol. XXIII No. 3 1961.
The Human Factor:	*The Hindu*	11 April 1978.
The Human Factor:	*The Times of India*	1 April 1979.

6. Criticism (General)

Abercrombie, L. *Principles of Literary Criticism*. London: Martin Secker, 1927.

Thomas Hardy. London: Martin Secker, 1912.

Abrams, M.H. *A Glossary of Literary Terms*. Madras: Macmillian, 1978.

Allen, Walter. *The English Novel*. London: Phoenix House, 1954.

Tradition and Dream. London: Phoenix House, 1964.

Berdyaev, Nicolai A. *Christian Existentialism*. London: Allen & Unwin, 1965.

Bergonzi, Bernard. *The Situation of the Novel*. Harmondsworth: Pelican Books, 1972.

Blistein, Elmer M. *Comedy in Action*, Durham: Duke Univ. Press, 1965.

Booth, Wayne C. *The Rhetoric of Fiction*. Chicago: Univ. of Chicago Press, 1961.

Boulton, Marjorie. *The Anatomy of the Novel*. Lonon: Routledge and Kegan Paul, 1961.

Brereton, Geoffrey. *Principles of Tragedy*. London: Routledge & Kegan Paul, 1967.

Buckler, William E. *Novels in the Making*. Boston: Houghton Mifflin & Co., 1961.

Burgess, Anthony. *The Novel Now*. London: Faber and Faber, 1967.

Cecil, Lord David. *Hardy the Novelist*. London: Constable, 1954.

Church, Richard. *British Authors*. London: Longmans, 1948.

Collins, A.S. *English Literature of the Twentieth Century*. London: University Tutorial Press, 1951.

Colmer, John. (ed.) *Approaches to the Novel*. Edinburgh Oliver and Boyd, 1967.

Cooper, Lane. *Aristotle's Theory of Comedy*. New York: Harcourt Brace & Co., 1922.

Daiches, David. *Critical Approaches to Literature*. London: Longmans Greene & Co., 1957.

A Study of Literature. London: Andre Deutsch, 1968.

Dawson, S.W. *Drama and the Dramatic*. London: Methuen, 1970.

Echeruo, Micheal J.C. *Joyce Cary and the Novel of Africa*. London: Longman, 1973.

Eliot, T.S. *Selected Essays*. London: Faber, 1932.

Feibleman, James. *In Praise of Comedy*. London: Allen & Unwin, 1939.

Fowlie, W. (ed.) *Francois Mauriac: Five Novels*. London: Eyre & Spottiswoode, 1968.

Fraser, G.S. *The Modern Writer and his World*. Calcutta: Rupa, 1961.

Frye, Northrop. *Anatomy of Criticism: Four Essays*. Princeton: Princeton Univ. Press, 1973.

Gardner, Helen. *Religion and Literature*. London: Faber, 1970.

Gilman, R. *Common and Uncommon Masks*, New York: Random House, 1971.

Grierson, H.J.C. *The Background of English Literature and other Essays*. London: Chatto and Windus, 1961.

Halio, Jay L. *Angus Wilson*. Edinburgh: Oliver & Boyd, 1964.

Harvey, Sir Paul. *The Oxford Companion to English Literature*. London: Oxford Univ. Press, 1967.

Harvey, W.J. *Character and the Novel*. London: Chatto & Windus, 1965.

Hazlitt, William. *Lectures on Enlish Comic Writers*. London: Oxford Univ. Press, 1907.

Heilman, R.B. *Tragedy and Melodrama*. Seattle: Univ. of Washington Press, 1968.

Heiney, Donlad and Dawns, Lenthiel. *Contemporary British Literature*. New York: Barron's Educational Series, 1974.

Hinchliffe, Arnold P. *The Absurd*. London: Methuen, 1969.

Hoy, Cyrus. *The Hyacinth Room*. London: Chatto & Windus, 1964.

Iyengar, K.R.S. *Francois Mauriac*. Bombay: Asia Pub. House, 1963.

James, Henry. "The Art of Fiction," *The House of Fiction*. Ed. Leon Edel. London: Rupert, Hart-Davis, 1957.

Karl, Fredrick R. *A Reader's Guide to the Comtemporary English Novel*. London: Thames and Hudson, 1968.

Kazin, Alfred. *Contemporaries*. Boston: Little Brown & Co., 1962.

Kettle, Arnold. *An Introduction to the English Novel*. London: Hutchinson Univ. Library, 1969.

Krutch, Joseph Wood. *The Modern Temper*. New York: Harcourt Brace & Co., 1929.

Langer, Susanne K. *Feeling and Form*. New York: Charles Scribner & Son, 1953.

Laverty, Fredrick et al. *The Unity of English: Five Basic Focal Points*. New York: Harper & Rowe, 1970.

Leech Clifford. *Tragedy*. London: Methuen, 1969.

Lever, Katherine. *The Novel and the Reader*. London: Methuen, 1961.

Lewis, R.W.B. *The Picaresque Saint*. London: Gollancz, 1960.

Liddell, R. *The Principles of Fiction*. London: Jonathan Cape, 1927.

Lodge, David. *The Novelist at the Cross Roads*. London: Routledge and Kegan Paul, 1971.

Lubbock, Percy. *The Craft of Fiction*. London: Jonathan Cape, 1921.

Lucas, F.L. *Tragedy*. London: The Hogarth Press, 1957.

Mc Collan. *Tragedy*. New York: Macmillian, 1957.

Merchant, Moelwyn. *Comedy*. London: Methuen, 1972.

Meredith, George. *An Essay on Comedy*. London: Archibald Constable, 1906.

Megroz, R.L. *Francis Thompson: The Poet of Earth and Heaven*. London: Faber and Guyer, 1927.

Modern English Poetry. London: Nicholson & Watson, 1933.

Muir, Edwin. *The Structure of the Novel*. London: The Hogarth Press, 1928.

Murray, John M. *The Problem of Style*. London: Oxford Univ. Press, 1960.

Myers, H.A. *Tragedy*. New York: Cornell Univ. Press, 1956.

Neill, Diana. *A Short History of the English Novel*. New York: Collins Books, 1964.

Mc Cormic. *Catastrophe and Imagination*. London: Longmans, 1957.

Morris, Brian. *Ford's It's a Pity She's a Whore*. London: Benn, 1968.

O'Connor, William Von. *The Grotesque: An American Genre*. Carbondale: Southern Illinois Univ. Press, 1962.

O'Faolain, Sean. *The Vanishing Hero*. London: Eyre and Spottiswoode, 1956.

Palmer, John. *Comedy*. London: Martin Secker, Date of Pub. not printed.

Potts, L.J. *Comedy*. London: Thames and Hudson, 1966.

Praz, Mario. *The Hero in Eclipse*. London: Oxford Univ. Pres, 1956.

Prescott, Orville. *In My Opinion*. New York: Bobs Merril Co., 1952.

Priestley, J.B. *English Humour*. London: Longmans Green & Co., 1930.

Quennel, Peter. *The Sign of the Fish*. London: Colins, 1960.

Read, Herbert. *English Prose Style*. London: Bell, 1956.

Richards, I.A. *Principles of Literary Criticism*. London: Kegan Paul, French, Trubner, 1934.

Ristine, F.H. *Tragicomedy*. New York: Columbia Univ. Press, 1910.

Ross, Lawrence J. ed. *Cyril Tourner's Revenger's Tragedy*. London: Edward Arnold, 1967.

Schorer, Miles and Mckensie. Criticism, *The Foundations of Modern Literary Judgement*. New York: Harcourt, Brace & Co., 1948.

Scott James, R.A. *Fifty Years of English Literature*. London: Longmans, 1951.

Scott, Nathan A. (Jr.) *The Tragic Vision and the Christian Faith*. New York: Haddom House Book Association Press, 1957.

Sheed, Wilfred. *The Morning and After*. New York: Farrer, Strauss & Giroux, 1968.

Shipley, Joseph. (ed). *A Dictionary of World Literature*. New Jersey: Littlefield and Adams, 1972.

Smith, James. *Melodrama*. London: Methuen, 1973.

Stephens, John. *Seven Approaches to the Novel*. London: Harrap, 1972.

Stratford, Philip *Faith and Fiction: Creative Process in Greene and Mauriac*. Notredame: Univ of Notredame Press, 1964.

Styan, J.L. *The Dark Comedy*. Cambridge: Cambridge Univ. Press, 1968.

Sykes, Christopher. *Evelyn Waugh: A Biography*. London: Collins, 1975.

Sypher Wylie. *Comedy*. Garden City, New York: Doubleday Anchor, 1956.

Thomson, Philip. *The Grotesque*. London: Methuen, 1972.

Thorndike, Ashley H. *English Comedy*. New York: Macmillan, 1929.

Vinson, James. *Contemporary Novelists*. London: St. James Press, 1972.

Warrena and Brooks. *Understanding Fiction*. New York: Appleton, Century and Croft, 1959.

Watt, Ian. *The Rise of the Novel*. Harmondsworth: Pelican, 1972.

Weales, Gerald. *Religion in Modern English Drama*. Philadelphia: Univ. of Pennsylvania Press, 1961.

Weiner, Philip P. (Ed.) *Dictionary of the History of Ideas*. New York: Charles Scribner, 1973.

Wellek and Warren. *Theory of Literature*. Harmondsworth: Penguin, 1963.

West, Paul. *The Modern Novel*. London: Hutchinson Univ. Lib., 1967.

Whitman, Cedric H. *Sophocles: A Study of Heroic Humanism*. Cambridge, Mass.: Harvard Univ. Press, 1951.

Williams, Ian. *Meredith*. London: Routledge & Kegan Paul, 1971.

Winsatt, W.K. *Dr. Johnson on Shakespeare*. Harmondsworth, Penguin Shakespeare's Library, 1969.

Wright, Walter F. *Art and Substance in George Meredith*. Lincoln. Na.: Univ. of Nebraska Press, 1953.

Zabel, Morton D. *Craft and Character*. London: Gollancz, 1957.

7. Special Numbers of Journals

Modern Fiction Studies. Graham Greene Special Number Vol. III No. 3. Autumn, 1957.

Renascence Graham Greene Special Number XII Fall 1959.

8. Unpublished Dissertations

Carl, Edward Stenberg. *The Quest for Justice in the Fiction of Graham Greene*. Univeristy of Connecticut 1969.

Coroneou, Marianthi. *Suffering as Part of the Human Condition in the Fiction of Graham Greene, Albert Camus, and Nikos Kazantzakis*, University of Kentucky, 1967.

Handon, Robert Micheal. *Graham Greene's Religious Sense*. University of Massachusetts, 1971.

Lattinville, Ronald Edward. *Comic Characterization in the Fiction of Graham Greene*. University of Southern California, 1974.

Malagi, R.A. *The Problem of Evil in Graham Greene*. Karnatak University, 1966.

Paul, Richard La Chance. *Man and Religion in the Novels of Graham Greene*. Kent State University, 1970.